HISTORY OF THE 12th (EASTERN) DIVISION IN THE GREAT WAR 1914-1918

[*Elliott & Fry*

MAJOR-GENERAL SIR ARTHUR B. SCOTT, K.C.B., D.S.O.

HISTORY OF THE 12th (EASTERN) DIVISION IN THE GREAT WAR, 1914-1918

EDITED BY
MAJOR-GENERAL SIR ARTHUR B. SCOTT,
K.C.B., D.S.O.

COMPILED BY
P. MIDDLETON BRUMWELL,
M.C., C.F.

London
NISBET & CO. LTD.
22 BERNERS STREET, W.1

First published in 1923

Printed and bound by Antony Rowe Ltd, Eastbourne

Dedicated

TO THE MEMORY OF

THOSE WHO FELL IN THE RANKS OF THE
12TH (EASTERN) DIVISION

IN THE

GREAT WAR, 1914–1918

PREFACE

THE 12th (Eastern) Division was formed from the first of the Service Battalions raised in August, 1914. It retained this order of battle throughout the war, with the exception that, in February, 1918, three battalions were disbanded in the general reduction, and in April, 1918, the 1st/1st Cambridgeshire Regiment joined, absorbing the remnants of the 7th Battalion, the Suffolk Regiment.

In recounting this history, the aim has been to narrate the doings of the Division, and in no way to attempt a record for military study. The war of 1914–1918 necessitated the employment of such vast bodies of troops that, in a general history, it is probable only exceptional engagements of individual divisions would be recorded, the narrative of minor actions being omitted. Nevertheless, to the battalion, to smaller units, and to the individual, it is frequently the minor action which is more absorbing, and more strongly impressed on the memory.

As a consequence a great debt of gratitude is due to the Rev. P. Middleton Brumwell, M.C., through whose enthusiasm and zeal the details for the following account of the Division have been compiled. Mr. Brumwell was present with the Division from its formation to its demobilisation, and it is safe to say that but for his labour in searching records and collecting information, this history would possibly never have been published.

The pages now before us recall many brave deeds,

though perforce some have had to be omitted from lack of space; many glorious days from a soldier's point of view, as also, alas! many tragic ones. They recall the rough and the smooth; the indomitable will and cheerfulness with which all difficulties were overcome; the one aim that was always in view—the defeat of the Empire's enemies at whatever cost; the final triumph.

The 12th Division can be justly proud of its achievements. For those who served in its ranks I trust this book will be a valuable souvenir, and to their families a source of pride.

ARTHUR SCOTT

LONDON,
9th May, 1923.

COMPILER'S NOTE

THE compilation of this history has been a long and arduous task, involving the study of the war diaries of all units in the Division from the date of their formation to the close of the campaign. The task has not been rendered easier by frequent changes of stations both at home and abroad. But at last the labour of love has been accomplished.

Grateful acknowledgments are due to the Historical Section (Military Branch) of the Committee of Imperial Defence for placing at my disposal the documents and war diaries relating to the Division; to Colonel-Commandant H. W. Higginson, C.B., D.S.O., A.D.C., for his constant and unfailing help from the initiation of the work to its completion; to Colonel B. Vincent, C.M.G., and Lieut.-Colonel H. E. S. Wynne, C.M.G., D.S.O., for notes on important actions in which the Division was engaged; to others who have placed private diaries at my disposal; finally, to Mr. C. A. Hutson, of Colombo, Ceylon, who came, at much expense on his part in time and money, and took the photographs of the battlefields of the Division, some of which are reproduced in these pages.

The history does not set out to be a complete record of all the deeds performed by each unit, much less of each individual in the Division. It is more than probable that many important incidents have been omitted. But an endeavour has been made to make the record as complete as the space at disposal would permit, and it is hoped that the volume may prove to be of permanent interest to all who served in the Division, and at the same time serve as a memorial and tribute to those who made the great sacrifice within its ranks.

P. MIDDLETON BRUMWELL, C.F

CONSTANTINOPLE,
 March, 1923.

CONTENTS

		PAGE
PREFACE	. . . . . .	vii
COMPILER'S NOTE	. . . . .	ix

CHAPTER		
I.	EARLY DAYS	1
II.	"SOMEWHERE" IN FRANCE	5
III.	THE BATTLE OF LOOS	12
IV.	FIRST WINTER IN FRANCE	26
V.	THE BATTLE OF THE CRATERS	32
VI.	BATTLE OF THE SOMME—I. OVILLERS . .	47
VII.	BATTLE OF THE SOMME—II. POZIÈRES AND RATION TRENCH	62
VIII.	BATTLE OF THE SOMME—BETWEEN THE BATTLES	75
IX.	BATTLE OF THE SOMME—III. GUEUDECOURT AND BAYONET TRENCH	80
X.	AFTER THE SOMME—SECOND WINTER . .	86
XI.	PREPARATIONS FOR THE BATTLE OF ARRAS .	90
XII.	THE BATTLE OF ARRAS	97
XIII.	THE DEFENDERS OF MONCHY-LE-PREUX . .	114
XIV.	THE BATTLE OF CAMBRAI—I. THE ATTACK .	132
XV.	THE BATTLE OF CAMBRAI—II. THE GERMAN COUNTER-ATTACK	143
XVI.	OUR THIRD WINTER	161
XVII.	STEMMING THE TIDE	168
XVIII.	BACKS TO THE WALL	180
XIX.	THE ADVANCE TO VICTORY—I. . . .	190
XX.	THE ADVANCE TO VICTORY—II. . . .	202
XXI.	THE ADVANCE TO VICTORY—III. . . .	215
XXII.	FAREWELL TO THE 12TH	225

CONTENTS
APPENDICES

		PAGE
I.	Terms of Armistice with Germany	231
II.	(a) Original Order of Battle of 12th (Eastern) Division	237
	(b) Succession of Commanding Officers, Staff Officers, etc.	238
III.	(a) Summary of Honours and Awards Gained	250
	(b) Awards of the Victoria Cross	251
IV.	Summary of Casualties	254
V.	The Memorials	255
VI.	"The Spades"—The 12th Divisional Theatrical Troupe	257
	Index	259

LIST OF ILLUSTRATIONS

	FACING PAGE
MAJOR-GENERAL SIR ARTHUR B. SCOTT, K.C.B., D.S.O.	*Frontispiece*
DIVISIONAL HEADQUARTERS, NIEPPE	6
MAJOR-GENERAL F. D. V. WING, C.B., C.M.G.	16
AIR PHOTOGRAPH, HOHENZOLLERN CRATERS	38
HOHENZOLLERN CRATERS—I., II.	42
BARBED WIRE STOP GATE	76
TAKING UP AMMUNITION, SOMME, 1916	82
HOTEL DE VILLE AND PETITE PLACE, ARRAS	92
ENTRANCE TO SEWER, ARRAS	94
NEAR MONCHY-LE-PREUX	108
MONCHY-LE-PREUX	116
TANK WITH 12TH DIVISION EMBLEM	134
BARBED WIRE, HINDENBURG LINE	136
SONNET FARM } BATTLE OF CAMBRAI, 20TH NOVEMBER, LATEAU WOOD } 1917	138
AVELUY BRIDGE, 27TH MARCH, 1918	174
COLONEL (TEMP. MAJOR-GENERAL) H. W. HIGGINSON, C.B., D.S.O., A.D.C.	182
MALASSISE FARM, 19TH SEPTEMBER, 1918	
LITTLE PRIEL FARM, 20TH SEPTEMBER, 1918	210
MEMORIAL CROSS AT EPÉHY	256
THEATRICAL TROUPE	258

LIST OF MAPS

Drawn by MAJOR-GENERAL SIR ARTHUR SCOTT

MAP NO.		FACING PAGE
1.	PLOEGSTEERT	10
2.	LOOS	14
3.	THE QUARRIES	22
4.	BETHUNE	24
5.	HOHENZOLLERN CRATERS, FORECAST	36
6.	HOHENZOLLERN CRATERS	44
7.	OVILLERS	58
8.	POZIÈRES	72
9.	ARRAS FRONT	78
10.	GUEUDECOURT	84
11.	ARRAS TRENCHES	98
12.	THE BATTLE OF ARRAS	104
13.	THE SCARPE	112
14.	MONCHY-LE-PREUX	126
15.	CAMBRAI, 20TH NOVEMBER, 1917	140
16.	REVELON RIDGE	148
17.	CAMBRAI, 30TH NOVEMBER, 1917	158
18.	FLEURBAIX	164
19.	COUNTRY ROUND ALBERT	172
20.	ALBERT, MARCH, 1918	178
21.	MORLANCOURT	198
22.	NURLU	206
23.	EPÉHY	212
24.	ADVANCE FROM LENS (1)	218
25.	ADVANCE FROM LENS (2)	220
26.	ADVANCE FROM LENS (3)	222
	GENERAL MAP OF NORTH-WEST FRANCE.	

HISTORY OF THE 12TH (EASTERN) DIVISION

CHAPTER I

EARLY DAYS

August, 1914—May, 1915

THE 12th (Eastern) Division consisted of men from the Eastern and Home Counties. The rural population of these counties was not a whit behind the urban in response to the call of their country in August 1914. From every village and hamlet came men of all classes. Shoulder to shoulder, in the queues awaiting enlistment, were clerks and navvies, stockbrokers and farmers, porters and lawyers, masters, assistants, and messenger boys. The country man, however, is a little more clannish than the townsman; he wants to join his own county regiment. Consequently the men who ultimately formed the first of the Eastern Divisions proceeded to their county recruiting depôts to enlist. Training in the elements of drill and route marching commenced at once; but rifles and implements of war were not forthcoming to equip such large numbers, and improvised wooden rifles were used therefore to accustom the recruits to the handling of arms. When sufficient enlistments had been made to complete a battalion, it was moved to its Infantry Brigade centre, and there went through a more advanced course of training. Of this training it is unnecessary to speak.

It is described, in an inimitable manner by one who personally experienced it, in the well-known book " The First Hundred Thousand " (Ian Hay). The 12th Division formed part of that heroic force, and the experiences of one division during the period of instruction were practically those of another.

The Infantry Brigades forming the Division were the 35th, 36th, and 37th. The first of these, consisting of the 7th Battalion the Norfolk Regiment, 7th Battalion the Suffolk Regiment, 9th Battalion the Essex Regiment, and the 5th Battalion Princess Charlotte of Wales's (Royal Berkshire Regiment), formed near Shorncliffe. The second included the 8th and 9th Battalions of the Royal Fusiliers (City of London Regiment), 7th Battalion the Royal Sussex Regiment, and the 11th Battalion the Duke of Cambridge's Own (Middlesex Regiment), and was stationed at Colchester. The 6th Battalion the Queen's (Royal West Surrey Regiment), 6th Battalion the Buffs (East Kent Regiment), 7th Battalion the East Surrey Regiment, and the 6th Battalion the Queen's Own (Royal West Kent Regiment), constituted the 37th Infantry Brigade assembling at Purfleet.

The Royal Artillery of the Division, the 62nd, 63rd, 64th Brigades R.F.A. of 18-pounders, and the 65th Brigade R.F.A. of 4·5" Howitzers, formed and trained at Shorncliffe. Originally these artillery brigades were composed of three batteries of four guns each, but later on a fourth battery was added. An ammunition column was attached to each brigade, these eventually becoming the nucleus of the Divisional Ammunition Column.

The 69th, 70th, and 87th Field Companies, and Divisional Signal Company constituting the Royal Engineers of the Division, were quartered at Hounslow, subse-

it true ? Inspections of kits took place, iron rations were issued, and the prospects looked more hopeful. Suddenly one morning we awakened to the sounds of bands playing " It's a long, long way to Tipperary," and the tramp, tramp, tramp of troops on the march. The first division (9th Highland) of the First Hundred Thousand was on its way to the railway station.

Another short spell and a second division, the 14th, was despatched. At last the turn of the 12th came, and on the 29th of May, 1915, nine months after they had come into existence, the first units commenced entraining, leaving at all times of the day and night. The move had been rehearsed so often that few believed it genuine, until they found some pal had vanished with his battalion without a word, or until they themselves were well away.

To summarise the move : *Personnel*, with the exception of a few small units, went *viâ* Folkestone to Boulogne, transport *viâ* Southampton to Havre, the other side of the Channel being reached without accident or loss, a sufficient tribute to those responsible for the organisation and execution of the plan. By the early hours of the 1st June, all units of the Division were in France, and the dawn of their " Great Day " had arrived.

CHAPTER II

"SOMEWHERE" IN FRANCE

June—August, 1915

(*Map* 1)

AFTER two days' rest in camp near Boulogne, awaiting the arrival of the transport, the troops proceeded by train to a rendezvous near St. Omer. At first experiences of the French troop trains were amusing, although later on they were to become merely monotonous. Each railway waggon bore the significant inscription, " 8 horses or 40 men," but with forty men installed, there was little room for packs except on the knees of the owner or under him, neither position being exactly comfortable. However, as a first experience, and with keen enthusiasm pervading all ranks, the journey was endured with cheerfulness. By the 4th of June the Division had concentrated at its rendezvous, and on the following day, with the exception of the 5th Northamptonshire Regiment, which was attached to the Second Army and moved to the Ypres salient, marched to the Hazebrouck-Boeseghem area. On the 6th inst. the march was continued to the Meteren-Steenwerck area. These two marches are memorable ones for those who took part in them. The heat was intense, there was no breeze and no shade, the roads in a great part were *pavé*, and a march of twenty miles on *pavé*, with full equipment and packs, proved as severe a test as new troops could be asked to perform. All were relieved when the end of the journey was reached, and were thankful to bivouac anywhere, and sleep under hedges or in barns. On the next day the 36th and 37th Infantry Brigades moved to Pont de Nieppe and Armentières respectively, and the first headquarters of the 12th Division opened formally at Nieppe.

The Division now commenced its training in trench warfare, and for this purpose the 35th Infantry Brigade, with the 63rd and 64th Brigades, R.F.A., was attached to the 27th Division, the 36th Infantry Brigade and 62nd Brigade, R.F.A., to the 48th Division. The Field Companies of the Royal Engineers and the Field Ambulances likewise receiving instruction from these two divisions.

On the 23rd of June the period of instruction ended, the Division being ready to take its place in the fighting line, and to enter on those three and a half years of heroism in battle, which was to gain for it a lasting reputation.

The first system of trenches to be occupied were those north-east of Armentières reaching through Ploegsteert Wood. These were taken over from the 46th Division, the 37th Brigade going in on the right and the 36th on the left, the 35th being engaged in working on a reserve trench known as the G.H.Q. line. It is interesting to record that the first battalions to occupy the front line were the 6th Queen's and 6th Buffs of the 37th Brigade, and the 11th Middlesex of the 36th Brigade. In view of later days, an early entry in a war diary is worthy of notice here : "Except for thirty high-explosive shells fired at our trenches the day was quiet."

The Canadian Corps having relieved a portion of our troops on the left, the Division extended to the right, relieving the 27th Division, and holding from the River Lys to Ploegsteert Wood. On a trench map this well-known wood read like a bit of London. The northern

DIVISIONAL HEADQUARTERS, NIEPPE

extremity of our sector had been given the familiar name of "The Strand," and many reminiscences must have been recalled when journeying from there to Piccadilly Circus or Oxford Circus, and passing along tracts called Regent Street or The Haymarket. Though disguised by such familiar and pleasing references, it was, nevertheless, the most sinister portion of the divisional front, as it provided both opponents with that favourite form of exercise, sniping. Much ingenuity was shown in camouflaging sniper's posts in the trenches and trees, and, in consequence, enemy snipers were difficult to locate. Working in pairs was one of the most successful methods. The observer, concealing himself in a tree, watched for movement on the part of the enemy, and reported to a sniper below. It was by these means that a German, masked and clothed in sandbags, was discovered through raising his arm to fire his rifle, and was shot. Later on in the war a sniping school was instituted, in which every known device and camouflage for successful sniping was taught, and the Germans evidently appreciated the results, as they were issued with steel vizors to wear when employed on this duty themselves. But these were things of the future, and the 7th East Surrey Regiment were flattered when a notice board appeared in the German trench saying, "Don't fire, East Surrey; you shoot too well." As a matter of fact, this battalion showed considerable zeal in this direction, encouraged by the enthusiasm of Major A. H. Wilson, who had great experience as a big-game shot. Amongst others, Captain H. Patterson, adjutant of the 9th Royal Fusiliers, fell to a sniper's rifle on the 4th of August. A sure result of successful sniping was retaliation by shell fire.

On the 1st of July the Division had its first experience of a mine explosion, though, fortunately, the gallery had not reached the trench, and no damage was done. Later in the month two more attempts were made, one only eight yards away, but with no serious effects.

Aeroplanes were few and far between in these days, and every one, including the civil population, would turn out to watch their appearances.

On the 15th of July, the divisional front was extended to the south as far as due east of Armentières, making the total distance held 7,000 yards. This necessitated having all three infantry brigades in the trenches, the 36th on the right, with headquarters at Houplines, the 37th in the centre, headquarters at Armentières, and the 35th on the left, headquarters Pont de Nieppe. On completion of this alteration the Germans greeted the brigade in Houplines by firing 100 shells into the village in an hour. It sounds a small matter now, but in those quiet days it was considered as the herald of an attack, and all stood to, and for the first time excitement in the Division ran high. Divisional Headquarters likewise received its baptism of fire, but nothing happened beyond the fact that our artillery was allowed to retaliate with a fifteen-minute intense bombardment, a quite unheard of occurrence, in which the gunners rejoiced. A record of casualties for the month of July is interesting, as showing the toll taken for holding the trenches : killed, 7 officers, 64 other ranks ; wounded, 18 officers, 413 other ranks.

August passed fairly placidly except for one day, the 9th inst. At 4 a.m. on that morning the Germans commenced a heavy bombardment, lasting one and a half hours, on the trenches held by the 8th Royal Fusiliers. The front and support lines were considerably damaged and all the wires from company headquarters were cut. For some time the situation was uncertain but no attack developed. During this shelling, the heaviest hitherto experienced, the bearing of the troops was worthy of the best traditions of the Army.

On the 18th a new experience was undergone. The enemy, firing incendiary shells into Nouvel Houplines, set fire to a large factory and some houses, but, fortunately, no lives were lost.

The quietness on this front was no doubt partly due to the fact that the Saxons, reported as non-aggressive unless provoked, were holding the line opposite us. They were even inclined to fraternise on occasions, the following message being received : " To the opposition. We have sent by rifle grenades some newspapers over. When you get it, stick up a white flag and we don't shoot. Wait a minute and newspapers come by non-exploding grenades. Is peace in sight? Please answer." After the capture of Warsaw a large board was placed outside their trench : " Warsaw taken," and the next night two more were erected : " Russia is over " ; " Calais will follow soon " ; but a few nights later a party of the 9th Royal Fusiliers, creeping through the wire, brought back the Warsaw board in triumph, and on the 24th August our men sent by catapult the news of the Baltic naval losses. A large amount of night patrolling in No Man's Land also took place at this time, and, in view of his future career in the Division, it may be noted that a successful reconnaissance was carried out by Captain Dawson, assisted by Private King, of the 6th Royal West Kent Regiment. Both sides were likewise busy trying to tap each other's telephone messages by running wires across No Man's Land, and placing earth pins in the opponent's parapets. The results on our part were not very successful at this period, though later on, when delicate receiving instruments were installed, valuable information was obtained by this method.

At the end of the month, to the great joy of the men in the front line, the artillery achieved distinction by bringing down the large chimney of a *blanchisserie*, which was used as an observation post.

One of the constant troubles throughout the war was the presence of a considerable number of non-combatants in the forward areas, and very frequently in close proximity to the front lines. Towns like Armentières provided excellent opportunities for spies to locate themselves with a certain amount of safety, and all new divisions appeared to become quickly infected with the spy mania. Strange lights at night, or pigeons flying about, instantly awakened the " Sherlock Holmes " instinct. On occasions the spy was reported to be dressed as a Staff officer, and for several days the life of a Staff officer became unbearable. Then the spy was a brigadier moving about in the back areas in a motor car without a number, when woe betide a brigadier in a motor car either with or without a number. Another time the suggested impersonation was that of an officer of the Royal Engineers making sketches, and such an officer of ours was arrested four times one day, when he was trying to sketch the enemy's position. The Chaplains also had their turn of suspicion. But perhaps the most vivid recollection of the Division at that time would be in connection with the continual working parties, the comments made on the subject hardly leading one to think that the troops regarded the work in the nature of a rest. A new line of trenches having to be dug, battalions out of the line would find from 300 to 600 men a day for the work, and the following extract from a battalion war diary speaks for itself : " Quiet day without working party, the first since coming to Houplines " ; or this, from the diary of a private : " R.E. continually drawing on us for 600 men at a time

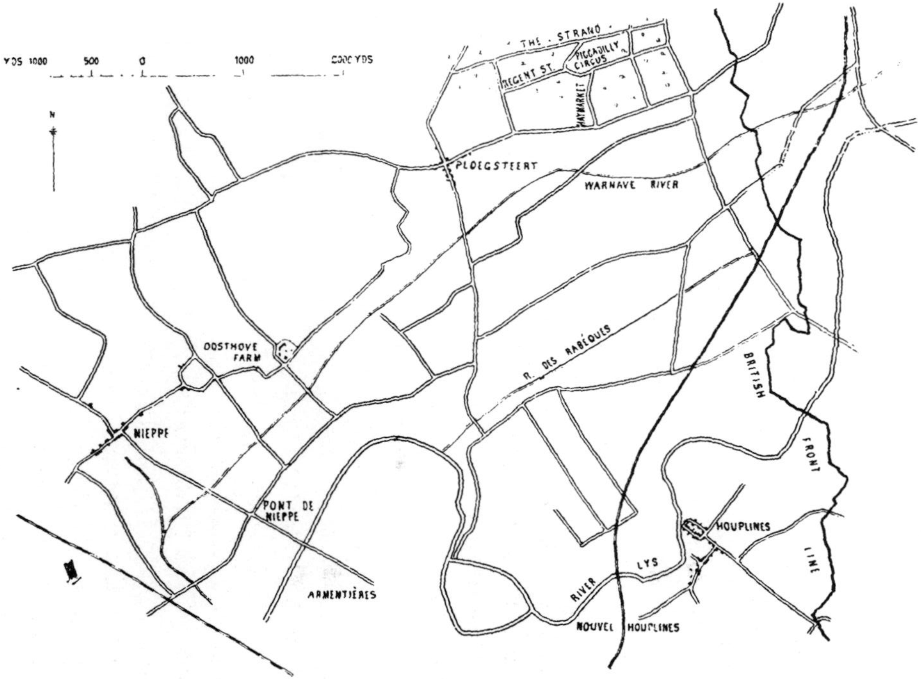

Map No. 1. Ploegsteert

to assist them in trench work, consequently our visit to Oosthove Farm (in the reserve area) instead of being a rest cure, proved just the opposite." With regard to this an order furnishes amusing reading : " In reference to the complaints of the battalion on the provision of working parties, it must be pointed out that it is necessary to make the line as comfortable and as safe as possible in case we have another winter."

Even as late as August, 1915, the supply of machine guns was very meagre, and on the 25th inst. the allotment was raised to four per battalion. There was also a shortage of ammunition of all descriptions, and very strict orders were issued as to its conservation, or any over expenditure of the fixed allowance.

Such was the routine of these early days. Relief was regular, two battalions of each brigade held the front line, one in reserve, and the other at rest, and life, on the whole, in the reserve area was not too dreary. The town of Armentières, although a few thousand yards from the front and within easy range of the enemy's guns, was only shelled intermittently, and troops were able to get rest and recreation there. A concert party had been formed, which entertained the units behind the line, providing them with merriment and fun, and receiving its own baptism of fire at Houplines. An institute and canteen were opened in Nieppe, baths and a laundry at Pont de Nieppe. Thus began those institutions which were to develop in later days and form such a distinctive feature of the administrative work.

Casualties were not heavy, and the experience gained in those three months inspired confidence in the troops, fitting them to take their places beside the Regular Army. The result showed Great Britain that the New Army could be relied on for steadiness, endurance, and heroic courage in the day of fierce battle. That day was not far off.

quently moving to the Infantry Brigade Centres for combined exercises.

The 116th, 117th, 118th and 119th Companies of the Royal Army Service Corps, from the training establishment at Aldershot, composed the 12th Division Train, and at the end of October, 1914, assembled on that historic spot, the cricket ground at Lord's.

The Royal Army Medical Corps field ambulances, the 36th, 37th and 38th, were stationed at Hounslow, moving in January, 1915, to Eastbourne.

At the end of November, 1914, the infantry brigades were concentrated in the neighbourhood of Hythe, coming under the command of Major-General J. Spens, C.B., and in February, 1915, the 5th Battalion the Northamptonshire Regiment joined them there as the Pioneer Battalion.

On the 20th February, 1915, the Division marched to Aldershot to complete its training before proceeding to the front, Major-General F. D. V. Wing, C.B., C.M.G., assuming command in March. "A" Squadron King Edward's Horse, the 9th Motor Machine-Gun Battery, the 23rd Sanitary Section, and the 23rd Mobile Veterinary Section joined up about this period.

At last the Division was complete, and it seemed as if the wearisome waiting must end. Each day brought fresh rumours of a move, which, however, never materialised. Still more training, more musketry, more manœuvres, and no order for the Front. Four of the new "K" Divisions were now concentrated at Aldershot.

Six months had been the general idea as the necessary time to render efficient the men of the New Army, but six months passed, seven and eight passed, and all ranks still waited patiently. Finally, word went round that one of the divisions had received orders to move. Was

CHAPTER III

THE BATTLE OF LOOS

September—October, 1915

(*Maps* 2, 3, *and* 4)

BY the beginning of September, 1915, the output of ammunition had been so greatly increased that an artillery bombardment on a large scale became possible, and an offensive by the Allies was planned to be carried out in the West before the arrival of winter.

This offensive, the Battle of Loos, was to consist of two attacks, the main one by the French in Champagne and the second by the combined French and British forces on a front extending from Arras to La Bassée. In addition, small subsidiary attacks were to be made on the Aubers Ridge, on a portion of the line immediately south of Armentières, and in the Ypres salient. The purpose of these latter attacks was mainly to prevent withdrawal of the enemy's troops, but all were ready to advance should any signs of retirement on the enemy's part be detected. The 12th Division, in the Second Army, holding the line east and north of Armentières, was therefore not actively engaged in the operations, although the artillery assisted in the general bombardment and cutting of wire, which, commencing on the 23rd of September, continued throughout the 24th and for several hours on the 25th. On the night of the 24th–25th bundles of damp straw were thrown over the parapets along most of the British front, and at 5.50 a.m. on the 25th these were lighted, and the wind being favourable a most effective smoke screen was formed, preventing the enemy from observing any movements, and mystifying him as to the probability of an attack. On our portion of the front this semblance of an impending offensive was maintained all day, but there was little retaliation, and after dusk parties of men bombed the German trenches with small response. On the 26th inst. the Division was relieved by the 1st Canadian and 50th Divisions, and received orders to proceed to the Lillers-Choques area, preparatory to taking part in the main battle.

News had arrived of successes gained in the opening phase of the Battle of Loos by the men of the New Army (9th and 15th Divisions), and the 12th Division was all enthusiasm and excitement at the prospect of joining in the fight. Some took their departure by train, some by bus, and some by road, but all went singing and in the highest spirits, concentrating on the evening of the 28th in the villages of Busnes, Robecq and Gonnehem; reaching Fouquières, Verquin, La Bourse, and Noeux les Mines by march the following day. On nearing the vicinity of these villages, signs of the battle became evident, and a great cheer greeted the first batch of German prisoners who went by, another cheer going up when captured guns at a gallop splashed our troops with, what they will never fail to remember, French mud.

The attack on this front, from Arras to La Bassée, had been carried out by the Tenth French Army (Foch), and the First British Army (Haig), the latter consisting of the IVth Corps (Rawlinson) on the right,. and the Ist Corps (Gough) on the left. The German position was exceptionally strong and well suited for defence, its main points being, on the south, Hill 70 and the village of Loos with its two tall pylons rising from the pithead of a colliery; on the north, the Quarries, Fosse 8, a large slag heap which dominated the surrounding country, and the Hohenzollern Redoubt, an outwork of the main line on a slight rise of ground giving valuable command.

At 5.50 a.m. on the 25th September gas was discharged, but the wind was not altogether favourable, and some of the gas drifted back causing casualties in our lines, nevertheless our troops succeeded in capturing all the positions enumerated above with the exception of Hill 70. The Germans counter-attacking on the 27th and following days regained the Quarries, Fosse 8, and practically all the Hohenzollern Redoubt. This was virtually the situation when the 12th Division, arriving on the 29th inst., received orders to relieve the Guards Division, on the line east and north-east of Loos. The relief was completed on the night of 30th September–1st October, the 35th Infantry Brigade (Straubenzee) being on the right in touch with the 12th French Division, the 36th Brigade (Borrodaile) on the left and the 37th Brigade (Fowler) in reserve at Vermelles, advanced Divisional Headquarters in Quality Street.

Fortunately, during the first week of October the Germans did not show much activity on our front, as a large amount of work was entailed in consolidating the lines, and in making communication trenches of 2,000 to 3,000 yards through the newly-captured area. The importance of this work was appreciated by the Commander-in-Chief (Sir John French) in his despatches, when he said : " Our troops all along the front were busily engaged in consolidating and strengthening the ground won, and the efficient and thorough manner in which this work was carried out reflects the greatest credit upon all ranks. Every precaution was made to deal with the counter-attack which was inevitable."

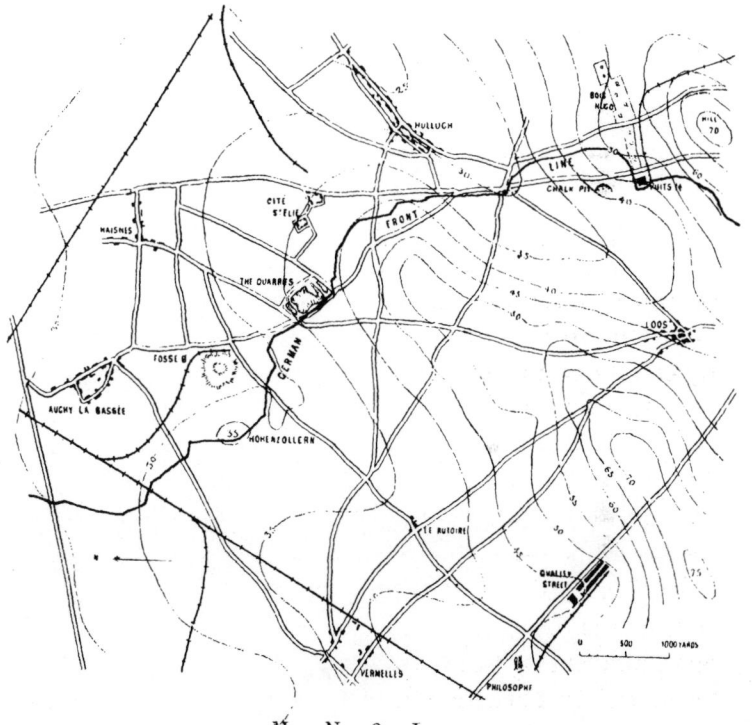

MAP NO. 2. LOOS

Many men were also employed in carrying forward ammunition and water. Artillery fire was incessant, and our field batteries had some difficulty in obtaining suitable positions free from the observation of the Germans. This artillery fire was, unfortunately, the cause of one of the heaviest losses of the Division in this battle. Major-General F. D. V. Wing, C.B., being very anxious about the gun positions, was on his way to inspect them on the afternoon of the 2nd October, when a German shell, falling just in front of him, he and his A.D.C., Lieutenant C. C. Tower, D.S.O., were killed.

General Wing joined the Royal Artillery in 1880, and, serving with distinction throughout the South African campaign of 1899–1902, was promoted Brevet Lieut.-Colonel and awarded the C.B. On the outbreak of the war he was commanding the artillery of the 3rd Division on Salisbury Plain, and accompanying that Division to France, was present throughout the retreat from Mons. Greatly distinguishing himself again, he was promoted Major-General, and eventually appointed to command the 12th (Eastern) Division. His daily round invariably included a visit to the front line trenches, where he had shown such personal interest in the welfare of the men, that he became one of the most familiar, most respected, and best beloved figures in the Division. All ranks mourned the loss of this distinguished officer at such an early stage of the campaign. The Commander-in-Chief, in his despatch of the 1st November, 1915, said, " I have to deplore the loss of a third most valuable and distinguished General of Division during these operations. On the afternoon of the 2nd October Major-General F. D. V. Wing, C.B., commanding the 12th Division, was killed." *

---

* Major-General Wing and Lieutenant Tower were buried in the cemetery at Noeux les Mines on 4th October, 1915.

Major-General A. B. Scott, C.B., D.S.O., who had arrived in France in October, 1914, as General Officer Commanding the Royal Artillery, Meerut Division, subsequently holding the appointments of Brig.-General, Royal Artillery, Indian Corps, and Major-General, Royal Artillery, Third Army, succeeded General Wing, and assumed command of the 12th Division on the 3rd October.

Meanwhile fighting remained desultory, and only small infantry actions were undertaken to improve the line, the 8th Royal Fusiliers securing a better site on the Lens-La Bassée road on the 4th by bombing. The Division was now in the XIth Corps (Haking) with headquarters at Mazingarbe, and on the 5th inst. commenced side-slipping to the left, reaching a position from south of the Vermelles-Hulloch road to opposite the Quarries on the 7th inst. Plans were immediately made for the capture of Gun Trench on the 8th inst.

The possession of Gun Trench, sited on a low crest, gave great advantages in observation of the country either towards Cité St. Elie on the east or towards Vermelles on the west, and that the Germans attached great importance to it was evident both from their determination to regain it on the 26th September, and their subsequent strong opposition to any attempt to capture it. The 6th Royal West Kent Regiment, supported by one company of the 7th East Surrey, one section of the 69th Field Company, Royal Engineers, and two companies of the 5th Northamptonshire, were to carry out the operation at 6.15 p.m., preceded by an artillery preparation. Unfortunately the 8th inst. had also been selected by the Germans for their counter-attack, and early in the afternoon an intense bombardment commenced on our front, extending from the portion held by the left of the French Army to as far north

[*Walter Gardiner*

Major-General F. D. V. Wing, C.B., C.M.G.

THE BATTLE OF LOOS

as Fosse 8. This attained its maximum between 3 and 4 p.m. A considerable number of tear shell being used against the batteries, compelled the wearing of gas masks for two hours, thereby rendering the service of the guns more difficult. In consequence of an air report, a concentration of the enemy in Bois Hugo was nevertheless successfully engaged by the divisional artillery. Probably heavy casualties were inflicted, for great confusion was observed and the break up of the attack was materially assisted.

At 4 p.m. the Germans, advancing in massed formation, were repulsed with tremendous losses, and failed to gain a footing in any portion of the line. They were caught by artillery, machine gun and rifle fire, and it is computed some eight or nine thousand dead were left on the battlefield in front of the French and British trenches. The attack was delivered by twenty-eight battalions in the first line with larger forces in support.

It will be evident that this German bombardment and attack was somewhat upsetting for the operations planned to be carried out by the 37th Brigade against Gun Trench. All communication wires to the front had been cut, but the officer in command of the attack decided to carry out his orders, and at 6.15 p.m. two platoons of the Royal West Kent under Captain Margots, advanced to form a screen for the bombers, led by Captain Carre. Captain Margots was severely wounded a few yards from our parapet, and Lieutenants Heath and Yates were killed, the majority of the leading platoon becoming casualties. The bombers, however, secured a footing in the trench, reaching the gun pits, from which it derived its name. Running out of grenades, and the failure of the reserve bombers to reach them, compelled the party to retire. Private S. Phyall greatly distinguished himself on this occasion by carrying on across the open under heavy fire for over an hour, when the majority of the chain of men supplying the grenades had been killed or wounded, and only gave up when the attack had failed. The 6th Royal West Kent Regiment lost 5 officers and 103 other ranks in killed or wounded in this operation. A message from the Corps Commander stated, "they showed fine military qualities in undertaking the attack after sustaining such a heavy bombardment throughout the day."

At this period of the fighting bombing was a leading feature, the method of supply during an attack requiring very careful organisation in consequence of the large number of grenades used. On the 9th October the Guards on our left had used 9,000 in a few hours.

On the 10th of October orders were received for the continuation of the offensive, and the task of gaining the Quarries and Fosse 8 was allotted to the XIth Corps. The capture of Fosse 8 was very important owing to the commanding position it held over our trenches. It was argued that while this position remained in German hands, winter in the British trenches would be unendurable, an opinion that must have changed subsequently, as not till the end of the war did we get possession of Fosse 8.

The 12th Division objectives were Gun Trench and the Quarries, and those of the 46th Division on the left the Hohenzollern Redoubt and Fosse 8. The 1st Division were co-operating on the Hulloch Road to the right. The assault was to take place at 2 p.m. on the 13th inst., preceded by an artillery preparation of two hours, and the formation of a smoke screen. The latter was to be maintained on a front of 1,200 yards, and formed by Threlfallite grenades and smoke candles. For this purpose 1,000 Threlfallite grenades were issued to the troops holding the trenches, two grenades being thrown into No Man's Land every four minutes, 25 yards apart. The candles were to be grouped together at the same distance and thrown over the parapet every two minutes. As results had been unsuccessful on previous occasions through the failure of the supply of bombs, 2,000 of the latter were issued to each battalion in the front line, and special dumps of 5,000 formed in convenient centres, special parties being detailed to fuse the bombs and "feed" the advancing troops. To ensure communication, cables were buried, visual signallers established at fixed stations, relays of runners arranged for, pigeons issued to each brigade, and the squadron of King Edward's Horse and the Cyclists stood by.

After careful consideration the following equipment was carried by the troops: greatcoat, waterproof sheet, filled waterbottle, gas helmet ready for use, goggles on peak of cap in case of tear shell, sand-bags, 250 rounds of small-arm ammunition, and a proportion of wire cutters, periscopes, and entrenching tools. The divisional artillery was augmented by that of the Guards and 7th Division, and was to commence an intense bombardment at 12 noon, pause for three minutes at 12.57 p.m., reopen with a rapid burst for one minute, and then resume as before until 2 p.m. It was hoped that this three minutes' pause would cause the enemy to man his trenches, expecting an attack, and get caught by the rapid fire. It was also thought when the lift came at 2 p.m. he might suspect another trap, and hesitate to leave his shelters until our assaulting troops were in his trenches. Unfortunately these hopes were not altogether fulfilled.

During the morning of the 13th inst. the advanced Divisional Headquarters moved to Philosophe, and the bombardment to be followed by the attack commencing at noon, the enemy immediately retaliated along our front, and on the main communication trenches, causing heavy damage though not many casualties. In addition, the smoke screen clearing away too quickly did not provide the curtain desired, and as it lifted, the enemy, observing the approaching troops, manned his trenches and stood ready.

The attack on the right was carried out by the 37th Brigade (Fowler), the 7th East Surrey, with the 6th Royal West Kent in support, against Gun Trench, and the 6th Buffs against a trench to the north of it. Two platoons of " B " Company, East Surrey, under Lieutenant Hewat, leading the advance, succeeded in securing Gun Trench, closely supported by two platoons of " A " Company under Captain Tomkins, although the latter suffered severely from machine gun fire from the left. The bombers under Lieutenant Findlay pushing through, blocked the communication trench leading to Cité St. Elie, materially assisted by a party of the 5th Northamptonshire. " C " Company, 7th East Surrey, immediately reinforced the advanced troops, and later on " D " Company, and a company of the 6th Royal West Kent under Captain Dawson, went forward to strengthen the position, the latter company sustaining severe casualties on account of the enfilade fire from the left. Still later Lieutenant Pike led forward a platoon of the 6th Queen's and assisted in maintaining Gun Trench against a counter-attack which eventually developed. Bombing continued for a considerable time, and Sergeant Evans, 7th East Surrey, rendered valuable services by throwing grenades from a sap head until midnight, when he was relieved in an exhausted condition. Nevertheless, after a short rest, he returned to the task, and continued most of the following day. For this heroic conduct he received the French Croix de

Guerre. The attack had been entirely successful, 16 prisoners, 1 machine gun, 3 trench mortars, and a large quantity of ammunition being captured, besides heavy losses inflicted on the enemy. Our casualties were 4 officers and 212 other ranks killed and wounded.

The objective of the 6th Buffs, a trench lying over the crest and out of sight of our line, apparently escaped our artillery fire, the three attacking companies to top the rise being met with a terrific fire from this trench, and also from the south-eastern face of the Quarries, which practically mowed them down, bringing the advance to a standstill. It was a very severe first action for the battalion; 9 officers were killed and one wounded, amongst them being Majors Furley and Soames, D.S.O., Captains Davidson and Brodie, and over 400 other ranks killed and wounded. Though unsuccessful in itself, however, this attack was undoubtedly of assistance to the others. Owing to these heavy losses a company of the 6th Royal West Kent was moved to assist "B" Company in holding the original line.

To the 35th Infantry Brigade (Straubenzee) was allotted the capture of the Quarries, a somewhat unknown quantity, although it had been in British possession for a short period on the 25th and 26th September. In the attack by the 7th Norfolk on the south-western face, the right company failed to gain the enemy's trench owing to heavy fire, but Captain Ottar and about sixty men, entering it further to the left, established themselves there. "A" Company, 5th Royal Berkshire, under Major Bailey, with half a company of the Norfolk, advancing to reinforce the attack and regain touch with Captain Ottar, was unable to reach the position, although Lieutenant Pollard and some men, struggling on a little later, succeeded in crawling under a barricade and joining in the fighting. "B" and "D"

Companies now reinforced the advanced troops, the remainder of the battalion being employed in passing forward grenades, and about three hundred yards of the southern end of the German position was captured. Conspicuous in this fighting was Lieutenant Pollard, who, although wounded at the outset, led his men forward, and continued throwing grenades until, unable to stand, he supported himself against a parapet, and still directing his party, was killed in this position ; also Private L. W. Perris, by his courage and determination, aiding the original advance of the party, and Lance-Corporal Day and Privates Branch and Rumball, who, though wounded, continued to throw bombs.

"D" Company, 7th Suffolk (Captain Henty), and "B" Company (Major Currey), attacked the northern portion of the position. "D" Company, on gaining a footing in the enemy's trench, were held up by a block, which was eventually overcome, and Lieutenant Deighton (Captain Henty and other officers having become casualties) pushed on along the trench to gain touch with the 7th Norfolk on the right. That battalion, however, was held up, and Lieutenant Deighton, having only fifteen men remaining, fell back along the trench to a suitable position where a barricade was made. "B" Company, advancing along the line of the St. Elie Avenue, experienced much opposition, losing their commanding officer amongst others, and were stopped by a barricade. However "A" Company and a party of bombers of the 7th Norfolk arriving in support, carried this obstacle and drove the Germans along the northwestern face of the Quarries.

The day's fighting resulted in the capture of Gun Trench, the south-western face of the Quarries, with the exception of a portion in the centre, and the greater

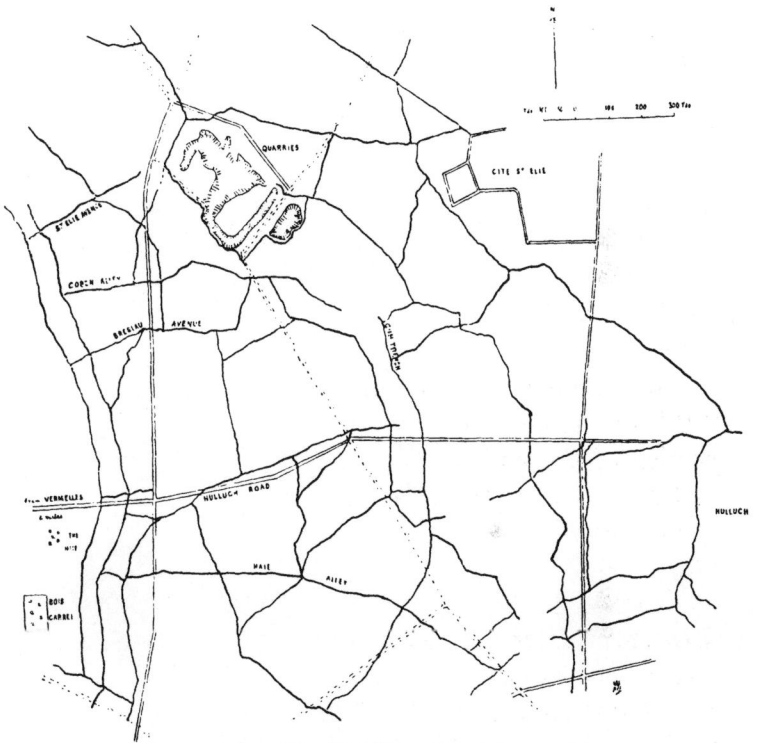

MAP NO. 3. THE QUARRIES

part of the north-western face, to be known later as the Hairpin Trench.

During the night the 9th Royal Fusiliers, of 36th Brigade, took over the captured trenches of the Quarries on the right, and the 9th Essex those on the left.

The following message was received by the General Officer Commanding the Division from the Corps Commander : " Please convey to the officers, N.C.O.'s and men of the 12th Division, my appreciation of their successful attack against Gun Trench on the 13th inst. and also the efforts to gain the Quarries, where they have made an important and successful advance. This advance was carried out by troops who had been for some days in the trenches and reflects great credit on all."

On the 14th October the 36th Infantry Brigade relieved the 37th, and during the three following days only small local bombing actions, without result, took place. It being essential that we should gain the entire trench on the south-western face of the Quarries, an attack by one platoon of " D " Company of the 9th Essex, under Lieutenant Walters, accompanied by bombing squads, was made at 5.30 p.m. on the 18th inst. to effect this purpose. Strong resistance was met, but the enemy was driven back along the trench, and, although all the officers became casualties, the N.C.O.'s carried on and erected a barricade just short of the furthest point aimed at.

At 4.30 p.m. on the 19th inst. Captain Green, 9th Essex, whilst inspecting the newly-captured trench, observed some German officers pointing out various positions in our line, and suspecting an attack, he at once ordered his men to stand to. Three squads of German bombers advancing shortly afterwards from the edge of the Quarries confirmed his suspicions. These were all killed, but as our front had been fairly heavily shelled during the day, and the enemy was reported massing in the Quarries, an attack seemed inevitable. Our artillery, joined by that of the Guards Division, concentrated on the Quarries, and when later on the attack developed, the Essex battalion completely repelled it with heavy loss to the enemy by means of machine-gun and rifle fire. During this action Corporal Butcher performed invaluable service by moving his machine gun to the rear of the trench, from which position he swept the ground in front, inflicting many casualties. At 8 p.m. all was quiet, and during the night the IVth Corps relieved the 36th Brigade, that brigade in turn relieving the 35th.

On the following day some German bombers captured a post held by the 7th Royal Sussex, but they were promptly counter-attacked by the bombers of " D " Company, 11th Middlesex, under Lieutenant Leach, who were in support, and driven out in confusion. For his promptness, bravery, and initiative, Lieutenant Leach was awarded the Military Cross, and Lance-Corporal Smart, Privates Brown and Davies the Distinguished Conduct Medal.

The 21st was a peaceful day, and by 9 p.m. the 36th Brigade had been relieved by the 15th Division. The Division was now wholly withdrawn from the line, and billeted in the vicinity of Fouquières lez Bethune, where headquarters were established.

The 12th Division had thus passed through its first important engagement, gaining great experience from the twenty-one days on the battle front. It had been successful in attack and in defence, had withstood heavy casualties, 117 officers and 3,237 other ranks having been killed or wounded, and given proofs of heroism in action. With increased training and experience, its future as a fighting unit seemed assured.

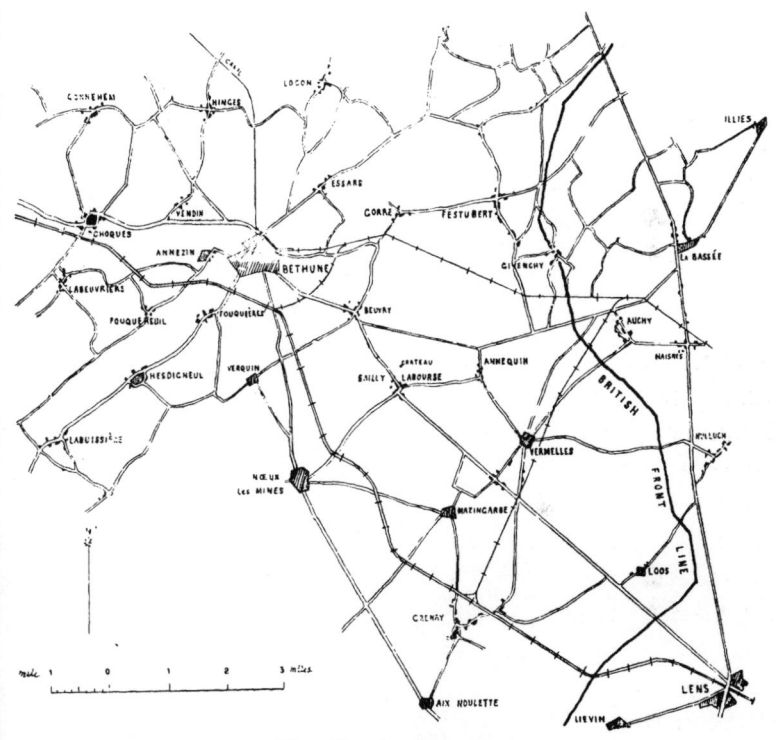

MAP NO. 4. BETHUNE

Before closing this account, reference must be made to the invaluable services rendered by the artillery, in which the infantry already placed supreme confidence; by the Field Companies and Signalling Company of the Royal Engineers, and the 5th Northamptonshire Regiment, who shared with the above the duties of consolidating newly won ground and other trench work; also by the officers, stretcher bearers and all ranks working with the Royal Medical Corps, who received a great tribute of praise from the fighting units. Nor can the work of the Divisional Ammunition Column and Royal Army Service Corps, who under adverse circumstances never failed to get up supplies from Philosophe to Loos, ever be overlooked or forgotten by any who passed along that shell-stricken road. Littered with broken-up waggons, dead bodies of men, and horses recently killed, lying side by side with those who fell in the original attack on the 25th of September, it was scattered everywhere with all the refuse and horror of war. It took days to clear the battlefield of these sights, bearing such tragic witness to the bravery and devotion of all units. Credit must also be given to the ceaseless work of those whose duty it was to direct operations.

CHAPTER IV

FIRST WINTER IN FRANCE
November, 1915—January, 1916
(*Maps 2 and 4*)

HAVING spent five days in the reserve area, during which time the battalions reorganised, refitted, and received reinforcements, the Division moved forward, and on 26th October took over from the Guards Division the line facing the Hohenzollern Redoubt; headquarters being at Sailly La Bourse.

The trench system was in a very bad state. The ground was low lying and much knocked about by the heavy fighting that had occurred there; the few dug-outs were waterlogged; there were no shelters; there was about a foot of water in the trenches which were not boarded; the communications were long, and the churned up clay made progress slow and exhausting. Though at night the troops moved over the top, during the day that was impossible as every movement was observed from Fosse 8. To add to all this, there was heavy rain. Practically the men had to remain on the fire step day and night. Fortunately there was little infantry activity, as undoubtedly both sides were trying to improve conditions for the winter. But we were on fresh ground, and the Germans on what they had held for over a year.

Work was therefore concentrated on improvements, and large parties laboured incessantly to that end. Early in November long rubber boots were issued, and these helped to better conditions, but often they would be pulled off by the sticky mud. Artillery fire was systematic.

On 30th October the Russian, Italian, and Japanese attachés visited Divisional and Brigade Headquarters.

On 1st November the Division passed to the Ist Corps (Gough). A problematical attack was being rehearsed, but the weather and state of ground eventually disposed of it. The Germans now caused annoyance by a new weapon, the aerial torpedo, with which they blew in trenches and interfered with working parties.

It was the first winter for the Division, and a large number of men suffered from exhaustion, bronchitis, pneumonia, and "trench feet." To counter these, stores for dry socks and clothing, soup kitchens, and hot baths were installed. A canteen was opened at Sailly la Bourse by Lieut.-Colonel Collen, A.A.Q.M.G., on 10th November, as well as much appreciated coffee-stalls closer to the front.

The Divisional School, with Lieut.-Colonel G. A. Trent, 5th Northamptonshire Regiment as Commandant, was opened by Major-General Scott on 22nd November at Fouquières.

The Division was relieved on the 24th November by the 15th Division. By now a great improvement had taken place in the trenches, the front line, and a greater portion of the communication trenches having been boarded.

The Division moved to the reserve area near Lillers, Divisional Headquarters at Ham, 35th Brigade Bosenghem, 36th Brigade St. Hilaire, 37th Brigade Ecquedecques. It was a welcome relief, as the troops had been in the line since the 30th September with the exception of five days.

Brig.-General A. Solly Flood, 4th Dragoon Guards, now commanded the 35th Infantry Brigade, *vice* Straubenzee, who had been invalided, and Brig.-General L. B. Boyd-Moss, the 36th Infantry Brigade, *vice* Borrodaile.

Such a period as now ensued has, for some strange reason, been called " rest." It is about the last word that describes it. The merry gibes of the Divisional Concert Party faithfully portrayed the general opinion of the man in the line, and any humorous reference to the state called " rest " invariably " brought down the house." If a fond mother in the Old Country imagined her boy spending his time sleeping and resting in the generally accepted term, she was very far wrong. " Rest " commenced with inspections of kit, rifles, billets, and of all and everything belonging to the make-up of a soldier; it followed with parades, drills, and route marches; it included constant practice on the rifle range, and last, but not least, the provision of fatigues, guards, and, not infrequently, working parties for a division in the line. Yet it had its lighter side in football tournaments and boxing contests, and the Divisional Concert Party kept us merry at night with songs that reminded us that we " had only signed on for three years." This jest somehow or other fell off in popular appreciation towards 1917–18. But there is no doubt that if the peculiar description " rest " invariably caused fun, these periods of training, exercise, and recreation did fit men for the days ahead, and were thoroughly enjoyed, though sometimes groused at.

On the 7th December the 9th Royal Fusiliers went for special duty to Bethune, where a raid for spies was about to take place. At an appointed time men suddenly sprang up with fixed bayonets at every street crossing, and no one in the street was allowed to leave. Other parties under selected officers searched the houses. The search was thorough, and though there were no results in the section allotted to the 9th R.F., some success was achieved in other parts of the town.

On the 10th December the Division moved up and relieved the 33rd Division on the Givenchy sector, headquarters at Bethune. If the last front was bad, this one beggared description. In the Festubert section, the country, principally water meadows, was intensely wet and water-logged, the rain had filled the trenches, and pumping had not overcome this trouble. Along a large portion of the front line the parapet appeared in the form of islands above the water. These islands became small defended posts, holding from five to ten men, and were called keeps. They could not be approached during daylight, and life was so intolerable on them, that reliefs took place every twenty-four hours under cover of darkness. On the other hand, they were immune from attack except by artillery, and to that they offered a very small mark. Each keep was provided with bombs and ammunition, and the N.C.O. had two Verey light pistols at his disposal. The actual islands were dry, though in many places the sentries stood in the water with their waders on. In other portions of the line the trenches were more or less normal, but inclined to be very wet.

Drying-rooms and soup kitchens were installed close to the front, and from 1,200 to 1,500 bowls of soup a day from each would be issued to the men in the front system of trenches.

At this time a divisional cinema was started, and the Divisional Institute, managed by the Rev. P. Middleton Brumwell, extended its sphere of action.

Infantry activity was at a discount, even raids and night patrols being almost impossible. However, the enemy made a small raid on one of our saps on the 15th December. It failed to inflict any damage, but was chiefly memorable for the endurance of a N.C.O. of the 7th Norfolk, who continued bombing for eight consecutive hours in his determination to keep the enemy from entering the sap. Mines were the chief source of enemy activity. On 21st December one was exploded north of Givenchy, but the crater was too far away for occupation by us. At 7.15 a.m. on 23rd a mine was exploded about fifty yards south-east of Rifleman's Crater, and caused 25 casualties in our ranks. The next day the Germans made two bombing attacks on the same front, but were driven back by rifle and machine gun fire. As a parting present of the old year, they exploded another mine on the 29th at 7.5 a.m., and attempted to occupy their own side of the crater, but were driven back by rifle grenade and machine gun fire. This mine blew in the end of our sap and buried some of the 7th Royal Sussex, who, however, managed to extricate themselves, and under Lance-Corporal J. Austin prevented the enemy from gaining any advantage from the explosion. During this attack the Germans bombarded our line with an instrument of war, new to us at that time, but since rendered familiar, a mechanical thrower, or catapult.

On the 30th December, it is interesting to record, 2 officers and 25 men of the Royal Navy were attached to the Division. After a night in the trenches, however, they considered gunnery more in their line and went to the batteries.

At Christmas time Captain Bayard, A.S.C., and his troupe, successfully produced "Aladdin" in the Bethune Theatre.

Beyond artillery and trench mortar fire, the early part of January was quiet. The Germans blew a negligible mine on the 13th. The 35th Infantry Brigade carried out two useful rifle grenade and trench mortar attacks on 14th and 16th, which had a very quietening influence on the enemy.

It must not be supposed, however, that during this period of infantry inaction the only losses suffered by the Division were due to sickness. Fire from artillery and trench weapons very rarely ceased, and day after day some part of the front received its turn of bombardment, and casualties occurred. The casualties from 12th December to 18th January may therefore prove useful to any one studying this aspect of the war.

	Killed.	Wounded.	Missing.
Officers	5	17	—
Other ranks	97	647	6
Total	102	664	6

On the night of 18th–19th January the Division was relieved by the 2nd Division and marched to the reserve area near Busnes.

On 20th General Joffre, accompanied by General Sir Douglas Haig, inspected the 36th Infantry Brigade and details from divisional units near Lillers.

All ranks were thankful to get a short respite from the trying winter conditions through which they had just passed. When it is remembered that these men of the New Army were accustomed to the comforts of home life, and many of them habituated to office routine, it is surprising how well they withstood the extreme hardships they had to undergo. But severe as these had been they were soon to be exceeded by conditions calling for even greater endurance, for some of the stiffest, fiercest, and bloodiest fighting of the campaign, and about which the British public knew little or nothing, was ahead of them, and has now to be recorded.

CHAPTER V

THE BATTLE OF THE CRATERS

February—April, 1916

(*Maps* 2, 5, *and* 6)

DURING the period in the reserve area the troops had been trained in open warfare, and two days were spent by the Division on manœuvres, the Corps Commander (Gough) directing a Staff exercise.

The football tournament, causing a great deal of excitement, had been won by the 9th Royal Fusiliers.

Changes which had taken place in the higher ranks were:—Brig.-General E. H. Willis, *vice* McLeod as C.R.A.; Brig.-General A. B. E. Cator, Scots Guards, *vice* Fowler, in command of the 37th Infantry Brigade; Lieut.-Colonel Silver, *vice* Wilson as Assistant Director Medical Services.

But this period of relaxation, thoroughly enjoyed by the Division, eventually had to end, the 36th Brigade being the first to go into the line, near the Quarries, on the night of the 12th–13th of February. The troops of this brigade had scarcely settled into their positions when at 5.20 p.m. on the latter date, after heavy shelling for an hour, and the explosion of three mines, the Germans attacked with bombs. The 11th Middlesex, who were holding the line, suffered 80 casualties from the shelling and mines, but successfully drove back the enemy. At one point Sergeant Moorhouse, almost single-handed, held up the attack by bombing until our counter-attack developed. Lance-Corporal H. T. Boyden, in charge of a Lewis gun, was buried three times by shell fire, and though slightly wounded, carried on. The 11th Middlesex Regiment (Ingle) were congratulated by the First Army Commander (Monro) for steadiness in the bombardment, and promptness in counter-attack.

By the 15th inst. the Division, with headquarters at Sailly la Bourse, had relieved the Dismounted Cavalry Division, and held the line from the Quarries to north of the Hohenzollern Redoubt, about 3,500 yards, and practically the same front that had been handed over in November, but the conditions were vastly improved, and the Division was to benefit from the hard work it had expended at that time.

Now followed a trying period of mine fighting. Mining had become a science requiring careful organisation, much forethought, great caution, and heroic action. The Germans were calculated to have had a six weeks' start of us, and it will be understood what that meant when a short description of the normal methods is given. The main objects being to blow up the enemy and his trenches, or to counter-mine against his underground attack, the question was, how to get there and do it without his knowledge or interference. Firstly, a shaft was made inside our trench system so as to be well protected. The excavated soil, in this case chalk and easily seen, had to be removed and placed where it could not be observed by the enemy or discovered from air photographs. Taken away in sandbags, a comparatively small amount being used for building up parapets, the bulk was carried back through the trenches. This meant large fatigue parties. The shaft having reached the requisite depth, the main gallery was driven forward and branch ones made in necessary directions. When nearing the enemy, great care had to be taken in excavating the soil, so that the noise of the mining was not heard by a listener. Most accurate plans of the work were kept, and these, with the probable galleries of the enemy, gathered from mines already blown, and from listeners' reports, formed an absorbing study. On discovering the near approach of the enemy to our system, a small mine or *camouflet* would be blown to damage his gallery. This would not show on the surface. It was then for the expert to settle how our advance was to proceed. Having reached the desired position, a chamber was formed, and charged with explosive, which was eventually fired. The strain on those carrying on this underground work was incalculable. The near approach of an enemy's gallery, the breaking in on an enemy's gallery, the listening in the galleries, and the moment of waiting to know that the mine was successful, were all calculated to try the endurance of the strongest, while it can be realised how nerve-wracking it was for troops in the front trenches to have to contemplate the possibility of a mine being exploded under them at any moment. There is something uncanny about being mined, and this method of warfare is particularly repellent to human nature.

The uncertain location of the German system of mines made it advisable to hold the front line by posts, so as to minimise the loss to *personnel* when mines were blown. By his operations in the vicinity of the Hohenzollern the enemy had formed four large craters in No Man's Land marked Nos. 1 to 4. The near lips of these craters were held by the opposing forces. Active mining was also in progress at the Quarries, and south of Fosse 8. Both we, and the enemy, frequently exploded mines which normally entailed a struggle, sapping out to the crater, and occupation of the near lip. But our mining operations were rapidly overhauling those of the Germans, and a scheme was in preparation to destroy their system and give us the lead underground. It was for the purpose of this operation that the 12th Division had gone into the line.

Four mines were prepared in the Hohenzollern sector. These were to be exploded simultaneously, and it was hoped that we should be able to gain the German front trench, the Chord, and hold the entire craters so as to obtain command of the enemy's trenches, and counteract the advantage he had in observation from Fosse 8. The destruction of the main galleries of the enemy's mining system was also contemplated. It will be interesting to note the size of the three principal mine charges, at this period of the war the largest the British had used. "A" contained 7,000 lbs. of ammonal, "B" 3,000 lbs. of blastine and 4,000 lbs. of ammonal, and "C" 10,550 lbs. of explosive. By the end of February these mines were ready and apparently unknown to the enemy. The 36th Infantry Brigade (Boyd-Moss) had been ordered to carry out the attack, and the plans and details of organisation were most carefully worked out. Large dumps of grenades were formed well forward, men were detailed for various duties and conveniently located in the trenches, while special arrangements were made for supplying hot soup to the men after capturing the position.

On the night of the 29th of February the 37th Brigade, which had done a large amount of the preparatory work, was relieved by the 36th Brigade, to enable the latter to make its final preparations for the attack. This was to be carried out by the Royal Fusiliers, the 9th Battalion (Gubbins) on the right, and the 8th (Annesley) on the left.

Before the operation the Officer Commanding the **170th Tunnelling Company, Royal Engineers (Daniels)** made a forecast of the probable result of the explosions. This was reproduced and issued to the troops taking part, greatly assisting them to realise beforehand what the alteration in terrain would be. The forecast of the new craters was practically correct: "A" crater was 100 feet in diameter and 35 feet deep, " C " crater 130 feet across and 35 feet in depth, and " B " similar to " A." The fourth mine, which was smaller than the others and under the side of No. 2, enlarged the existing crater and slightly altered its position.

The Divisional Artillery, with the 59th and 81st Siege Batteries attached, and one section of 9·2″, two sections of 8″ howitzers, and two sections of 60-pounders of the Ist Corps Artillery co-operated. Although there was no artillery preparation, ten trench mortars opened fire at 5.10 p.m. on No. 1 crater and the Chord, and on commencement of the attack formed a smoke screen.

The garrisons had been withdrawn from the craters before the operation, and on the explosions of the mines at 5.45 p.m. on the 2nd of March, the attacking troops left their positions of assembly. There had been much snow, sleet and rain during the previous week, and the ground was heavy, and the men sank over their ankles in the loose soil thrown up by the mines. " C " Company, 9th Royal Fusiliers, under Major Elliott Cooper, rushed craters 1, 2, and " A," also Triangle Crater, which was uncharted on our maps. Sergeant Cromyn and his party, who were to block Big Willie, dashed down the south-east face of the crater, into that trench and killed several of the enemy, bombing the dug-outs said to be full of Germans. This party, after a fierce grenade fight against reinforcements, was driven back to Triangle Crater. Captain the Hon. R. Phillips with fifty men of " B " Company, assembled in west face. Unfortunately the *débris* from " A " crater buried

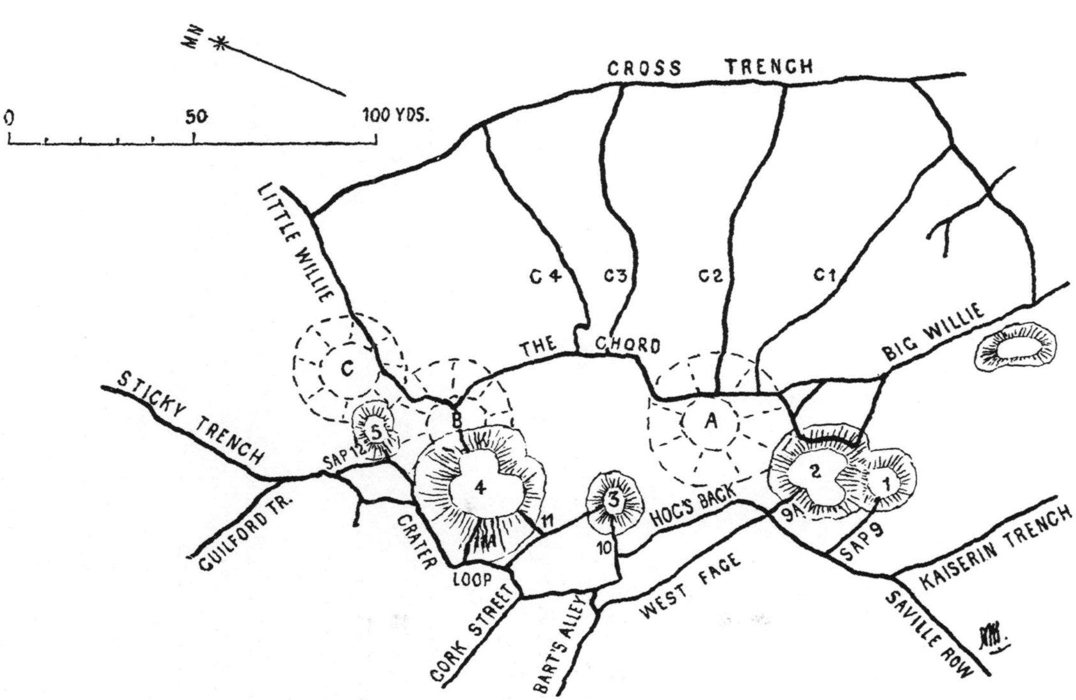

MAP No. 5. HOHENZOLLERN CRATERS—FORECAST

twenty of this party, who were eventually extricated. With the remainder, however, he gained the Chord from crater " A " to near trench C4, where heavy bombing attacks were withstood. Captain Phillips, originally wounded in the face by the *débris* from crater " A," was now wounded in the chest, and forced to give up his command to Lieutenant Beck.

On the left the 8th Battalion gained No. 4 crater in its altered condition, and " B " and " C " craters, but of the party told off to capture the Chord from crater " B " to " C4," only one officer (Lieutenant Wardrop) and one man appeared to have survived to reach their objective. They were joined on the way by Captain Mason and twenty men from the supports, but as the Chord was practically obliterated near the newly-formed crater, and heavy shelling and bombing ensued, this party was compelled to withdraw to the crater line, where, Major Cope arriving with twenty other men, the position was held. Major Cope, though wounded, remained to direct the consolidation, which was carried out by Company Sergt.-Major M. Sharp in No. 4, Lieutenant Upward in " B," and Captain R. A. F. Chard in " C " craters respectively. During the night the Germans indulged in constant bombing attacks, but these were driven off, and the consolidation made satisfactory progress, considering the difficulties of communication due to the sticky state of the ground.

At 9.37 a.m. on the 3rd of March the General Officer Commanding the 36th Infantry Brigade reported : " The general situation very satisfactory. We hold all the craters and great progress has been made in the work on consolidation. We also occupy an uncharted crater south-east of No. 2 (Triangle Crater), the main shaft of enemy mining system is situated in this crater. We hold a portion of the Chord. Greater portion originally held by us has been destroyed by artillery fire. Very heavy bombing took place between 6 and 8 a.m. this morning. Casualties rather heavy, most of which occurred after position captured."

The 8th Royal Fusiliers lost: officers, 2 killed, 5 wounded; other ranks 247 killed and wounded. The 9th Battalion lost 1 officer and 14 other ranks killed, 4 officers and 141 other ranks wounded.

The possession of these craters gave us excellent observation of the German lines as far as Fosse 8, and this was evidently recognised by the enemy from his oft-repeated attempts to drive us back. The possession of Triangle Crater, and one of his main mining shafts, likewise led him to make very determined attacks in that direction.

Before passing from the fighting of the 2nd of March, the gallantry shown by the Royal Army Medical Corps and the stretcher bearers must not be forgotten. The craters became full of wounded men, who, from the loose nature of the soil, slid down the sides to the bottom. These craters were naturally " cockshies " for the German artillery and trench mortars, and became veritable death-traps. Removal of the wounded was a difficult matter, and it was mainly owing to the indefatigable efforts of Captain J. H. Fletcher, and the stretcher bearer parties under his command, that they were successfully got away. Private S. McKenna, responding to the call for volunteers, carried a man on his back out of crater " A," but on his way to No. 2 crater came under such heavy bombing that he had to lie down for over an hour before he could proceed. He then got his man safely to Northampton Trench, a distance of about 400 yards, assisted by Private S. A. Smith. On the completion of this McKenna immediately volunteered to return to " A " crater and brought

Royal Air Force official] [Crown copyright reserved

HOHENZOLLERN CRATERS

back a second man. Sergeant Langley, of the 38th Field Ambulance, hauled up wounded men from the bottom of the craters by means of stretcher slings, and carried them across the open to safety. These are but a few of the instances of what was done on this occasion to rescue the wounded under dangerous conditions.

On the 3rd of March the 11th Middlesex Regiment and the 7th Royal Sussex relieved the 9th and 8th Royal Fusiliers respectively, German activity becoming general immediately afterwards, with an intense artillery bombardment on the craters. On the 4th inst., at 6 a.m., an attempt by the enemy to debouch from the Chord and Little Willie was driven off, as also were two more attempts at 7 and 9 p.m. At 4.15 p.m. a heavy bombardment commenced on the right craters, and after three attempts the Germans regained possession of Triangle Crater. During these two days' fighting, conducted under terrible conditions of snow, rain, and intense cold, the 36th Infantry Brigade had suffered 905 casualties.

The 37th Brigade (Cator) relieved the 36th on the 5th inst., the 6th Buffs and the 7th East Surrey taking the places of the 11th Middlesex and 7th Royal Sussex. Bombing attacks by the enemy continued throughout the day, and definite attacks were made on "C" crater at 8 p.m., 9.22 p.m., and 10.35 p.m. These were all repulsed, the divisional artillery rendering material assistance.

The German possession of the Triangle Crater, with their main shaft so close to our new positions, made the holding of these somewhat precarious owing to the likelihood of mines being exploded. After the large explosions on the 2nd of March, time was required to clear our galleries and push forward. It was therefore decided to regain Triangle Crater and a portion of the

Chord, and to block Big Willie, and "C1" and "C2." The attack was entrusted to the 6th Buffs, and consisted of three parties; the first to proceed from No. 2 crater, attack the south face of Triangle Crater, and secure the east lip, and block Big Willie; the second to proceed from the same crater, attack the north face of Triangle Crater and seize the Chord; the third to start from crater "A," gain the Chord and block "C1" and "C2."

The attack was delivered at 6 p.m. on the 6th of March by "C" Company. Number 1 party advanced along the south edge of Triangle Crater, but it was hampered by the terribly sticky condition of the ground, in many places the men sinking up to their knees, and whilst floundering through this mud and slush being caught by enemy's bombs and machine gun fire. The Germans, counter-attacking at once, compelled this party to retire on No. 2 crater. The fight became very confused and disorganised, and Corporal Cotter, who was in charge of the party, was severely wounded, his right leg being blown off just below the knee; he was also wounded in both arms. Regardless of these injuries, he took up a position on the side of the crater, issued orders and controlled the fire. He remained in this position for two hours, and not until the attack had been repulsed and matters had quieted down did he allow his wounds to be roughly dressed. It was impossible to evacuate him till fourteen hours later. There is no doubt that the fine example he showed, his endurance under great suffering, his coolness under heavy fire, and his keen sense of responsibility, helped materially to save what might have developed into a critical situation. For this brave act Corporal Cotter was awarded the Victoria Cross. Unfortunately he died before the award was published, though he had been informed of the recommendation.

THE BATTLE OF THE CRATERS

Parties numbered 2 and 3 had joined up in the Chord, but coming to the end of their grenades, were compelled to retire. Meanwhile No. 1 crater had been heavily attacked and most of the garrison were casualties. Lieutenant Lea Smith and Private Bradley, rushing from No. 2 with a Lewis gun, held up the Germans until reinforcements arrived. At 6.55 p.m. the Officer Commanding the Buffs reported the failure of the attack and the fact that the old positions were only being maintained with great difficulty. A company of the 6th Royal West Kent was sent up, and, with the assistance of the Divisional Artillery, the counter-attack came to a standstill. The casualties in this Infantry Brigade for the 6th and 7th March amounted to 331.

On the 7th of March the 170th Tunnelling Company, working from No. 2 crater, broke into the German mining system leading from Triangle Crater. The galleries were unoccupied but had been cleared by the enemy. The tension was now relieved, and the possession of Triangle Crater became less important, as we were masters underground. This system of galleries was destroyed by us on the 12th March.

Attacks on the craters were made repeatedly for several days, and all were repulsed, although about this time our artillery ammunition had been curtailed. On the 15th inst. a new trench weapon, the *minenwerfer*, was used by the Germans. The fire therefrom was accurate and effective in destroying defences, and the explosions of its projectiles in the craters were somewhat demoralising.

With reference to the fighting on the 2nd of March and succeeding days, the following communications were received : " The General Officer Commanding the Ist Corps (Gough) wishes to place on record his great appreciation of the way in which the whole operation was conducted. The points deserving particular credit are :

" 1. The very thorough and careful preparations previously made by your Divisional Staff, 36th Infantry Brigade Staff, Commanding Royal Engineer, and 170th Tunnelling Company, Royal Engineers.

" 2. The dash and great gallantry displayed by the attacking troops and their leaders, both officers and non-commissioned officers.

" 3. The devotion, hard work, steadfast resolution and cheerfulness under miserable conditions displayed by all ranks of the battalions and Royal Engineers who consolidated the position and held it against so many counter-attacks and bombardments, and the excellent support which the artillery gave them in repelling these counter-attacks and minimising hostile artillery fire.

" Courage and resolution was shown in plenty and to a very high degree by our young officers and non-commissioned officers in the operation, and the General Officer Commanding would like all ranks to be informed of the value of their services.

" The work of the Royal Engineers, both Field Companies and Tunnelling Companies, also deserves very high praise."

In publishing the above remarks of the Corps Commander, the Divisional Commander (Scott) " expressed his gratitude to all ranks for the good work displayed in the arduous and difficult fighting, in the exhausting task of consolidating the ground won, in the maintenance of communications, and in the supply of ammunition, grenades, and stores of all kinds for the fighting troops.

" In these duties practically all the units of the Division have been employed, and the work has been carried out with a determination and a cheerfulness which have never failed."

Hohenzollern Craters. I

Hohenzollern Craters. II

"The Army Commander (Monro) will be glad if you will convey to Brig.-Generals Boyd-Moss and Cator, and the troops who have been engaged in the recent operations at the Hohenzollern Redoubt, his appreciation of the determined and gallant spirit in which they have held to the craters under exceptionally arduous conditions."

The Commander-in-Chief (Sir Douglas Haig) "considers that the recent operations at the Hohenzollern Redoubt were well arranged and conducted. He agrees in the opinion of the Army Commander that though the losses were heavy the results gained justify the undertaking."

On the 18th of March, at 5 p.m., the Germans opened a violent bombardment on the craters, blew some mines and attacked. Vermelles was heavily shelled, and in two hours some 2,000 shells fell in it and in its vicinity. One, unfortunately, hit the divisional canteen, and biscuits, chocolate, cake and cigarettes went sky high. A barrage was placed on our communications as far back as Annequin and Noyelles, a large number of lachrymose shell being used. The *minenwerfers* did much damage to the craters and front line defences. All communication wires were cut, and initiative passed to the lower commanders and frequently to non-commisioned officers.

On the right of the line, held by the 6th Buffs, the garrisons of Nos. 1 and 2 and "A" craters were all killed or buried, and confusion rendered worse by the fact that West Face and the top end of Saville Row, Saps 9 and 9a, had been filled in by the *débris* from the explosions. The Germans seized the craters, and our counter-attack was delayed until these saps were cleared. Eventually three companies of the 6th Royal West Kent delivered a counter-attack and regained the near lips of these craters. The 7th East Surrey were holding the left of the line, and here " C " crater was blown up, and the Germans rushed " B " and No. 4, and for some time held Sap 12 and Russian Sap, penetrating to Sticky Trench. Company-Sergt.-Major Palmer and three others appear to have been all that were left of the garrison of " C " crater after the explosion. They continued bombing and firing until driven back to " B," and thence to No. 4, and finally out of that. A very gallant counter-attack by a party of the 7th East Surrey, led by Captain Scott, bombed the enemy out of No. 4, and established posts overlooking " B," somewhat restoring the position in this sector. Meanwhile blocks had been established in Sap 12 and Russian Sap, and by 9.25 p.m. these positions had been consolidated. No. 3 crater had been held throughout the attack. At 3.15 a.m. on the 19th inst. some of the 6th Queen's, under Captain Cannon, regained the near lips of " B " and " C " craters, but had to withdraw from the latter at daylight. The position therefore on the morning of the 19th was that we held all Nos. 3 and 4, and the near lips of 1, 2, " A " and " B " craters. By 10.30 p.m. on that day we had gained the near lip of " C," and the Northamptonshire Regiment had joined it up with Russian Sap.

Our main trouble on the 18th inst. was caused by the explosion of two mines, which was an actual surprise, and of which we had no suspicion. These had been driven through the clay on the top of the chalk, and so our listeners had failed to hear the Germans working. The final position of this big counter-attack resolved itself into each side holding the lips of the craters nearest them. Our casualties had been heavy, and there is every reason to think that the Germans had suffered even more. When it became evident that neither side

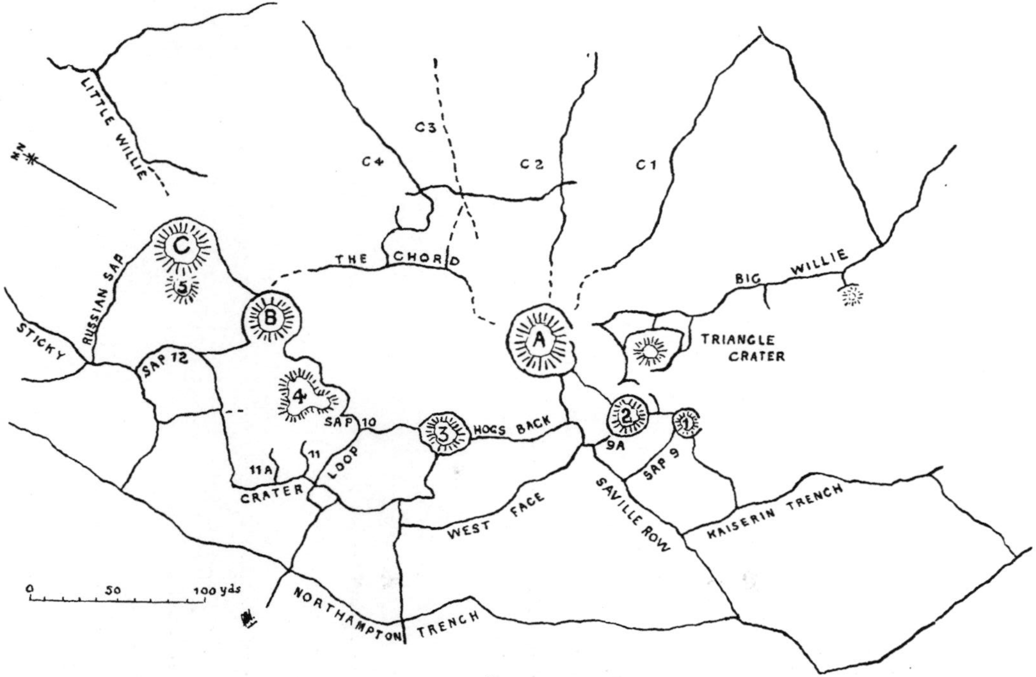

MAP No. 6. HOHENZOLLERN CRATERS

was going to continue aggression, this portion of the line quieted down, but the close proximity of the bombing posts made it an unpleasant locality. Experience in this fighting taught that the best method of holding a crater was either by an entrenched line in advance of it or by occupying the near lip.

On the 19th March the 35th Infantry Brigade (Solly Flood) relieved the 37th, and the severe crater fighting ended. All that England ever knew of this fierce and heavy fighting was a couple of lines in the summary, " we sprung three mines under the German front in the Loos sector, and occupied the craters." Yet in that brief period, March 2nd–19th, the 12th Division suffered over 3,000 casualties. But the work achieved was recognised by the higher command and in the Commander-in-Chief's despatch of 19th May, 1916, of the ninety-six units specially mentioned, nine belonged to the 12th Division.

After the attack on the 18th inst. quiet reigned for a few days, but the Germans started activity again on the 24th by blowing two mines in the Quarries sector, in answer to one we blew on the 19th. Mining operations were rigorously continued, and mines were exploded by us on 26th, 27th March, 5th, 13th, 20th, 21st, and 22nd April, and by the enemy on 31st March, 2nd, 8th, 11th, 12th and 23rd April. Though no action on a big scale ensued, these explosions entailed fighting and consolidation, leading to casualties. The greater portion of this front was a continuous line of craters. No one knew when or where the next would make its appearance, and each devoutly hoped that it would come on some one else's front. But relief was not far off, and the troops were well due for a rest, the Division having been in the trenches since the 12th of February. Any rumour of relief was warmly welcomed. Army Service Corps drivers were cross-examined, French interpreters in the inspection of billets were treated as birds of good omen, even Staff officers of other divisions doing a tour of the front line were regarded with pleasure. All these portents were seen, noted and approved, and finally the Division was relieved on the 26th of April, having suffered casualties amounting to 4,025 in this period of crater warfare.

During this fighting the work of the Tunnelling Companies of the Royal Engineers gained the unstinted admiration of all ranks, their ceaseless toil underground, their tedious hours spent in listening galleries, their initiative in combating the enemy's mining and the constant danger to which they were exposed therefrom, their success in blowing mines, secured for us that ascendency in mine fighting which commenced in the attack on the 2nd of March and remained with us for the remainder of the war.

Occasionally there was a lighter side to this terrible underground work. Canaries were taken down the mine galleries to detect the presence of gas, and twice a particular bird gave the necessary warning by dropping off his perch. Having recovered on both these occasions, he evidently considered he had done his " bit " as on the next and future visits he habitually fell off his perch immediately he entered the galleries, although there was no suspicion of gas. Consequently he had to be relieved of further duty, and took his place as the Commanding Officer's pet.

CHAPTER VI

BATTLE OF THE SOMME—I. OVILLERS
May, 1916—July 9th, 1916
(*Maps* 19 *and* 7)

THE troops got out of the Hohenzollern line just in time to avoid an unpleasant day. Divisional Headquarters were not due to leave until early on the 27th of April, but the three infantry brigades were already well on their way to the rest area, when at 5 a.m. on that morning the Germans opened an intense bombardment on the Ist Corps front. The 15th Division, which had relieved us, had a very severe handling, and the 16th (Irish) Division on the right an experience it is not likely to forget. The rear areas likewise came in for the bombardment. Artillery positions were searched with lachrymose shell, and a gas attack followed. Wind and temperature conditions were in favour of the enemy, and the gas clouds reached Divisional Headquarters at Sailly la Bourse, the use of P.H. helmets being necessitated as far back as Bethune. The enemy succeeded in penetrating our line on the right and for some time it appeared as if the 12th Division would be recalled, but a gallant counter-attack restored the position, and by 10 a.m. the Divisional Headquarters was able to move back to near Lillers and opened at Philomel.

A few days were occupied in overhauling kits and drafting in reinforcements, after which the first week in May was spent in battalion training. Afternoons and evenings were free for recreation, and battalion, brigade, and divisional sports were arranged; football leagues inaugurated, boxing tournaments started, and concerts, thoroughly well organised and most efficiently staged, helped to keep alive the interest of the men and provide them with healthy amusement. Who in the Division will ever forget the divisional boxing tournament at Lapugny, when the first prize was " ten days' leave." There never was a tournament like it before or since. Every win was a " knock-out," and the memory of it remains as one of the most vigorous, if not the most scientific, contest of any tournament. During this time the divisional band improved to such an extent as to be competent to play in the Market Square of Lillers.

On the 8th of May instruction became more strenuous, and the 35th and 37th Infantry Brigades moved still further back to the First Army training area, the 36th Brigade remaining as a reserve to the front line. On the 10th inst. the Divisional Artillery moved to this area also, and then commenced that intimate work between artillery and infantry which led to such efficient co-operation in later days. The poor " maids of all work," the Royal Engineers, and the 5th Northamptonshire Regiment (Pioneers) returned to duty under the Ist Corps on the reserve lines. On the 22nd the 36th Brigade moved back, having been relieved by the 35th. Training in open warfare proceeded steadily, though on the 27th May, information from a German prisoner leading to the belief that an attack on the Loos salient was imminent, the whole Division moved nearer to the front. However, no attack developed, and the Division continued its instruction in the neighbourhood of its billets. But the best of good things come to an end, and the most ideal of rests seem short when orders arrive to return to the line. It was the longest period of rest and the most pleasant the Division ever experienced. The French civilians did their best to make every one comfortable, and it is fitting to record the kindness and tolerance shown to the troops, who must have seriously incommoded the French households. The rest and recreation and strenuous training had all tended to make the Division as fit a fighting force as it was at any time in its history.

On the 12th of June one field company, Royal Engineers, moved south to the IIIrd Corps near Albert, for already the Somme battlefield was casting its shadow before. Two more were to follow, and the General Officer Commanding the Divisional Artillery and some Staff officers of the Division were ordered in that direction too. Our future destination, hitherto kept secret, was therefore revealed, and between the 16th and 18th the Division detrained at Longeau, two miles east of Amiens, marching to the Flesselles area, at which latter place the headquarters were located. The Division now belonged to the IIIrd Corps (Pulteney) of the Fourth Army (Rawlinson). The other divisions of the Corps were the 8th (Hudson), 19th (Bridges), 34th (Ingouville-Williams), and final training for the expected rôle of the Division took place, viz., the capture of Martinpuich, a village some three miles behind the German front line. A suitable portion of the country to represent our objective was selected; the German trench system, obtained from air photographs, was marked on the ground, and the troops were practised over it. On the 23rd June the Division carried out this exercise, which was, unfortunately, never to mature.

Kits were now reduced to a minimum, and on the 27th inst. the Division commenced moving up to the front to take part in one of the biggest battles of the British Army, known to future history as the Battle of the Somme. The attack was to be made by the Fourth Army (XIIIth, XVth, IIIrd, Xth and VIIIth Corps) on a twenty-five-mile front, extending from Maricourt in the south to Gommecourt in the north. The Sixth French Army was attacking on our right. In the opening phase the 34th and 8th Divisions of the IIIrd Corps were to attack La Boisselle and Ovillers, and the 19th and 12th Divisions were to pass through and push forward. The supply of artillery ammunition had been still further increased, permitting of a long bombardment which was to commence on the 25th June, and planned to continue until the 29th inst., but the inclement weather causing a postponement of the attack for forty-eight hours, the bombardment continued until 7.30 a.m. on the 1st of July.

It was hoped that this heavy bombardment would pulverise the German defences and demoralise his troops, but the enemy had established a marvellous defensive system with deep dug-outs, 30 feet below ground, and good communications. There was ample sleeping accommodation, and the supply of electric light made underground existence possible, so that loss in *personnel* was reduced to a minimum. And though the villages of La Boisselle and Ovillers, as villages above ground, had disappeared, the *débris* was honeycombed with machine gun emplacements, as also were the banks of the Mash Valley.

On the 30th June Divisional Headquarters moved to Baizieux, and the infantry, marching after dark, reached Hénencourt and Millencourt by 10 a.m. on 1st July. Meanwhile the attack had commenced. The 34th Division had gained some success south of La Boisselle, but the 8th Division had suffered very heavy casualties, mostly from machine guns, and was back in its original position. Late in the afternoon of that day orders were received to relieve the 8th Division, and headquarters opened at Hénencourt at 11.50 p.m. Fortunately a certain amount of reconnaissance of the trenches had been carried out, and the relief was completed during the night of 1st–2nd July.

On the 2nd orders were received for the attack to be continued, the 19th Division was to push on in La Boisselle, the 12th to capture Ovillers, and the Xth Corps on the left to gain the Leipzig salient.

The attack, preceded by an intense bombardment of one hour, and under cover of smoke on our left, was to be delivered at 3.15 a.m. on the 3rd. At 3 a.m. a message was received at Divisional Headquarters to say that the Xth Corps attack was postponed. It was obviously impossible at this stage to make any alterations in the dispositions. This delay of the Xth Corps attack was most unfortunate, as it freed the German machine guns on that flank to pay attention to the 12th Division.

The Division attacked on a two-brigade front, the 35th on the right with the 5th Royal Berkshire and 7th Suffolk Regiments in the front line, the 9th Essex in support, and the 7th Norfolk in reserve; the 37th Brigade on the left with the 6th Queen's and 6th Royal West Kent Regiments in front, the 6th Buffs in support, and the 7th East Surrey in reserve. The 36th Infantry Brigade held the extreme left of the front line and was in divisional reserve. At 3 a.m. or soon after, the attacking troops left the trenches, crept across No Man's Land, and at 3.15 a.m., when the artillery fire lifted, rushed the German front line.

The 5th Royal Berkshire (Willan) suffered hardly any casualties whilst crossing, and maintained good direction, being materially assisted thereto by the Sunken Road leading straight to Ovillers. Going was good until near the German front line, where the large shell holes, made by our bombardment, caused some congestion. The wire had been almost completely destroyed and formed no obstacle to the advance.

The leading " waves " passed over the first line to the second, and through the second to the third, bringing them nearly to the ruins of the western houses of the village. Here they became involved in a heavy bombing attack, and with the failure of further supplies to reach them, the bombers were overwhelmed and practically the whole of the two leading companies became casualties. A report said that during this confused state of fighting an officer gave the order to retire, and the rumour spread that it was a German in British uniform, but whoever he was he received short shrift, and did not live long enough to issue further orders. The 7th Suffolk (Major Henty) met with very little resistance in the front line, and, after overcoming a determined opposition in the second, passed to the third. This was strongly held, and the majority of the casualties in the battalion occurred here owing, in a great measure, to the fact that the 6th Queen's on its left had not got so far forward, thus permitting the enemy to attack on that flank.

The 9th Essex (Lewes) had considerable difficulty in getting up into our front line, heavily shelled as it was by the German artillery, and the Royal Berkshire and Suffolk Regiments had disappeared in the darkness before the Essex companies began to cross No Man's Land, by this time swept by machine gun fire from both flanks. Considerable casualties were sustained, and the waves of the attack becoming a series of small parties not strong enough to give any material assistance to the forward formations, the 35th Brigade attack broke down, and the remnants of the battalions were driven out of the German lines. A party of two officers and about 100 men, however, dug itself in on the Sunken Road, some sixty yards from the German position, and held on until dark, when it was withdrawn.

" C " Company of the 9th Essex left our trenches from a portion facing south-east. This caused a loss of direction, and the company, taking with it the rear platoon of " B " Company, crossed the Mash Valley and struck the German line north-west of La Boisselle. Having carried the front and support lines without much difficulty, they proceeded through the village of La Boisselle and came in touch with the 19th Division, attacking from the opposite direction. Some 200 Germans surrendered to this company, which was under the command of Lieutenant E. H. Kennifick, who, with Second Lieutenant Karn and Company Sergt.-Major J. Collins, distinguished themselves in the fighting. This loss of direction of " C " Company, mainly due to the orientation of the departure trench, the darkness, and the fact of not having had sufficient time to get acquainted with the surroundings, though leading to a success on another front, was a misfortune for its own brigade, which was compelled to give ground owing to lack of support.

The 6th Queen's (Warden), on the right of the 37th Brigade attack, only gained the front line in one place. Elsewhere the battalion was held up by uncut wire and machine gun fire from Mash Valley.

" A " and " C " Companies, Royal West Kent (Owen), gaining the first line, commenced consolidating, when the Germans fired a red rocket, bringing heavy artillery fire on this line. Nevertheless, " B " and " D " Companies, pushing through, captured the second line, when the enemy again fired a red rocket, this time bursting into two flares, and attracting artillery fire on to that line.

Shortly after our original bombardment had lifted, the enemy opened with intense machine gun fire from the Leipzig salient (apparently the same position from which the 8th Division attack had been brought to a standstill on the 1st inst.), sweeping down all supporting waves not already across No Man's Land, and thereby making it impossible to reach the leading battalions, as carrying parties with bombs and material for consolidation were shot. There was also very heavy shelling on our trenches.

" A " and " C " Companies of the 6th Buffs (Cope), in support of the Royal West Kent, suffered heavily in crossing to the German trenches, and none of them reached the advanced West Kent position. This position was strongly counter-attacked and only a few survivors came back to the first line. The casualties were very heavy, and the want of grenades, which could not be got forward, forced the remnants now in the first line to give way and fall back on our own trenches about 5.30 a.m. The Royal West Kent Battalion lost in this action 19 officers and 375 other ranks.

The capture of the position had failed, and the failure was undoubtedly affected by the flanking machine gun fire, which was unmolested, and raked the excessive distance between the opposing front lines over which supports had to cross. Also by the attack being carried out in the dark by troops who were hurried into the fight without being well acquainted with the terrain, leading to loss of cohesion ; by the artillery bombardment destroying the wire and trenches, yet failing to reach the deep dug-outs, which remained unharmed ; and by the recent storms making shell holes and trenches in places almost impassable.

The casualties in the two brigades, 35th and 36th, amounted to 97 officers and 2,277 other ranks.

On the 4th July the 19th Division made further progress in La Boisselle, thus affording the 35th Brigade machine gunners some effective shooting at the retiring Germans on the left. A direct hit, on this day, on one of our trench mortar ammunition stores caused an explosion which formed a crater 30 feet by 15 feet. Fortunately there were no casualties. Meanwhile the units were mostly employed in clearing the trenches and getting back the dead and wounded. The 7th East Surrey brought in 250 in two days, many of them belonging to the 8th Division. Search parties were out all night, and it is impossible to speak too highly of the work done by the Royal Army Medical Corps and the stretcher bearers.

The 69th Field Company, Royal Engineers, under Second Lieutenant Kelan, the 5th Northamptonshire (Captain Cathcart), and a party of the 8th Royal Fusiliers dug a new trench from our right to join up with the 19th Division in La Boisselle. The 12th Divisional Artillery now came into action relieving that of the 8th, and it was only natural that the troops were glad to have their own artillery covering them again.

The following order of the day was received from the IIIrd Corps : " As the 12th Division is leaving the IIIrd Corps, the Corps Commander wishes to thank all ranks and to express his appreciation of the gallantry and dash shown in the attack on Ovillers. He is also grateful for the very efficient support which the Division rendered to their comrades of the 19th Division, who were fighting in La Boisselle. The Commander-in-Chief desires Sir William Pulteney to convey his congratulations to General Scott and the brigadiers of the 12th Division, and all ranks should be informed of his satisfaction."

On the 5th July the Division was transferred to the

Xth Corps (Morland) of the Fifth Reserve Army (Gough), and the front was extended to include La Boisselle. The 74th Brigade of the 34th Division was attached to the 12th and held this extension. The 36th Brigade moved back to Albert, the line being held by the 7th Suffolk, 9th Essex, 7th East Surrey, and 6th Buffs. On the 6th inst. orders were received to again attack Ovillers, and the task was allotted to the 36th Brigade. Notwithstanding the terrible casualties incurred by the 8th Division on the 1st, and by our own brigades on the 3rd July, the troops of the 36th Brigade were anxious to have a chance, and in the diary of one of the 9th Royal Fusiliers the following extract shows the keenness of the men, the brigade having been relieved the previous day: " Hear our brigade is to have a chance to take Ovillers. Hurrah ! . . . So we join the remainder of our own brigade and do without twelve hours of our rest to do so. We are all proud to know the G.O.C. has given us this task. Boys are determined not to fail, and no grumbling is heard when our rest is cut down to twelve hours." This gives an example of what the men of the service battalions were made of.

The attack was to take place by daylight on the morning of the 7th July. Zero hour was fixed at 8 a.m. for the 74th Brigade on the right, and 8.30 a.m. for the 36th Brigade on the left. The difference in time being to allow the 74th Brigade to get forward and capture the machine gun positions in Mash Valley, from which the fire had been so destructive on the 1st and 3rd instants, before the 36th Brigade left the trenches. On this occasion the left of the 36th Brigade was kept on the south side of the spur to avoid as much as possible the machine gun fire from the Leipzig salient. Grenade dumps were formed well forward, one of 15,000 being made where the Sunken Road left our trenches. A buried cable was laid two-thirds of the way across No Man's Land. The 36th Brigade took over the trenches on the afternoon of the 6th inst.

At 4.45 a.m. on 7th the French artillery fired gas shell for two hours, the bombardment by the 12th, 25th, and 36th divisional artilleries, the heavy artillery and the trench mortars commencing at 6.45 a.m. The 74th Brigade attacking as ordered made some progress, but failed to reach the machine guns in Mash Valley. On the commencement of this attack the Germans bombarded the trenches held by the 36th Brigade, and heavy casualties were suffered before the assault started, the 9th Royal Fusiliers having 225. At 8.30 a.m. the 36th Brigade assaulted, the 8th Royal Fusiliers (Annesley) on right, 7th Royal Sussex (Osborn) in centre, and 9th Royal Fusiliers (Overton) on left, the 11th Middlesex being in reserve. Immediately " D " Company, forming the first line of the 8th Royal Fusiliers, left our trenches, it came under heavy machine gun fire from Mash Valley, and was momentarily overwhelmed, but the advance of the second and third lines carried it on. With the third line was Lieut.-Colonel A. C. Annesley, who, seeing the confusion arising from the heavy casualties, took personal command, and waving his stick in the air shouted the familiar words of a field day, and led the men on. He was wounded in the hand and leg, but continued leading to the enemy's front line, where he was hit in the thigh. Shortly afterwards he fell, being hit for the fourth time, shot through the heart. His gallant conduct infected his battalion, and the fourth line coming up, the second and third objectives were carried. During the bombardment of the trenches previous to the assault, and whilst crossing to the German trenches, Private F. Warren played his mouth-organ to cheer on his comrades.

The 7th Royal Sussex succeeded in gaining three objectives, and the 9th Royal Fusiliers, who had suffered heavily from the enemy's artillery fire, gained the first and second objectives. Communications were again a difficulty. Lieutenant Redford, though wounded, succeeded in taking the wireless apparatus to the German front trenches, but on arrival he found the accumulators so damaged as to be useless. Pigeons, or the men carrying them, had all been shot, and the telephone cables were broken. Smoke and dust prevented visual signalling. Messengers attempting to cross No Man's Land were shot down. In consequence no reports of the situation were received by the Brigade Headquarters until the afternoon, and all attempts during the morning to send over supplies of grenades or reinforcements failed on account of the enemy's artillery barrage. But, fortunately, the men had been instructed in the use of the German rifle and the German grenades, and were able to handle material captured in the enemy's trenches.

The 37th Brigade had assisted the attack by making a smoke screen on the left and by machine gun fire.

About 12 noon Lieut.-Colonel Osborn took command of the forward troops and deciding, in view of his numbers, that he could not hold all the gains, withdrew the men of the 8th Royal Fusiliers and 7th Royal Sussex who had reached the third objective, and consolidated positions in the first and second objectives.

At 2.30 p.m. eight volunteers of "A" Company, 11th Middlesex Regiment (Lance-Corporals Kearney and Dale, Privates Tutt, Caterer, Dunsly, Nossworthy, Jackson and Hale), tried to cross to the captured trenches with bombs, but the six men were wounded. At 3 p.m. Captain Lewis, Lieutenant Moore, and sixty other ranks of "A" Company, Middlesex, with a

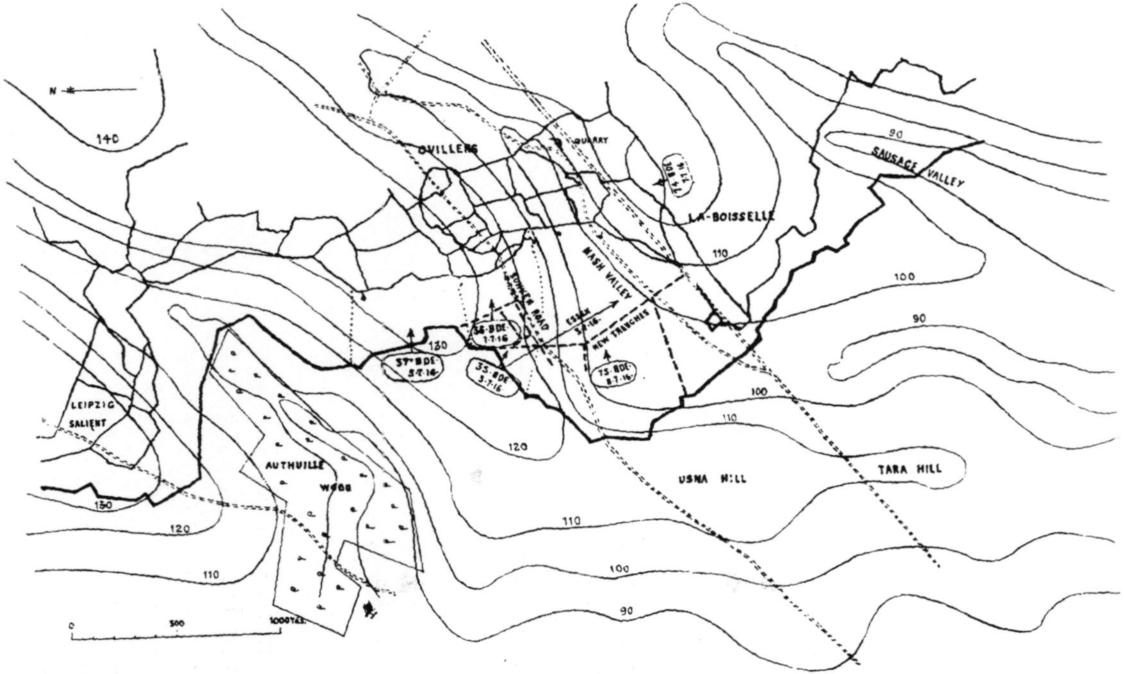

Map No. 7. Ovillers

BATTLE OF THE SOMME—I

platoon of the 7th Royal Sussex under Sergeant Leach, each carrying twenty grenades, attempted the crossing. Captain Lewis was killed, but Lieutenant Moore and about forty men succeeded in getting over with one Lewis gun. Two hours later, fifty men of " B " Company, under Captain Crombie, reached the left flank of the captured position with grenades and a Lewis gun, suffering little loss.

The 74th Brigade had made no headway, so at 11.30 a.m. the 7th Suffolk Regiment (35th Brigade) were sent up as reinforcements to La Boisselle. The 75th Brigade (25th Division) being placed at the disposal of the 12th Division at 12.50 p.m., two battalions were moved to the Tara Usna line and two battalions to Albert.

At 5 p.m. the 7th East Surrey and 9th Essex Regiments of the 35th Brigade reinforced the 36th Brigade.

At 8 p.m. the 2nd Manchester Regiment (14th Infantry Brigade, 32nd Division) was placed at the disposal of the Division and was moved to the reserve trenches of the 36th Brigade.

About 6 p.m. definite information of the position in Ovillers began to arrive, and immediately it was dark the East Surrey and Essex Battalions were sent forward and the holding of the captured positions was assured. Bombing attacks and hand-to-hand fighting had gone on all day, but no organised counter-attack on a big scale had been made by the enemy, probably because of his losses, which were no doubt heavy, the rapidity of the infantry advance, following closely on the artillery lift, causing many to be caught in the dug-outs, which were systematically bombed.

As direct communication between the 74th and 36th Brigades had not been established, the 75th Brigade was ordered to take the intervening German trench.

During the night the 74th Brigade made some progress on the right and gained touch with the 19th Division; at 3.45 a.m. on 8th inst. the inner flanks of the 74th and 36th Brigades having been marked by lights, the 8th South Lancashire Regiment, of the 75th Brigade, captured the intervening trench, which was only lightly held, and passed on to the second line, thus bridging the gap; the 9th Royal Fusiliers also gained some 90 yards of trench by bombing on the left.

The 36th Brigade front was now held by the 7th East Surrey, with portions of the 8th Royal Fusiliers and 11th Middlesex, under Lieut.-Colonel Baldwin, on the right, and the 9th Essex, with remnants of the 9th Royal Fusiliers, 7th Royal Sussex and 11th Middlesex, under Lieut.-Colonel Osborn, on the left. On the 8th further progress through the village was made by the 7th East Surrey and Essex Battalions, and touch was gained all along the front. The captured position had brought us to the summit of the spur on which Ovillers stood and provided a good starting point for a further advance.

The 12th Division troops were relieved by those of the 32nd Division during the early hours of the night, and on the 9th inst. the Headquarters of the Division moved to Contay, the 35th Brigade to Varennes, 36th to Senlis, and the 37th to Warloy, the artillery remaining in action.

Thus came to an end one of the severest fights the 12th Division was called upon to take part in.

One of the main difficulties the troops had had to contend with in the attack was the mud, which was very deep and sticky, in many places men being unable to move without assistance. A factor, undoubtedly aiding the 36th Brigade in their success, was that each man carried twenty grenades. On capturing the enemy's trenches a large quantity of tinned meat, cheese, butter, etc., was found, also mineral waters and packets of "Iron Crosses" done up in pink tissue paper.

The casualties of the three battalions making the attack on the 7th were very heavy. Out of 66 officers, 60 became casualties. In other ranks, out of a total of 2,100, 340 were hit by shell fire before leaving our trenches, 1,260 were hit by machine gun fire in No Man's Land, and of the 500 who reached the village, 150 became casualties during the subsequent fighting.

The total casualties of the Division from 1st to 8th July inclusive were officers 189, other ranks 4,576.

CHAPTER VII

BATTLE OF THE SOMME—II. POZIÈRES AND RATION TRENCH

July 10th—August 18th, 1916

(Maps 19 and 8)

THE Division had now been transferred to the VIIIth Corps (Hunter-Weston), and on the 10th July Headquarters moved to Bus-les-Artois. During the next ten days drafts were received, and re-organisation carried out, very large numbers of men being employed on working parties. On the 20th inst. the Division, relieving the 4th Division (Lambton), returned to the line near Beaumont Hamel, with headquarters at Betrancourt Camp. Nothing of importance took place, and on the night of the 24th–25th the Division was relieved, and marched to the Hédauville-Bouzincourt area, coming under the IInd Corps (Jacob), on its way to the sector from which it had been withdrawn on the 8th July.

Meanwhile this portion of the line had been advanced, the Australians having captured Pozières and the British Divisions having moved forward in co-operation on the left. The line now faced north, and the future plan of operation was to advance systematically northwards, and securing the high ground north and northeast of Pozières, to destroy the German garrison in the Thiepval area. For this purpose the 12th Division, with the Australian Corps on their right, were to push forward, whilst the 49th Division (Perceval) on the left was to hold the Germans to their position.

Accordingly, on the morning of the 27th inst. the 37th Brigade relieved a brigade of the 48th Division (R. Fanshawe) on the left, and in the evening the 36th Brigade went in on the right, the 11th Middlesex sustaining heavy casualties on the way up. Divisional Headquarters remained at Bouzincourt. During the four succeeding days, several minor attempts against German strong points having failed, an operation on a larger scale to capture 4th Avenue Trench, was planned and carried out at 11 p.m. on the 3rd of August.

After an artillery preparation by heavy and field guns, and trench mortars on the points to be attacked, and on the adjoining strong points and communications, and also by an intense bombardment of five minutes immediately preceding the attack, the 8th Royal Fusiliers (Elliott-Cooper) and the 6th Buffs (Cope) assaulted the 4th Avenue and gained all the objectives, the trench from point 95 to point 20, and a strong point at 23. Owing to loss of direction in the dark, some of the 8th Royal Fusiliers captured the trench 23–93, and were joined by men of the Buffs. This party then bombed along about 200 yards of the trench and made a block.

As the attack had been so successful, it was thought possible to exploit the success, and the 8th Royal Fusiliers were ordered to bomb up Ration Trench to point 77, the 7th Royal Sussex, who were in Pozières Trench, being ordered to capture the strong point there, and bomb down towards the 8th Royal Fusiliers. A message having been received that the whole of Ration Trench was captured, a company of the Royal Sussex in reserve was ordered up to Ration Trench, and arriving in the south-west portion, Lieut.-Colonel Cope, who was in command there, ordered patrols to be pushed out along 6th Avenue from point 99 to point 81. Two patrols went forward, one from 7th Royal Sussex under Second

Lieutenant Rolfe, and the other from the 6th Buffs under Second Lieutenant Routley. They reported 6th Avenue as thinly held by the enemy, without wire or deep dug-outs. Many dead and wounded Germans were seen, showing the accuracy of the artillery preparation and the severe losses that could be inflicted on the enemy when there were no deep dug-outs. A captured prisoner stated that his company was "half an hour" away in Thiepval. A small gap had evidently been found, but it was impossible to exploit further as machine guns now opened fire from a position about 200 yards to the west, and a body of some 200 Germans advancing from Mouquet Farm, forced the patrols to retire from the vicinity of points 81 and 14. Valuable information had been gained for the future however. The attack on point 77 by the Sussex was met by heavy machine gun fire and grenades and failed.

The report of the capture of Ration Trench was incorrect, but the result of the night's fighting had effected the complete capture of the 4th Avenue, a firm footing in Ration Trench at point 93, and 2 officers and 93 of the enemy had been taken prisoners.

In order to complete the capture of Ration Trench the attack was to be continued on the night of the 4th–5th August with the Australians on the right. In the 36th Brigade the 7th Royal Sussex were to attack the strong point 77 and 250 yards of Ration Trench to the south-west, the 9th Royal Fusiliers the centre portion, and the 8th Royal Fusiliers to bomb up from the post they held in it. In the 37th Brigade the 6th Royal West Kent were to capture the strong point 90 and join up with our own post at 47, the 6th Queen's co-operating by a bombing attack from this latter point. The artillery preparation was similar to that of the preceding night, and zero was at 9.15 p.m. The attack with the exception of that on point 77, which again defied capture, was entirely successful and completed by midnight. The Australians likewise gained their objectives.

At dawn on the 5th inst. a considerable number of Germans were discovered in bits of old trenches and shell holes between the 4th Avenue and Ration Trench. They had evidently taken refuge there during our bombardment of Ration Trench, and had been over-run in the attack. Some appear to have attempted to escape through the gap between points 85 and 77, but were turned back by reinforcements of the 7th Royal Sussex on their way up to Ration Trench. The 5th Northamptonshire (Pioneers), who were making communication trenches to the captured position during the night, had reported at the same time that they had been fired at from somewhere between the lines. Consequently machine guns, Stokes mortars and rifle grenades were pushed forward, and at 2.30 p.m. the area between the 4th Avenue and Ration Trench was subjected to an organised bombardment from these weapons. Lance-Corporal Camping and one or two of the 8th Royal Fusiliers who could speak German also crept out, in spite of the risk, and told the enemy it would be better to surrender, and at about 3 p.m. small parties began to come in. By 3.50 p.m. 3 officers and 112 men had surrendered, besides 35 previously captured. The following messages were received by the General Officer Commanding the Reserve Army (Gough): "The Commander-in-Chief warmly congratulates you and the commanders, staffs and troops of all arms under you who organised and carried out the attack last night. The success gained is of very considerable importance and opens the way to further equally valuable successes to be obtained by similar careful methods of preparation and gallantry and thoroughness in execution."

"The 12th Division and 2nd Australian Division have not been mentioned by name in the congratulations telegraphed to you this morning in accordance with the Commander-in-Chief's instructions.

"The reason for not mentioning them is that there is a risk of conveying information to the enemy. . . .

"The Commander-in-Chief desires, however, that the divisions concerned may be informed that they are specially included in his congratulations. . . .

"5.8.16. CHIEF, GENERAL STAFF."

The Germans, having shelled our front and support lines intermittently throughout the 5th inst., and very heavily between midnight and 3 a.m. on the 6th inst., followed up the latter at 3.15 a.m. by a determined attack on our block at the north-east end of Ration Trench. They employed eight *flamenwerfers*, the men using them being clothed in shiny black oilskins. The range of the flame was about 25 yards. These were followed by some forty bombers. The trench became untenable, and about 150 yards of it were evacuated. Whereupon Captain G. L. Cazelet and Second-Lieutenant E. L. Fifoot, of the 9th Royal Fusiliers, extended their men in the open on either side of the trench, and, counter-attacking, drove the enemy back, regaining all the lost trench except 40 yards, and establishing a new block. Lance-Corporal C. Cross helped considerably in this counter-attack by taking his Lewis gun into a shell hole and inflicting many casualties on the enemy. Privates T. Crowe and L. Rouse showed entire disregard of the new weapon, one bombing from the edge of the flames and the other effectively sniping. The Germans had now introduced an "egg" grenade, which was smaller and less cumbersome than his stick bombs, and gave him a longer range than our men got with our "Mills" grenades.

On the night of the 6th–7th August the 35th Brigade relieved the 36th, the 7th Suffolk Regiment taking over on the right and the 5th Royal Berkshire on the left. The Germans shelled our trenches throughout the period of relief, and only desisted on the appearance of our aeroplanes in the morning. At 3 a.m. on the 8th the Germans made further *flamenwerfer* attacks on both flanks of the portion of Ration Trench, now held by the 5th Royal Berkshire Regiment. The bombers of each attack gained a footing in our trench but were immediately driven out by counter-attacks. At 5 a.m. a large party of the enemy made a second attack with liquid fire on the same points, and succeeded in capturing about 50 yards of our trench on the south-west side of the block previously erected by the 9th Royal Fusiliers. Lieutenant F. A. L. Edwards, Company Sergt.-Major A. W. Waite and Sergeant J. Faulkner, of the Berkshire, showed considerable courage and initiative on both these occasions, rallying the men and organising counter-attacks, thereby preventing further loss of trench, and recapturing a portion of that lost. At 7 a.m. the enemy made another attack on one of our blocks on the extreme left of our front held by the 37th Brigade, but here the attack was repulsed.

The next operation was the capture of the German strong point at 77 in conjunction with the 4th Australian Division on the right. After a heavy bombardment during the day of the 8th inst., and a three-minute intense bombardment preceding the attack, three-companies of the 7th Suffolk Regiment went forward from the trench 95–85, but were immediately stopped by machine guns from a German trench 96–86, which, from its close proximity to our line, had been untouched by our bombardment. Of these three companies only 1 officer and 13 other ranks returned unwounded.

"C" Company, under Captain Isham, attacking on the left, rushed the German barricade and machine guns and gained about 350 yards of Ration Trench, but was brought to a stop about 20 yards from point 77 by uncut wire and machine guns. Meanwhile the Australians had succeeded in gaining point 89, but decided it was impossible to remain there unless the 35th Brigade gained 77, which they were unable to do until a fresh bombardment had destroyed the very heavy wire.

On the 9th August the troops were withdrawn from the vicinity of trench 95–85 so as to permit of a heavy bombardment on trench 96–86, and with a further bombardment of 77 and its surroundings, the Australians gained all the objectives, and the 7th Suffolk joined up with them in Ration Trench. On the 10th August, Lieut.-Colonel Cope, commanding the 6th Buffs, reported that one of his patrols had proceeded to point 20 and bombed the German dug-outs, and asked permission to attack this strong point. General Scott approved of his plans, and, sanctioning the attack, our trenches were cleared, and the trench mortars bombarded this point. Unfortunately one of the trench mortar bombs fell short into the store of grenades, collected for the attack at the head of our sap, and exploded them, and one of these, dropping back into our main trench, wounded the two officers, Captain R. O. C. Ward and Lieutenant Sir Robert Onslow, who were to lead the attack, which consequently had to be abandoned.

On the afternoon of the same day the 36th Infantry Brigade (Boyd-Moss) had the honour of being inspected by H.M. the King, with whom was H.R.H. the Prince of Wales. The Brigade was formed up on each side of a country road just north of Senlis, and about a mile west of Bouzincourt, which village the Germans frequently shelled. His Majesty and H.R.H., accompanied by General Sir Hubert Gough, Commanding the Fifth Army, Lieut.-General C. Jacob, Commanding the IInd Corps, and Major-General A. B. Scott, Commanding the 12th Division, walked down between the lines. It is needless to say how greatly this honour was appreciated by the Division.

On this day also the Trench Mortar Batteries were greatly elated at the fact that nine Germans surrendered to them as prisoners.

From 3 p.m. on the 11th to 2 a.m. on the 12th inst. the enemy shelled our trenches and communications intensely, more especially Ration Trench, causing much damage and many casualties in the 9th Essex and 7th Norfolk Regiments, also seriously hindering the preparations for an attack arranged to take place on the night of the 12th. Long-range guns were also more aggressive on Bouzincourt, the Divisional Headquarters, and so many casualties occurred in billets that the troops were sent to bivouac outside the village.

The task allotted to the 12th Division in the operations to be carried out on the night of the 12th-13th August, was the capture of the 6th Avenue and the German front line opposite the 37th Brigade. The Australians meanwhile attacking the trenches south of Mouquet Farm, and the 49th Division making a subsidiary attack on a German strong point on the left. In view of this advance and in consequence of the distance between Ration and 6th Avenue Trenches, and the importance of early communication to a newly-gained position, the Field Companies, Royal Engineers, and the 5th Northamptonshire Regiment (Trent) had been steadily sapping forward from Ration Trench since its capture.

The artillery preparation for this attack consisted of a

steady bombardment for forty-eight hours, the batteries of the 12th, 25th, and 49th Divisions, assisted by the IInd Corps heavy artillery, and heavy and medium trench mortars, taking part. An innovation in artillery and infantry co-operation was attempted in this attack. An 18-pound battery was placed under the orders of each battalion commander for use if required, at fifteen minutes after zero, a forward observation officer from the battery concerned being in close touch with the battalion commander, a procedure that met with some success.

In consequence of the enemy's shell fire, Ration Trench became impossible for assembly, and the troops were formed up in advance of it. In order to avoid loss of direction in crossing the extensive No Man's Land to the 6th Avenue, the battalions of the 35th Brigade taped out assembly positions well forward.

Zero hour was 10.30 p.m., and after three minutes' intense bombardment the 7th Norfolk Regiment (Walter), with " A " and " B " Companies in front and " B " and " C " in support, dashed forward, and captured their portion, the right of 6th Avenue, at 10.40 p.m. So rapid was their advance that touch on the flanks was temporarily lost. " C " Company, however, worked down the trench to the left and gained touch with the 9th Essex at about 11.40 p.m., and at midnight touch was also obtained with the 4th Australian Division, which had gained its objective, at point 81. Patrols pushed forward, but were held up by our artillery barrage. Few casualties had been incurred and seventeen prisoners were taken. The 9th Essex Regiment (Richards) attacking on the left of the Norfolk Regiment, with " C " and " D " Companies, and " A " in support, captured their objective, the 6th Avenue, as far south as point 78, with little opposition.

Patrols were sent to the left to obtain touch with the 7th East Surrey. Trench 78–74 was found to be almost obliterated, and after advancing about 75 yards along 78–55 strong opposition was met and a barricade made. A bombing party from 99 reached 59 and formed a block there.

At 11.30 p.m. the Germans counter-attacked point 78 from 55 and were repulsed. At the same time 59 was attacked, and the bombers, running out of grenades, fell back on 99. At 3 a.m. on 13th the enemy made a further heavy attack on 78, and the 9th Essex kept them at bay until their grenades ran short, when they were driven back about 50 yards. Fresh ammunition arriving they regained their lost ground. Touch had not been gained on the left, and the situation was for some time obscure, failure on the part of the East Surrey to capture their objective having exposed the Essex to the counter-attacks they had so gallantly defeated. During the night the 35th Brigade made four strong points in the captured trench, and suitable garrisons with machine guns and trench mortars were established in them, the two communication trenches, begun beforehand, were also completed. Before daylight the line was thinned out in order to avoid losses from the inevitable bombardment.

The attack of the 37th Brigade on the left had not met with success. In connection with this failure it must be remembered that this sector was part of the original German system and full of deep dug-outs, and although the communication trenches had now become fire trenches, they easily adapted themselves to their new rôle. The ground was very much cut up by shell holes from the many bombardments, and consequently attacks became broken up and cohesion lost. The task of the 7th East Surrey (Baldwin) on the right was the capture of the quadrilateral 74, 62, 44, 55, and to maintain touch with the Essex at point 78. " D " Company (Second Lieutenant Evans), attacking on the right, advanced on 74, but, owing to large shell holes and heavy artillery and machine gun fire, became scattered and lost direction. Small groups of two or three men appear to have reached 44, and a few got in touch with the Essex at 78, but the majority apparently pushed through with their commander and were reported missing. " B " Company (Captain G. F. Garnet) attacked point 62, and immediately coming under machine gun fire and a barrage of grenades was unable to make headway, and forced to retire, Captain Garnet being wounded. Captain Cook, with the support company " C " and the remnants of " B," made a second attempt but with no better success. Captain Hubbard then brought up the reserve company " A " and a third essay also failed.

Meanwhile, the 6th Royal West Kent Regiment (Owen) on the left were assaulting strong points 20 and 81.

Immediately the attack commenced, the Germans put a heavy barrage on our front line, manned the parapets from 62 to 81, and opened with machine guns. The right attack reached a point about 15 yards short of point 20, where a barricade was built, overlooking trench 62–03. The left attack was brought to a standstill. The Germans kept up their fire, which became intense at intervals, until 3 a.m. on the 13th inst. The trenches attacked by the 37th Brigade were, according to several reports, full of Germans, many of them with packs on, as though about to attack themselves or carry out a relief. The battle of the night had resulted in the capture of the German position on a front of 1,000 yards to an average depth of 400 yards. At 7 a.m. 13th inst. air reports stated that the Germans were

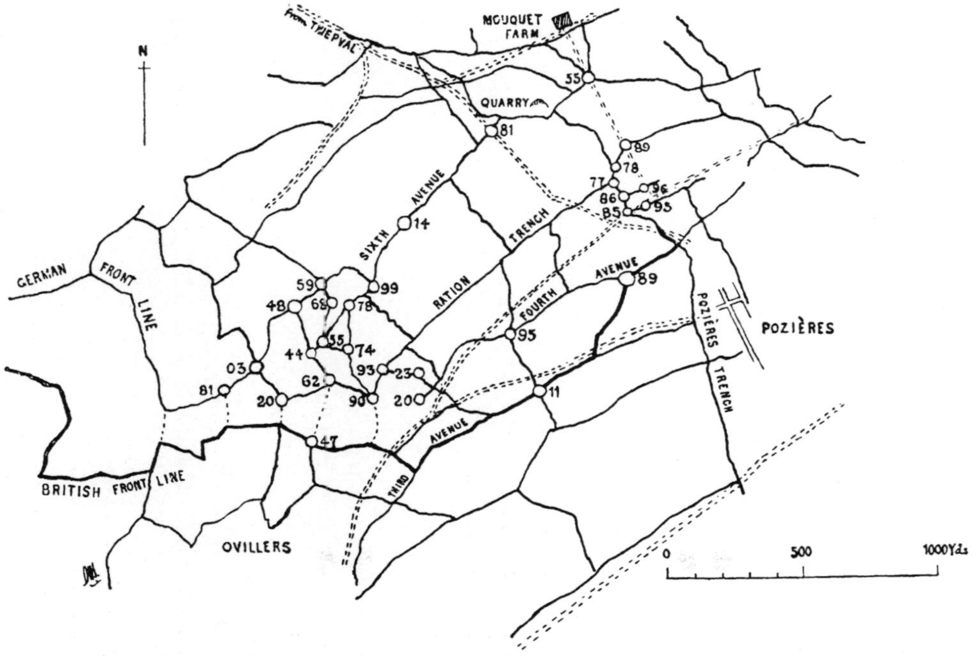

MAP No. 8. POZIÈRES

massing to counter-attack. The artillery, however, soon scattered them and nothing materialised, and at 10 a.m. the 35th Brigade was relieved by the 145th Brigade of the 48th Division. Great credit is due to the Royal Engineers and Pioneer Battalion, whose work on the communication trenches, one at least 500 yards long, could permit of a daylight relief the morning following on a successful night attack.

The General Officer Commanding the 48th Division (R. Fanshawe) took over command at 3 p.m., and Divisional Headquarters moved back to Doullens. The 37th Brigade was relieved about midnight and marched to Hédauville and Forceville, with the 35th Brigade at Bouzincourt and the 36th at Puchevillers.

Since going into the line on the 28th July the Division had gained three lines of enemy's trench on a front of 1,500 yards to a depth of 1,000 yards on the right and 500 yards on the left. In the method of fighting which we had just experienced, nibbling and pushing on over ground on which trenches and strong points sprang up like mushrooms, the Air Force rendered us invaluable assistance by their photographs, as also in observing for our artillery.

The Division was now to leave the IInd Corps and the Fifth Army, and a special order of the day was received from the G.O.C. Fifth (Reserve) Army, as follows :

" On the departure of the 12th Division to join the Third Army, the G.O.C. Reserve Army desires to place on record his appreciation of the good work done by the Division while under his command.

" On both occasions on which the Division has been in the line it has borne its full share of the fighting with gallantry and determination, and the best records of its achievements is to be found in the considerable area of ground now in our possession, in the capture of which it has played so important a part.

"The G.O.C. parts with the services of the Division with regret and wishes all ranks the best of good luck in their new sphere of action.

"13.8.16.   H.Q. Reserve Army."

The casualties in this second tour in the Somme battle were:

Officers	126
Other ranks	2,739

The Division, marching to the Arras Sector, now joined the VIth Corps (Haldane) of the Third Army (Allenby), and prepared to take up a line again, prolonged rest being out of the question in these stirring times.

CHAPTER VIII

BATTLE OF THE SOMME—BETWEEN THE BATTLES
August—September, 1916
(*Map* 9)

AFTER marching for five successive days the Division arrived in the vicinity of Arras on the 19th August, and on the following day the brigades commenced the relief of the 11th Division (Woollcombe), completing, on the 22nd inst., with headquarters as follows : Divisional, Warlus ; 37th Brigade on the right at Brétencourt ; 36th Brigade in centre at Dainville ; and 35th Brigade on the left in Arras.

The front now held was an interesting one, involving the defence of the southern suburbs of the city of Arras, and was some 9,000 yards in extent. The attitude of the enemy was reported quiet. The battle on the Somme occupied most of his attention, and this portion of the line was held by those of his troops, who had been withdrawn from that struggle to recoup and enjoy a period of comparative rest. In a large measure this was likewise true of the British troops, but with one great difference, the general attitude of the enemy was non-aggressive, whilst our policy was one of constant raids in order to obtain identifications of the opposing units, such information being of the utmost value to the intelligence branch of General Headquarters, and by which means the " wear and tear " on the enemy's forces was ascertained. Our position, running along the valley of the Crinchon, was very much dominated by that of the Germans on the rising ground to the east, and especially by Beaurains, and, whereas our communication trenches were all on the forward slope of the hill and so in full view of the enemy, his were over the rise and practically unseen. It was here that the French attack in September, 1915, had failed.

Portions of Arras were shelled daily and the inhabitants were not allowed out of their houses till 9.30 p.m., at which hour they proceeded to do their shopping. Brétencourt, Wailly, and Dainville also came in for attention, and the railway line was "watered" by machine guns at night. Arras Railway Station was at all times considered an unhealthy spot.

On the 28th August about twenty Germans raided a portion of the 35th Brigade line but failed to enter our trenches. Our men retaliated by erecting large notice boards announcing that Roumania had entered the war on the side of the Allies, thereby giving the enemy some useful rifle practice.

On the 4th September 1 officer and 18 N.C.O.'s and men of the 9th Essex, supported by artillery fire, left our trenches at 10.40 p.m. and crawled to within 10 yards of the German wire. The night was extremely dark, and the wire, though cut, was very broad, and progress was difficult and slow. Our artillery barrage lifted at 11.3 p.m. and the party reached to within 8 yards of the German front line, when it was met with heavy rifle fire and compelled to return. Three Germans were shot and we sustained two casualties who were got back. Next evening another party proceeded to investigate a sap and tunnel discovered the preceding night, and, if possible, to secure a prisoner. In the two former tasks they were successful, but not in the latter. On the night of September 8th–9th Second Lieutenant Ketteringham and some men of the 7th Norfolk Regiment made a raid following an artillery bombardment at

Imperial War Museum] [*Crown copyright*

BARBED WIRE STOP GATE

2 a.m. The German wire was found knocked about and difficult to negotiate, as it was very broad, but assisted by some special wire cutters they worked through it. They came upon a party of five of the enemy lying in the wire, probably a listening patrol, whom they shot, and proceeded on to the front line. Here some dead were found, but no shoulder straps or means of identification, with the exception of two caps, were forthcoming. On the same night an officer and 20 men of the 6th Buffs made a similar raid on the 37th Brigade front at 3 a.m. They entered a sap, and finding no one in it, proceeded some 25 yards down it, when they came to masses of coiled wire preventing any further advance, and in consequence they returned unrewarded. At 8.45 p.m. on the 10th inst. an officer and eight men, with a Lewis gun detachment, went out to secure a prisoner. They took up a position in the long grass, near a gap that had been recently cut in the German wire. After waiting for three-quarters of an hour, in the hope that the enemy would come to repair his wire, the officer decided to increase the gap, and moving the party forward to the front line, wait on the parapet for any one who might pass along the trench. But before this could be completed, some Germans were heard approaching, and the party took up their original position. Unfortunately this movement had been detected, and the enemy fired Verey lights and opened fire, forcing the patrol to withdraw. The Verey light was a brilliant fire ball, fired into the air from a single or double-barrelled pistol, illuminating the ground as the light descended. On occasions, when the Germans were extra anxious, their front line assumed the appearance of a Brock's benefit at the Crystal Palace.

On the 17th inst. the 6th Queen's raided a sap and reconnoitred some trenches without success, and

Lieutenant Robson being severely wounded in the head by a grenade, Sergeant Pentelow withdrew the party in good order and brought Lieutenant Robson in.

On the 23rd a raid was carried out by the 5th Royal Berkshire. An attempt at 9 p.m. was delayed by a German patrol, which was dispersed, leaving their grenades in sandbags behind them. At 1.48 a.m. on the 24th the attempt was renewed and a Bangalore torpedo was employed as a wire cutter. The torpedo consisted of a long pipe filled with explosive, and being laid under the wire was exploded by a time fuse. The noise of the explosion was similar to that of a trench mortar, and so did not attract particular attention. It successfully cut a practicable lane in the wire, and the raiding party got through this gap, but was held up by more wire, during the destruction of which they were discovered and fired upon and forced to retire. On the night of 25th–26th inst. a raid by the same battalion under Second Lieutenant Taylor, using Bangalore torpedoes, was discovered by the enemy, and unfortunately Lieutenant Taylor was killed. A party of Germans attacking them on a flank caused some casualties which could not be withdrawn.

Our efforts at obtaining identifications had not met with success, but the fact was, that the German wire was anything from 20 to 50 yards broad, the front line was only held by posts, the remainder of it being filled up with wire, and the troops were located in the support line. On the other hand our activities, which included at least one patrol from each brigade every night, had made us masters of No Man's Land, the result being that with the exception of the one on the 28th August which failed, no raid was ever carried out against our line. In addition the junior officers and other ranks received a most valuable training in night work, and great confidence was inspired.

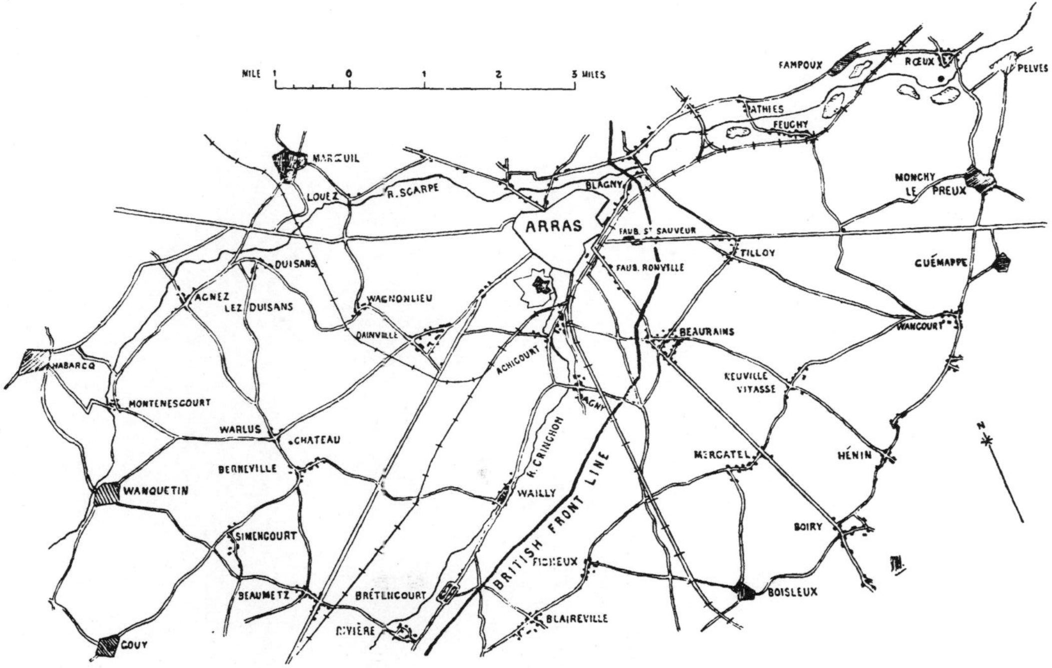

Map No. 9. Arras Front

On the 26th and 27th September the Division was relieved by the 14th Division (Couper), and on the next day left the VIth Corps for the XVth Corps (Du Cane) of the Fourth Army (Rawlinson).

Notwithstanding the length of front held, the system of reliefs permitted one battalion of each brigade to enjoy a fixed period out of the line in turn. The City of Arras and the villages behind the front afforded these battalions convenient centres for recreation in which the Divisional Concert Party ably assisted, and this period of comparative rest, in the Arras sector, gave the 12th Division the necessary respite to enable it to renew its part in the battle of the Somme.

CHAPTER IX

BATTLE OF THE SOMME—III. GUEUDECOURT AND BAYONET TRENCH

1st—19th October, 1916

(*Map* 10)

IT was now the fate of the 12th Division to experience yet another portion of the Somme battlefield. As a result of the capture of Flers on the 14th September, when tanks were used for the first time, the British line had advanced to Gueudecourt, and practically reached the bottom of the valley, with the attendant disadvantages arising from very long communications down a forward slope.

The Division relieved the 21st Division (D. Campbell) on the night of 1st–2nd October, the 37th Brigade taking over the right, including the northern and eastern extremities of Gueudecourt, and the 36th Brigade the left, occupying Grid and Grid Support Trenches as far west as the Flers-Ligny-Thilloy road. The 35th Brigade was in reserve at Bernafay Wood, and advanced Divisional Headquarters at Pommiers Redoubt. This was a captured German strong point, famous for its mud and the size of its rats, which could only be kept in subjection during the night by means of a light. The state of the country, including the roads, was deplorable, and the rain in October made it, in fact, indescribable. One of the main arteries to this sector was the road from Fricourt to Montauban, a road no wider than an ordinary country road, and which at times had to take a double line of up traffic, slow moving and fast moving. It was forbidden to proceed against this traffic, and to get from Montauban to Pommiers Redoubt involved a long round. Men on point duty at the various cross-roads had a hard task these days, and it can be easily understood how a breakdown, or an upset in the mud, meant considerable delay. The rain was so incessant that the ground became a quagmire, and even artillery ammunition limbers could not get across country, and shell were taken up by pack horses, which often sank in over their hocks. On two occasions men were found drowned in the thick mud in shell holes. Probably during the darkness of night, worn out with fatigue, they stumbled in and were unable to get out again. The great needs were : floor boards for the communication trenches to save the excessive fatigue entailed by struggling through the mud ; and dug-outs to protect the forward troops from the incessant shelling, causing an average of twenty-five casualties a day in each of the four battalions in the front trenches. A very considerable amount of labour was expended in digging one communication trench for each of the two brigades in the front line, and also in repairing the road from Longueval to Flers to make it passable for wheeled transport. The Field Companies, Royal Engineers, the Pioneer Battalion, Labour Companies, and all available men from other sources, worked continuously on this task.

An offensive had been planned for the 5th inst., but, owing to the inclement weather, it was postponed for forty-eight hours until the 7th inst., when the Fourth Army attacked, with the Fifth Reserve Army co-operating on its left, and the Sixth French Army on its right. The objectives of the 12th Division were Bayonet Trench, and then a further advance of some 500 yards. The 20th Division (Douglas Smith) was on the right, and the 41st Division (Lawford) on the left. After an artillery bombardment, the infantry advanced at 1.45 p.m. under a " creeping " barrage commencing 150 yards in front of our trenches, and proceeding at 50 yards a minute. Unfortunately, a few minutes before zero the Germans opened with machine gun and shell fire, which, becoming intense, greatly hindered the advance, and appeared to indicate a previous knowledge of our operations.

" A " " B " and " C " Companies of the 6th Buffs (Cope), with " D " in support, attacked from the north-eastern edge of Gueudecourt, and, though suffering heavy casualties, gained their first objective. This success was largely due to the bravery of Lieut.-Colonel Cope who, when the advance was momentarily checked, went forward under heavy fire and reorganised the attack. Unfortunately he was very seriously wounded, and Captain Pagen, R.A.M.C., in endeavouring to attend to him, was killed. Private Gregory made a similar attempt, and eventually protected him from further injuries by building up some cover round him. Five men became casualties in attempting to remove their colonel to a place of safety, but, finally, Corporal Tamblin and Lance-Corporal Alexander succeeded in getting him in. Meanwhile, Company Sergt.-Major Maxstead distinguished himself in organising the defence of the captured ground, after all his company officers had become casualties. Further advance was held up. The 6th Royal West Kent Regiment (Owen) attacked on the left of the Buffs, but owing to machine gun fire only a few made any progress, and these few could not maintain their position, and had to withdraw after dark.

In the 36th Brigade, the 9th Royal Fusiliers (Overton) advanced from the new trench in front of Grid Support, but was met by very heavy fire from a line of old gun

Imperial War Museum] [*Crown copyright*

TAKING UP AMMUNITION. SOMME, 1916

pits, with deep dug-outs, in advance of the German front line, and which had been apparently unaffected by the creeping barrage. The casualties were heavy, about 300, and the attack was brought to a standstill. The 8th Battalion (Elliott-Cooper), on the left of the 9th, also suffered considerable losses from the enemy's fire, and only a corporal and twenty men on the left managed to reach Bayonet Trench. The Germans in that portion surrendered, but being unsupported on either flank, this small party were compelled to retire later. With the exception, therefore, of the slight gain made by the 6th Buffs the attack had failed, the casualties amounting to 40 officers and 1,300 other ranks. The stretcher bearers on this day performed splendid deeds, and one of them, Private F. J. Brown, 6th Royal West Kent, the only one left in his company, did heroic work in getting thirty wounded into shell holes, eventually moving them to some disused dug-outs where he attended to them until dusk, when, getting further assistance, he brought them back to our trenches. During the night the 6th Queen's took over the 36th, and the 11th Middlesex the 37th Brigade fronts. The 20th and 41st Divisions each made small gains.

On the 9th October the German aeroplanes were much in evidence and repeatedly flew over our front line, at times firing machine guns. On the 10th, the 88th Infantry Brigade (Cayley), of the 29th Division (De Lisle), was attached to the 12th Division, and relieved the 37th Brigade, the 35th Brigade (Solly Flood) relieving the 36th. Preparations were now pushed forward to renew the attack, and shell holes were joined up in No Man's Land, forming a new trench 100 yards in advance of our front line. On the 11th inst. the 64th Brigade, R.F.A. (Barton), which had been attached to the French, returned to the Division, and some of the Divisional artillery came into the line. On the afternoon of this day a " Chinese " bombardment was carried out, the object being to get the enemy to man his trenches and, perhaps, disclose his machine gun positions without our making an attack. The only result was a heavy retaliation on our position.

The artillery preparation for the forthcoming attack was carried out by the guns of the 30th, 41st, and two Brigades of the 12th Division, together with the 15th Corps Heavy Artillery. The bombardment continued from 7 a.m. to 5 p.m. on the 11th and again from 7 a.m. to zero on the 12th inst. The attack was launched at 2 p.m. on the latter date, and two battalions of the 88th Brigade, the Newfoundland on the right and the 1st Essex on the left, gained their first objective. The latter were forced back by a bombing counter-attack, the Newfoundland Regiment retaking a portion of this position later. Two officers and 120 men were captured by this brigade. In the 35th Brigade, the 7th Suffolk on the right and the 7th Norfolk on the left, reached the enemy's wire, which was found uncut except in one place, where a small party of the Suffolk got into the trenches but were promptly bombed out from both flanks. After dark the remnants of these battalions returned to our trenches.

Strenuous work now continued on dug-outs, communication trenches, and keeping the roads in repair. Following a reconnaisance on the night of the 14th by by a party of the 9th Essex and the 4th Worcester Regiment (88th Brigade), the gunpits, which had proved such an obstacle to the attacks of the 7th and 12th October, were captured on the night of the 15th, and they were at once connected up with our front system. In a deep dug-out in one of these pits were found two of the enemy and one of our men, all wounded.

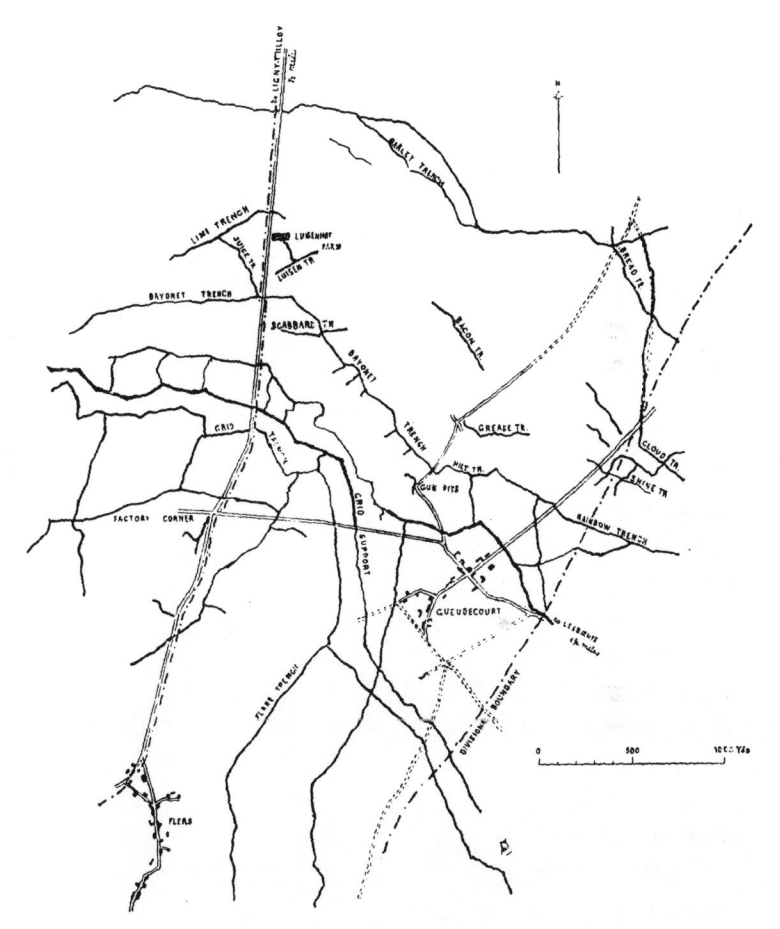

MAP NO. 10.   GUEUDECOURT

The Germans were still very active in the air, the result of this being that our trenches and battery positions were successfully shelled.

The attack was renewed at 3.40 a.m. on the 19th inst. with a more limited objective. In the 88th Brigade the 2nd Hampshire Regiment, and the 1st Essex advanced as far as Grease Trench, capturing 2 officers and 88 men. The 9th Essex (B. O. Richards), meeting with uncut wire, was unable to advance, and so for the third time the attack on this particular part of the German line was unsuccessful, owing to the undestroyed wire. A tank had been allotted to the Division but failed to reach the rendezvous.

The Division was relieved by the 29th Division on the 19th inst. and returned to the VIth Corps near Arras.

The third effort of the Division on the Somme battlefield had not met with success, but the conditions were of the worst, and, it may be remarked, that no advance on this sector of the line took place until the Germans commenced falling back in the spring of 1917. The casualties of this period were officers 135, other ranks 3,176, making a total of 10,941 for the forty-three days' fighting in which the Division had taken part in the Battle of the Somme.

CHAPTER X

AFTER THE SOMME—SECOND WINTER

November, 1916—January, 1917

(Map 9)

THE 12th Division, with the exception of the artillery which remained in action in the Somme battle, returned by French motor buses to the Arras area, and on the 25th and 26th October took back from the 14th Division (Couper) the sectors that had been handed over at the end of September. Divisional Headquarters were at Warlus. Raids and patrols were again the order of the day, as identifications were still important. On the 31st inst. two Germans, having crept through our wire, waited near the parapet and attacked an officer and non-commissioned officer who were going round the sentries. The N.C.O. was wounded, but the officer killed his opponent, being, in turn, wounded by the other German, who escaped. The dead man gave no identification beyond the fact that he was wearing a cap with the Prussian cockade.

On the 7th of November Brig.-General A. Solly Flood left the 35th Brigade in order to assume command of the Third Army school, and Lieut.-Colonel G. A. Trent, 5th Northamptonshire Regiment, took over the brigade temporarily. On the 8th inst. about fifteen of the enemy raided the 37th Brigade front and reached the wire where they were fired at, a wounded prisoner remaining in our hands.

On the 13th November the 37th Brigade liberated some gas from their front line, drawing a certain amount of fire from the enemy. Incidentally, it should be mentioned that this method of trench warfare was most unpopular with the soldier, and he cordially disliked anything to do with it. The discharge of gas from the trenches meant much digging and disturbance of the fire steps, it also entailed large fatigue parties to carry up the gas cylinders. Often the cylinders remained undischarged in the trenches for a considerable time waiting for favourable wind and weather conditions, and during these periods there was always the risk of an enemy shell exploding a cylinder and the " gasser " getting gassed. The soldier also never knew what real damage was done by this method, and it certainly seemed to him as not worth the trouble.

At this period the German airmen were very active, German officers were seen observing our lines, and our wire was frequently cut. A combination leading to an expectation of some form of aggression, but nothing materialised, in spite of the suggestions by the mysterious " IT " that the enemy was preparing a gas attack. In this connection it should be explained that a listening instrument had been installed in the trenches from which wires proceeded along our front line and out into No Man's Land. The main object was to tap the enemy's telephone messages, but, incidentally, it tapped our own telephones as well, revealing that forbidden conversations on military matters sometimes took place. As no mention of this apparatus was allowed, the nickname " IT," the awe-inspiring, the mysterious, the chief spy, came into use.

On the 5th of December a raid was attempted by the 6th Queen's. The wire had been successfully cut by the artillery and trench mortars, and the raiders were forming up under a cloudy sky when, at about 9 p.m., the moon came out brightly, and, being discovered, they came under heavy fire. The officer in command decided to withdraw till the moon had gone down, but, unfortunately, just as our own trenches were reached, two German heavy trench mortar shells burst in the trench, killing Lieutenant Pim and six men, others being buried and wounded. In consequence the raid was abandoned. During the same night, at 3 a.m., on the 6th, a sentry of the 7th Norfolk Regiment observed a party of about thirty Germans 20 yards from our trenches. Lance-Corporal W. G. Turner at once ordered the parapet to be manned, and, controlling the rifle and grenade fire, drove them off. The enemy had two officers and one man killed, and one officer and one man, both of whom died later, severely wounded. The raiders had blackened their faces and were armed with automatic pistols. The next day a dummy bomb, with a streamer attached, was sent over into our lines carrying a message enquiring for news of the wounded officer. On each of the two following days a German was wounded and taken prisoner reconnoitring our wire. On the 11th inst. an enemy aeroplane was brought down close in front of our trenches. The observer, in trying to gain his own lines, was killed, and the pilot surrendered. The Germans immediately shelled the area near the fallen plane, kept machine gun fire on it all night, shelled it all next day, and it was not till the 13th that the body of the observer could be brought in to our lines; the plane was, of course, completely wrecked.

Lieut.-Colonel E. H. Collen (A.A. and Q.M.G.) had been instrumental in having a large hut built for recreation purposes in Berneville. This hut held an audience of about 800, and was opened on the 13th of November, an excellent performance being given to a crowded house by the Divisional Concert Troupe under the direction of Lieutenant Howe. On the 20th November Brig.-

General Boyd Moss proceeded to England for three months, and was succeeded by Lieut.-Colonel C. Owen, the Royal Welsh Fusiliers, commanding 6th Royal West Kent Regiment.

On the 17th of December the Division was again relieved by the 14th Division and proceeded to the Grande Rullecourt and Ambrines areas, with Divisional Headquarters at Le Cauroy. This was the first real rest since the opening of the Somme battle on the 1st of July, and as it meant Christmas out of the line all ranks thoroughly appreciated the fact. The usual cleaning up, refitting, and reorganising took place, and the country was scoured for the orthodox necessities for Christmas dinners. A ton of divisional Christmas cards arrived for despatch to our friends. Tournaments, races, and various competitions took place, the most successful being a horse show, a regimental drum competition, and a Marathon race, in which 117 out of 140 competitors finished the course.

The divisional artillery was now reorganised and consisted of two brigades, each composed of three batteries of six 18-pounders and one battery of six 4·5" howitzers.

On the 13th January Lieut.-Colonel C. J. C. Grant (Coldstream Guards), who had been G.S.O. (1) since December, 1915, left the Division to take up the same appointment on the Third Army Staff. He was succeeded by Lieut.-Colonel C. J. B. Hay (The Guides), who had been G.S.O. (2) of the Division for the past year.

CHAPTER XI

PREPARATIONS FOR THE BATTLE OF ARRAS
January—March, 1917
(*Maps* 9 *and* 11)

EARLY in the winter it had been settled that the offensive of the British Army in the spring of 1917 was to be carried out by the First and Third Armies on a front of about twelve miles, with Arras as the centre. In the beginning of January this information reached the divisions concerned, and on the 14th inst. the 12th Division took over a sector of 2,000 yards, extending from 700 yards south of Faubourg St. Sauveur to the River Scarpe. The enemy's trenches ran parallel to ours at a distance of about 200 yards, except on the extreme left of Blangy village, where, in one place, they approached to as close as eight yards. From this sector the attack of the VIth Corps (Haldane) was to be launched. The 37th Infantry Brigade (Cator) took over this portion of the line, which was immediately on the left of that handed over by the Division in December. The other two Infantry Brigades remained in the training area, Divisional Headquarters moving to Agnez lez Duisans.

Arras was a city built, in a large measure, on its own quarry. The stones for its houses, erected chiefly during the Spanish occupation, when wooden houses were forbidden, were taken from the ground on which they stood, thus forming large and deep cellars. The city possesses an intensely interesting history, going back to the days of Julius Cæsar, when Comius was made king of the Atrebartes, which people had as their chief town Atrebartum, the ancient name of Arras. It is significant that the city was first devastated by the Hun invasion under Attila. Peter the Hermit came to Arras and preached the first Crusade there, and the body of Robert the Second of Jerusalem, Count of Flanders, was brought back from the Crusades and buried in Arras. A cross on the Place de la Madeleine commemorates a visit paid to the city by St. Bernard. The Porte St. Nicholas and Porte Ronville, familiar to our troops, were built by Phillippe Auguste, son of Louis VII., " in honour of his victory over Othon the Fourth, Emperor of Germany," while the first " hand " artillery, later to become arquebuses, was used in an attack by Charles VI. against Arras in 1414. The Battle of Agincourt was fought in Artois, and many of the French lords killed in that battle were taken to Arras for burial, where also the Convention, bringing that campaign to a close, was signed by the English King, Henry V. Here, too, Jean d'Arc was made a prisoner in 1430, while for a hundred years in the Middle Ages Arras belonged to Spain.

There are few cities in France with a history so interesting, not only in those days of the dawn of European history, nor in the Middle Ages in which Arras was one of the leading cities of France in commerce, learning and religion, but even down to more modern times during the French Revolution, and these later days of the Great War, when Germany again battered at the walls of this ancient city. It is also safe to say that there is no town in France so closely associated with the 12th Division, and when the Division left this sector towards the end of 1917, the Mayor, in eloquent and generous terms, described the 12th Division as the " defenders and the deliverers of Arras."

The training for the forthcoming battle was most carefully and systematically carried on, and the German system of trenches, having been photographed from the air, were accurately plotted out, and to a great extent dug, in a part of the training area which somewhat resembled the terrain of the enemy's ground, all known positions of strong points, machine guns, dug-outs, etc., being especially indicated. The troops were then trained in the actual *rôle* they would have to undertake in the attack, special days being devoted to co-operation with the artillery and Air Force.

Besides guarding the front, the task of the brigade in the line was to prepare the sector for the occupation of the three Divisions, 3rd, 12th, and 15th of the VIth Corps, that were to carry out the attack. A comprehensive scheme was approved of by the corps, and work began in real earnest, the intention then being that the offensive should commence in March.

Amongst the multitudinous tasks to be undertaken space will only avail to mention some of the principal ones. In order to avoid loss to *personnel* from retaliation during our bombardment, which was to continue for four days, dug-outs were to be made in the front system to accommodate 2,400 men of each division, and to give them sleeping facilities; caves which had been formed by the excavation of the chalk, mainly to build the churches of the villages of St. Sauveur and Ronville, were to be adapted as dwelling-places and connected up, the cellars of the Petite Place and Grande Place in Arras being made intercommunicating; tunnels had to be constructed leading from the Main Sewer, along which there was a side-walk, to the caves, and from the caves extending underneath No Man's Land, and for these purposes tunnelling companies were employed, largely augmented by working parties from the troops

[*Imperial War Museum*] [*Crown copyright*

HOTEL DE VILLE AND PETITE PLACE, ARRAS

to do the carrying; light railways had to be laid; communication trenches to be greatly increased and some widened to take stretchers; positions prepared for the influx of batteries that would come into action at the last moment, and large stores of ammunition, which was now unlimited, installed for them; dumps of rations and ammunition of all descriptions had to be formed and water stored. It is not surprising, therefore, to know that working parties numbering 2,500 men were found daily. In consequence the allocation of the three infantry brigades resulted in one being in the trenches, one in the training area, and one providing working parties.

The war produced many inventions, but certainly one of the most outstanding was the sound-ranging apparatus, by which not only could the range of the gun firing be calculated, but its actual position determined. One of these was installed in Arras, and it was of great assistance in dealing with the enemy's guns.

On the 28th of January General B. Vincent, 6th Inniskilling Dragoons, assumed command of the 35th Infantry Brigade. On the 5th February the divisional guns having come into action, Brig.-General E. Willis took command of the artillery, and on the 7th the 36th Brigade relieved the 37th. In the third week of the same month the 3rd and 15th Divisions took over their sub-sectors of the trenches, the 12th retaining the centre one with a front of about 900 yards.

Although there was so much to be done in preparation for the main battle, an aggressive spirit had to be maintained, and as the command of No Man's Land was very important to us, raids were carried out frequently, and with somewhat stronger forces than previously. On the night of the 3rd of February, which was very dark, the Germans under cover of a bombardment, raided a sap manned by one N.C.O. and six men of the 6th Queen's. Two sentries on duty at the head of the sap observed the enemy approaching, and one ran back to warn those in the trench close by, but being wounded, fell dead in the trench. The N.C.O. and the other men then rushed up the sap and, opening fire with a Lewis gun wounded and took one of the raiders prisoner. The original sentry was missing, and was what was commonly called " winkled " (taken prisoner).

After careful training in the reserve area, six platoons of the 11th Middlesex Regiment under Captain Maynard raided the German trenches on the 26th inst. The plan on this occasion was to form an artillery " box " barrage to include portions of the front and support line. Inside this area all trenches were to be searched and the dugouts bombed. At 8.30 a.m. the troops left our trenches under cover of artillery fire, 18-foot Bangalore torpedoes being used to cut the wire, which they did successfully, making gaps about 12 feet wide. The trenches were then entered, and blocks made in selected positions to prevent any interference with the raiders while they were carrying out their task. The front, support line and communication trenches were thoroughly exploited and 25 prisoners taken back. Our casualites were 1 officer (Second Lieutenant Gilfillan) and 4 men killed, and 1 officer and 12 other ranks wounded. The raid was a complete success, Captain Maynard being awarded a bar to his Military Cross.

On the 14th March a small German patrol of about six men was found examining our wire, and on being fired at four were captured. On the 15th the enemy raided the junction of the 3rd and 12th Divisions and succeeded in killing five and wounding twelve of the 7th Suffolk Regiment, they also captured a Lewis gun. On the 17th a raid was carried out by the 5th Royal Berk-

ENTRANCE TO SEWER, ARRAS

shire Regiment under Major J. S. Sharp and Lieutenant W. C. Adams. It consisted of 10 officers and 200 other ranks, who were divided into six parties, three to deal with the front line and three with the second. The divisional and corps heavy artilleries co-operated successfully in maintaining the " box " barrage. Opposition in the trenches was not very serious, and when we got into the front line the Germans tried to escape by the communication trenches, but our men going over the top, reached the second line first and shot several of them. All the enemy inside the barrage were killed or taken prisoners and the dug-outs destroyed by exploding Stokes mortar bombs in them. The raid started at 7 a.m. and lasted twenty-five minutes. Up to the time for the return to our lines the casualties had been negligible, Lieutenant Fellowes being wounded going over the top and one soldier near the enemy's front line. However, whilst retiring the Germans put down a heavy barrage through which our troops had to pass, and casualties occurred, amongst them Major Sharp, who was killed 10 yards from our parapet. Our casualties were 7 killed and 29 wounded. We captured 6 prisoners and two machine guns, and 120 of the enemy were computed to have been killed, and in addition 300 yards of front and support line were thoroughly searched. Other raids followed these and it was evident that the Germans were holding their front line lightly, with their main strength in the support line.

The withdrawal of the German line towards St. Quentin, which had commenced in February, now (18th March) began to show itself near Arras. The 12th Division front was not affected, as the northern pivot of the movement was on the Arras-Cambrai Road, on the immediate right of the Division. Each day now saw one or other of the different tasks in hand finished.

In the trenches, in addition to the dug-outs, Brigade and Battalion Headquarters, trench mortar emplacements, aid posts, a dressing station, bridges to cross the trenches and various stores had been made. The caves were fitted with sleeping bunks, kitchens, water supply, sanitation, and electric light. A tunnel ran from the Main Sewer through the caves to the front, and in this a tram line was laid. The expert work naturally fell on the field companies of the Royal Engineers, and on the Pioneer Battalion (5th Northamptonshire Regiment) under Lieut.-Colonel Trent. The amount of wood required was enormous, and entailed the purchase of standing trees in the woods at Le Cauroy, from whence they were transferred to a saw mill at Frévent, which ran continuously with eight-hour shifts. The timbers were then taken to workshops at Louez and finished off. The control of all this work was under the Divisional Commanding Royal Engineer, Lieut.-Colonel Bovet, and to him and his adjutant, Captain Lee Norman, the highest credit is due.

During the first days of April the artillery, which had been largely augmented, came into position. Tanks were concentrated, reserve divisions closed up, and on the 3rd the 12th Division troops moved to their battle areas, Divisional Headquarters going to Wagnonlieu.

Every detail for the coming attack had been practised by the troops, every requirement for their accommodation, movement and supply had been arranged. The streets of Arras were smothered in direction signs, and it was possible to go from the entrance of the Main Sewer near the Petite Place to half-way across No Man's Land under ground. The final preparations for the Battle of Arras were complete.

CHAPTER XII

THE BATTLE OF ARRAS
April 4th—May 16th, 1917
(*Maps* 11, 12, *and* 13)

THE attack of the British forces, aiming at the capture of Monchy-le-Preux and the Vimy Ridge, and the breaking through of the German line, was to be launched on the 9th of April. On the right was the Third Army (Allenby), with the VIIth Corps (Snow), VIth Corps (Haldane), and XVIIth Corps (Fergusson); on the left, the First Army (Horne), with the Canadian Corps (Byng).

The task of the VIth Corps with the 3rd Division (Deverell) on the right, the 12th Division (Scott) in the centre, and the 15th (Reed) on the left, was to gain the Wancourt-Feuchy line, entailing an advance of over 4,000 yards. The 37th Division (Williams) was to take the important position of Monchy-le-Preux, the cavalry meanwhile being in readiness to push on and exploit the success. Of the 12th Division, the 37th Infantry Brigade (Cator) on the right and the 36th (Owen) on the left were to capture the black line (800 yards) consisting of the enemy's front system, as well as the blue line, a further distance of 1,000 yards, in which were a series of strong redoubts. The 35th Infantry Brigade (Vincent) was then to pass through and, going forward 2,600 yards, attack the brown line, including the Wancourt-Feuchy trench, well wired and containing the strong post known as the Feuchy Chapel Redoubt, on the Cambrai Road.

An artillery bombardment commenced along the whole line at 7 a.m. on the 4th of April, the main objects being the destruction of the enemy's wire and the battering down of his defences. On portions of the front line the wire extended to a depth of 75 yards; it was also very thick in front of the second line and surrounding the various strong points. Counter battery work did not start until the 7th inst., in order that sufficient time might not be available for the enemy to restore damaged material before the infantry attacked on the 9th. The whole of the machine guns in the Division were placed under the command of Captain Hayward, and twenty-four of these formed a barrage which synchronised with that of the artillery.

The dug-outs in our front line fully justified the labour expended; one of the battalions occupying them for the five days of our bombardment, which at times drew heavy retaliation from the enemy, did not suffer a single casualty. The caves and cellars also afforded safety enabling the troops to rest, and in consequence enter the fight fresh and physically fit.

As an idea was prevalent that the Germans might be withdrawing their troops on our front, a raid was carried out by two parties of the 6th Queen's at 9 p.m. on the 7th inst. The northern party was successful in capturing two prisoners, but the southern one went with such dash that it passed through our own barrage penetrating to the German third line, and suffered in consequence, Second Lieutenant Bourne and five others being reported missing. One non-commissioned officer managed to crawl back, and he stated that the first and second lines of the front system were hardly recognisable and presented little or no obstacle. It was good news to hear that the artillery bombardment had been so effective.

Arras Trenches

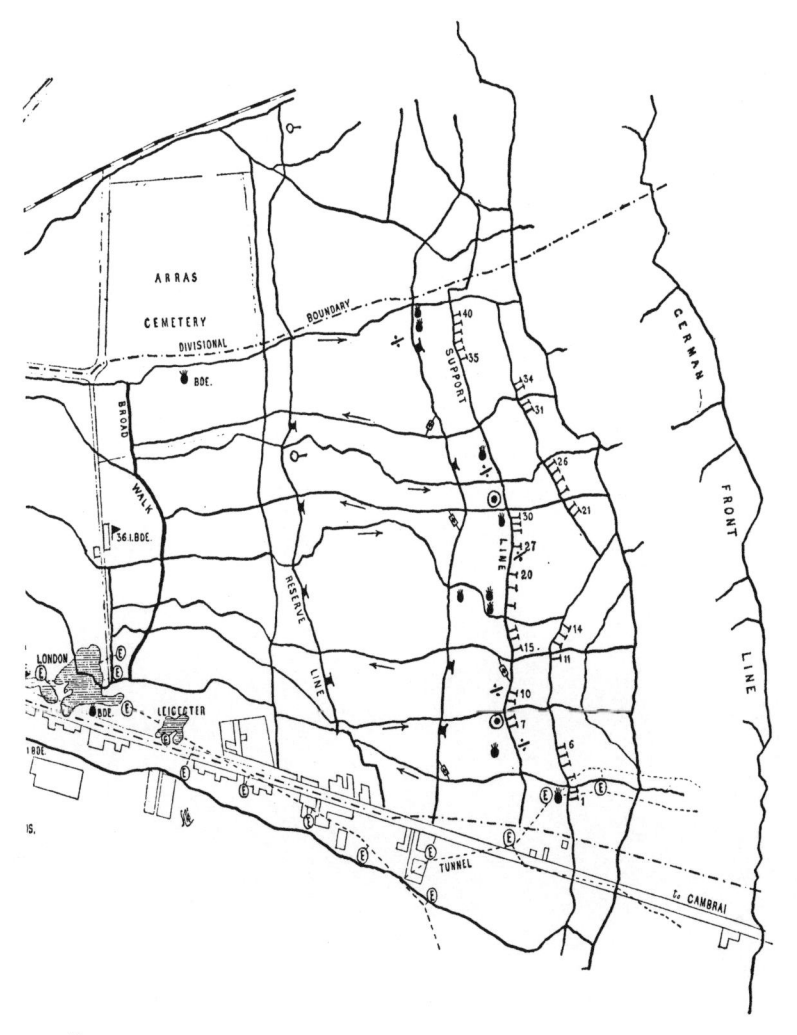

The underground way from Arras to the front culminated in two passages, and on the 8th inst. exits were made from them into No Man's Land. At the earnest request of the officer in charge of the Press (Major Faunthorpe, I.C.S.), one of these exits was placed at his disposal for the purpose of taking a cinema film of the attack. Unfortunately, some gas shell falling short he and the operator became affected, and no record was obtained.

Zero was fixed for Monday, April 9th, and sharp at 5.30 a.m. the leading waves of the infantry advanced to the assault under cover of a creeping barrage, stated by all units to have been most effective. Owing to the suddenness of the attack many of the Germans were unable to emerge from their dug-outs, which had very narrow entrances, in time to oppose our advance. Resistance was rapidly overcome and the front system (black line), consisting of four lines of trenches, was occupied to time. The battalions which carried out this operation were the 6th Queen's (Rolls) and 7th East Surrey (Baldwin) of 37th, the 11th Middlesex (Wollocombe) and 7th Royal Sussex (Sanson) of 36th Brigade. The counter battery work had practically silenced the German guns, and the leading troops halted on the black line to clear up the captured ground, and allow the supporting battalions to pass through and form up for the second phase.

At 7.30 a.m. the advance was continued by the 6th Buffs (Cope), 6th Royal West Kent (Dawson) of 37th, 9th Royal Fusiliers (Overton), and 8th Royal Fusiliers (Elliott-Cooper) of 36th Brigade, the creeping barrage again moving forward at 100 yards every four minutes. This further advance entailed the crossing of Scott's valley and the capture of Observation Ridge, on the western face of which the German second system consisted of a series of entrenched works, heavily wired and strongly defended by machine guns and brave fighters. The capture of this position did not prove such an easy proposition as anticipated, while of two tanks detailed for the attack on these strong points, one never reached the rendezvous, and the other failed to cross our trenches. As a consequence the infantry had to do without their assistance. Some portions of this system were carried by the assault, but some offered considerable resistance, only to be overcome by outflanking movements, initiated by individuals, or small parties working in co-operation. Houlette and Holt Works, however, held out.

Much opposition was encountered on the extreme left from the position known as Feuchy Switch. Here the 8th Royal Fusiliers, moving in conjunction with a battalion of the 15th Division on their left, worked to the north and overcame it. This movement resulted in cutting off the retreat of the enemy holding Hart Work, and 200 prisoners were taken there, Second Lieutenant Beames being awarded the Military Cross for his bravery and leadership. During this operation Corporal G. Moakes crawled forward and, reaching a German trench, secured a prisoner and took him back to his commanding officer, who thereby gained valuable information as to the enemy's disposition, materially assisting in the success. On the capture of Heron, Hamel and Hart Works, the 9th and 8th Royal Fusiliers pushed on, gaining Habarcq and Hem Trenches. Here their advance was delayed by machine gun fire from Observation Ridge.

The 7th East Surrey, which had gained its objective in the first phase, was consolidating its position, when Sergeant H. Cator of that battalion found his platoon was suffering severely by machine gun fire coming from Hangest Trench. On his own initiative, and taking another man with him, he advanced across the open. The other man was killed after going about 50 yards, but Sergeant Cator, continuing by himself, picked up a Lewis gun and some drums of ammunition on his way, and succeeded in entering the northern end of the trench. Having discovered the position of the machine gun which was causing the casualties, he opened fire, eventually killing the whole team and the officer in charge, whose papers he afterwards brought in. He continued to hold that end of the attack until Sergeant Jarrott and a bombing squad arrived, and attacking the enemy in flank, drove them out. This action greatly assisted the advance of the Royal West Kent Regiment, which had been temporarily held up, and Sergeant Cator, for this deed of daring, received the Victoria Cross.

Owing to the strong resistance met with, the blue line had not been completely captured in the scheduled time. Nevertheless, General Scott ordered the 35th Brigade to advance according to the plans laid down, considering its appearance on the battlefield would force the Germans, still holding out, to surrender. This brigade, which had been located in the cellars in Arras, proceeded through the tunnel to the caves, and thence, as the enemy's artillery fire on our trenches was negligible, it debouched and, moving over the top, closed up to the leading troops of the 12th Division. At 12.15 p.m. the 7th Norfolk on the right with the 5th Royal Berkshire echeloned on the left, followed by the 7th Suffolk and 9th Essex Battalions, passed through the 37th and 36th Brigades.

The 7th Norfolk (Walter) rapidly overcame the remaining opposition in Haucourt Trench and Houlette Work, and a platoon of "B" Company, 5th Royal Berkshire, outflanking Holt, that stronghold, with a garrison of thirty-five men with a machine gun, surrendered. Thus at 1.5 p.m. the blue line was definitely in our possession. The real task of the 35th Brigade, the capture of the brown line, now commenced. There was no intervening system of trenches, but opposition was expected at Maison Rouge, and the enemy's batteries were known to be in the valley that had to be traversed. The plan was to capture Feuchy-Chapel Redoubt and its surroundings, and to pierce the line just west of Orange Hill.

On the capture of the blue line the Germans, becoming disorganised, were caught on the run, and the 35th Infantry Brigade had the joy of seeing them retreating in disorder. Those overtaken were only too willing to obey instructions and move down the main road to Arras to report as prisoners. The 7th Norfolk pushed forward to level with the Bois des Bœufs, and Captain Gethin, giving the enemy no time to think, dashed on and, seizing the Maison Rouge, which was the completion of his task, continued until brought to a halt before Feuchy Chapel Redoubt. The 7th Suffolk (Cooper) and 9th Essex (Trevor) now proceeded to the final objective. The Essex gained Feuchy Chapel Redoubt, but the greater portion of this attack was stopped by Church Work, uncut wire, and machine guns. The tanks which had been detailed to assist in the capture of this position were out of action, two having been set on fire by the enemy's guns, and two having stuck in the mud. All attempts to cut the wire by hand and proceed were frustrated, and a line was taken up along the Feuchy Road, the 3rd Division on the right being held up in a similar manner. Meanwhile the 5th Royal Berkshire (Willan), advancing on the left, found itself in front of four German batteries of artillery, firing point blank at a range of about 400 yards. Undeterred, and, if anything, enthused by the sight, the troops charged forward, and by means of short rushes and concentrated fire, reached the batteries, and eighteen field guns, four howitzers, and forty prisoners, were captured. On this occasion Lieutenants J. M. Reday and G. P. Debeno, Company Sergt.-Major Arthur Blake, and Private McAllister distinguished themselves by their leadership and fearless courage. So keen were the men that, with the assistance of a Royal Artillery officer, who accompanied the battalion, they manned the captured guns and opened fire on the retreating enemy. The attack continued towards Orange Hill, but was held up by the uncut wire, and finally the 5th Royal Berkshire took up a line on the Feuchy Road in continuation of the Essex.

The artillery supporting the 12th Division attack was under command of Brig.-General E. Willis, and consisted of a Right Group (Hext), 63rd and 62nd (Wynne) Brigades, R.F.A., covering the 37th Infantry Brigade, and a Left Group (M. Smith), 17th R.F.A. and 15th R.H.A. Brigades of 29th Divisional Artillery, covering the 36th Infantry Brigade. Besides these batteries, there was Le Pelley's Group of VIth Corps heavy artillery, consisting of the 48th and 81st Groups, composed of twelve 6″ and eight 9·2″ howitzers. At 10 a.m. the 62nd Brigade, R.F.A., and at 11 a.m. the 17th Brigade, R.F.A., advanced to support the attack of the 35th Brigade on the brown line, timed to commence at 12.10 p.m. The 63rd Brigade, R.F.A., which had moved forward at 2 p.m. also came into action for the same purpose. The sight of the guns galloping into action was not one of the least thrills of the day.

The 37th Division (B. Williams), in accordance with its *rôle* to push through the 35th Infantry Brigade, when the brown line was captured, had advanced in rear of that brigade's attack, and the 63rd Infantry Brigade (37th Division) came up into line with the Essex and Berkshire battalions on the Feuchy Road. No further progress was possible before nightfall, and arrangements were made to destroy the wire by artillery fire, and renew the attack on the Wancourt-Feuchy line, on the morning of the 10th inst. The 15th Division (Reed), on the left, reached the brown line at about 6 p.m. and, with the assistance of a tank, gained a footing in the northern portion of the Wancourt-Feuchy Trench, and during the night extended the gap southwards. On ascertaining this fact, General Scott ordered a reserve formed by the 36th Infantry Brigade, consisting of three companies of the 7th Royal Sussex and three companies of the 11th Middlesex, to reinforce the 5th Royal Berkshire. This force, under the command of Lieut.-Colonel Willan, was to pass through the gap and work along the rear of the enemy's line, in conjunction with the artillery bombardment and frontal attack of the remainder of the 35th Brigade.

At daybreak the artillery fire opened on the Wancourt-Feuchy Trench, and Lieut.-Colonel Willan's force, crossing the trench in the 15th Division sector, passed along the slopes of Orange Hill, and caused the Germans who were still holding out in Church Work and its neighbourhood to evacuate their positions without fighting. By 12 noon the 35th Brigade had occupied the position, and the final objective of the 12th Division was captured. Patrols were pushed forward to Chapel and Orange Hills, and consolidation carried on.

The 37th Division then passed through to attack Monchy-le-Preux, the 8th Cavalry Brigade waiting close by.

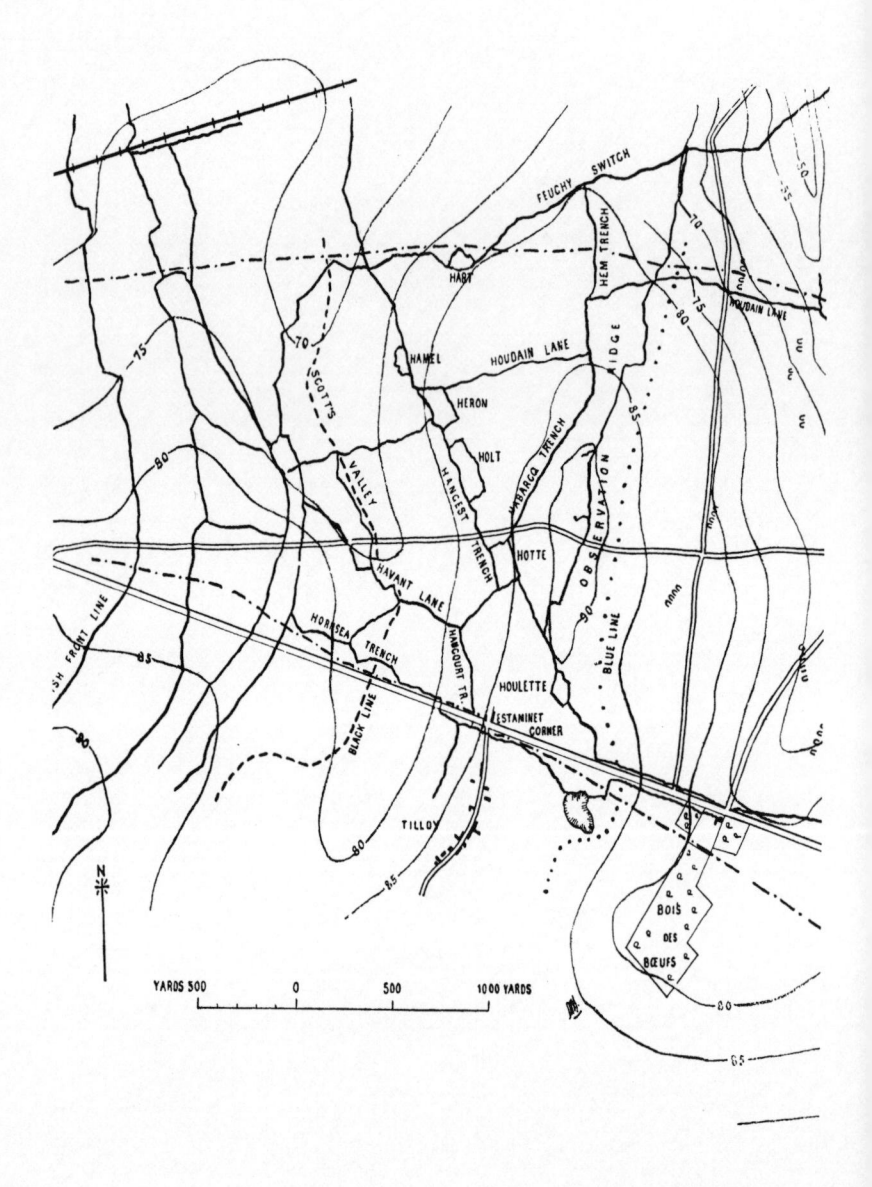

MAP No. 12. THE BAT

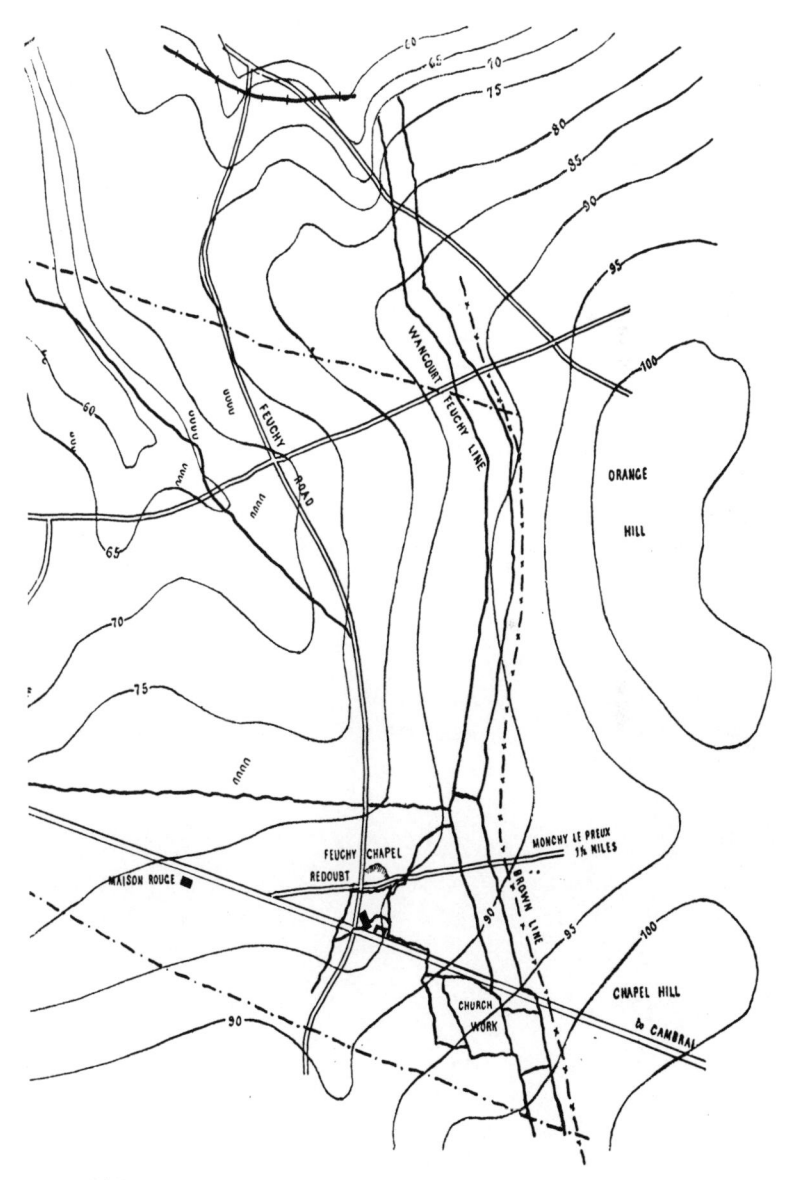

TLE OF ARRAS

The 12th Division now became VIth Corps Reserve, the troops remaining where they were. The weather on the 9th was very inclement, but during that night and on the 10th inst. it was far worse, owing to much sleet and snow. This inclemency was greatly aggravated by the fact that an order had to be issued forbidding the occupation of German "dug-outs," necessitated by the enemy having left "booby-traps" in these places. These traps were operated by various methods, a violent explosion being the inevitable result. The signallers of the 11th Middlesex fell victims to one such trap, and the above order was immediately given—fortunately as it turned out, six explosions taking place in the first twelve hours after the capture of the position. Of these traps two might be mentioned in detail. In one the eating through of a piece of metal by an acid released a weight which actuated the explosion. This was an unpleasant form, as the apparatus could be easily overlooked. The other was a warning to "curio" hunters. An attractive souvenir would be attached to the mechanism, and on being lifted or pulled the explosion occurred.

On the 11th inst. the 37th Division succeeded in capturing the greater portion of Monchy-le-Preux, and the 8th Cavalry Brigade, going to its assistance, completed the operation, although suffering heavy casualties. During the night of the 11th–12th the 36th and 37th Brigades of the 12th Division relieved the cavalry brigade, and the 37th Division, east of Monchy, the 35th Brigade being in reserve. Beyond some intermittent shelling and sniping nothing of note took place on the 12th inst., the principal work of that day being performed by the 37th Field Ambulance (Captain J. H. Fletcher) and the stretcher bearers. A German dressing station, two tiers deep, was discovered, and into this a large number of cavalry officers and troopers were moved, and many a life must have been saved by this gallant officer (Fletcher) and his stretcher bearers, foremost amongst whom were Privates H. P. Stansfield and E. A. Rider.

On the night of the 12th–13th the Division was relieved by the 29th (De Lisle) and, with the exception of the artillery, 69th Field Company, Royal Engineers, and 5th Northamptonshire Regiment, moved back to the caves and to Arras. The following day the Division was transferred to the XVIIIth (Reserve) Corps (Maxse) and Headquarters returned to Wagnonlieu from Arras, where it had gone on the 11th inst., the troops marching to the delightful villages between Arras and Doullens. Divisional Headquarters eventually reached Couturelle, 35th Brigade Halloy, 36th Pommera, and 37th Humbercourt.

The Battle of Arras was a memorable one, the VIth Corps having advanced 7,500 yards; on its own front the 12th Division penetrated to a depth of over 4,000 yards. Thorough training and careful attention to the minutest details in organisation had brought its reward. Nothing was left to chance, and all ranks worked with this end in view, while compared with other battles our casualties were not large, a total of 2,018, composed as follows : Killed, officers, 24, other ranks, 322 ; missing, other ranks, 242 ; wounded, officers, 67, other ranks, 1,363. The General Staff, under Lieut.-Colonel C. J. B. Hay, and the Administrative Staff, under Lieut.-Colonel E. H. Collen, carried out their duties brilliantly. Infantry, Artillery, Engineers, Pioneers, Signals, Trench Mortars, Machine Guns, one and all had contributed to the success ; and the Royal Army Medical Corps (Colonel Silver), Supply, Ordnance, and Military Police had also equally borne their share.

The following orders of the day were issued:—

"To the Officers, Warrant Officers, Non-commissioned Officers and Men of the 12th Division:

"Lieut.-General J. A. L. Haldane, C.B., D.S.O., commanding the VIth Corps, desires me to express to all ranks his grateful appreciation of the brilliant work carried out by the 12th Division whilst under his command.

"A. B. Scott, *Major-General,*
"*Commanding* 12th *Division.*"

"To the Officers, Warrant Officers, Non-commissioned Officers, and Men of the 12th Division:

"I desire to express my warm appreciation of the excellent work you have done, and at times under very trying circumstances, in the preparations and training for the attack on the 9th April, 1917.

"I also congratulate you on the brilliant and gallant manner in which you carried that attack through to such a successful conclusion. You have not only worthily upheld the reputation gained by the Division in its previous fighting, but added greatly thereto.

"The mutual confidence which exists between the different arms has formed a powerful combination which, I feel sure, will lead to further successes when occasions arise.

"I thank you one and all.

"The march of the troops from the battlefield, where the conditions had been very severe, was worthy of the best traditions of the Army.

"The Division captured about 20 officers, 1,200 other ranks, prisoners; 41 field guns and howitzers, 28 machine guns, and 2 aerial torpedo throwers.

"A B. Scott, *Major-General,*
"*Commanding* 12th *Division.*"

After an absence of ten days from the battlefield the Division moved towards the front again, and, reaching Arras on the 24th inst., rejoined the VIth Corps. On the following night the 35th Infantry Brigade relieved the 17th Division (Robertson) on that portion of the front extending from the north-east corner of Monchy to the River Scarpe. This was not a continuous line however, but a series of trenches which had been reached in an attack on the 23rd inst., when the VIth Corps had gained Guémappe in the south, and the XVIIth Corps (Fergusson) the outskirts of Rœux in the north.

In order to straighten the line before commencing a main operation early in May, the XVIIth Corps, on the north of the Scarpe, was to undertake the capture of the village of Rœux on the 28th April. The 35th Infantry Brigade, in conforming to this movement, was to gain a line on the south side of the River Scarpe. The first objective included Rifle and Bayonet Trenches, and the 7th Norfolk Regiment with the 5th Royal Berkshire, on its left, were detailed for the task. Zero was timed for 4.25 a.m., and at that hour an intense artillery bombardment commenced, lasting for two minutes. The Germans, who had been strongly reinforced with artillery, replied with a heavy barrage on our front and support lines at three minutes past zero. Nevertheless, the attacking troops moved forward, but the 7th Norfolk, being unable to reach its objective, was compelled to establish itself in a line of shell holes in front of its original position. The 5th Royal Berkshire captured the remainder of Bayonet Trench and some 150 yards of Rifle Trench, but further attempts to gain the whole of Rifle Trench, by bombing from both flanks, failed. During this operation Corporal J. Hedgman noticed an enemy's machine gun, about 150 yards away on the bank of the Scarpe, which was hold-

[Imperial War Museum] [Crown copyright]

NEAR MONCHY-LE-PREUX

ing up the attack. He thereupon collected a small party of men and, out-manœuvring the enemy, attacked their rear, capturing the gun, 1 officer and 21 men. From the officer he secured a map giving information as to the disposition of the German machine gun positions. The 7th Suffolk passed through the Berkshire to gain the final objective, but were unable to advance owing to the machine gun fire from Rœux, which had not been taken by the troops operating on the north of the Scarpe.

At 3 a.m. on the 29th, two companies of the 9th Essex succeeded in getting into the centre portion of Rifle Trench and repulsed a counter-attack, but later on the Germans, working up New Street, gained its junction with Rifle Trench, and our troops were driven back on either side to their original positions. At nightfall the 37th and 36th Brigades relieved the 35th.

Preparations were now made for an operation on a larger scale. This attack, in which the Fifth, Third, and First Armies were to participate, was to take place on the 3rd of May, being preceded by an artillery preparation commencing on the 1st. The task of the 12th Division entailed an advance of nearly 2,000 yards on the right and 3,000 yards on the left, the latter including the taking of the village of Pelves. There were three objectives, known as the brown, the yellow, and the red lines, and on this occasion the artillery barrage was not to advance from one objective to the next until orders were received from the Division, when a new zero would be fixed for the continuation of the attack.

In order to bring forward the left a preliminary attack was made by the 36th Brigade at 1 a.m. on the 2nd May. It was preceded by a discharge of gas from Lievin projectors, but unfortunately, the wind being unfavourable, some gas blew back and disorganised the troops, only a small portion of Rifle Trench being gained. A German prisoner, however, stated that in his battalion over 200 casualties had been incurred, and also a machine gun company had been almost entirely wiped out, from the effects of the gas.

From 10 p.m. on the 2nd to 3 a.m. on the 3rd the Germans subjected our batteries to an intense bombardment of gas and other shells. Several of our guns were put out of action and gas masks had to be worn all night.

The battle commenced at 3.45 a.m. on the 3rd of May.

The 37th Brigade (Cator) with the 6th Buffs (Cope) and 7th East Surrey (Baldwin) attacked on the right, and the 36th Brigade (Owen) with the 9th Royal Fusiliers (Overton) and 8th Royal Fusiliers (Elliott-Cooper) on the left. These battalions moved forward under the creeping barrage and the leading waves gained the brown line, but the left of the 8th Royal Fusiliers, coming under considerable fire from the direction of Rœux, only reached Scabbard Trench, from which they were driven back by a counter-attack. The supporting troops were unable to progress, being strongly opposed by the enemy, who had been passed over in the dark, probably in shell holes, and collected in Devil's Trench. Red flares, the signal for the presence of our troops, had been seen in Gun and Cartridge Trenches at 7.55 a.m., and so it appears the situation at that time must have been : our foremost troops in the brown line, and the Germans holding Devil's and Scabbard Trenches. However, the information was very uncertain as all communication over the open was impossible.

At 12.10 p.m. " B " and " C " Companies of the 7th Royal Sussex, attacking under a 4·5″ howitzer barrage, drove the Germans out of Scabbard Trench and past the brown line, the 36th Brigade thus practically gaining its first objective. On being counter-attacked 2 officers,

THE BATTLE OF ARRAS

45 men and two machine guns were captured by this battalion. Whilst clearing up the captured trenches one of the Sussex threw a bomb into the dug-out in which Sergeant G. Jarratt and a few of the 8th Royal Fusiliers, who had been in the leading wave, had been placed as prisoners. Without a moment's hesitation Sergeant Jarratt placed both his feet on the bomb in an endeavour to limit the explosion and save his comrades. In this he was successful, but both his legs were blown off. His comrades were safely removed to our lines, but Sergeant Jarratt died before he could be removed. For this act of supreme self-sacrifice the V.C. was awarded posthumously.

Some of the 9th Royal Fusiliers belonging to the leading troops had been made prisoners and were being marched along the road to Douai, when the party came under our machine-gun barrage. The guard immediately dispersed for shelter, and our men, taking advantage of this, escaped, regaining our lines during the night. This day the battalion suffered a serious loss in the death of Major Coxhead, one of its most valued leaders.

About forty men of the two leading companies of the Buffs, under Second Lieutenants P. A. Cockeram and Gunther, reached the southern end of Cartridge Trench, in the yellow line, or second objective, which was covered by the protective barrage on the brown line. Here they remained all day, and having consolidated their position, beat off three determined counter-attacks. Finding they were completely isolated, and having practically expended all their ammunition, they determined to fight their way back after dark. Whilst retiring, Lieutenant Cockeram on being called upon to surrender by a German officer shot him and continued the withdrawal. On reaching Devil's Trench it was discovered to be full of Germans, but the two officers and eight men, of the original forty, succeeded in getting over and reaching our own lines, though all were wounded.

An attempt to clear up the situation on the 37th Brigade front by the 6th Royal West Kent (Dawson) at 8.40 p.m. was frustrated at once by fire from Devil's Trench. Major Dawson, again conspicuous, as in the previous battle, was wounded, and received a bar to his D.S.O.

At 2 a.m. on the 4th inst. it was evident that the 37th Brigade had made no progress, and as the village of Rœux had not been captured, and Devil's Trench was strongly held by the enemy, General Scott ordered the 36th Brigade to withdraw from the northern end of Gun Trench and consolidate Scabbard Trench.

It had been a disappointing day, and the gain was small, but the cause must be attributed to the advance having been attempted at such an early hour over a portion of ground abounding in small valleys, banks, and shell holes, and where the objectives were ill defined, also to the unfortunate over-running and failure to "mop up" Devil's Trench in the dark. Owing to the certainty that our troops were forward in the brown line, and the uncertainty as to whether they occupied any portion of Devil's Trench, an artillery bombardment of this latter could not be undertaken.

In addition to the captures by the 7th Royal Sussex Regiment, thirty-five prisoners and one machine gun were taken.

For the next few days the German artillery was extremely active, and on the 8th, 9th, and 10th instants the fire became intense. On the 12th a local attack by the 3rd Division on our right and the 36th and 37th Brigades failed once more against Devil's Trench. It was sited on the far side of a ridge, and on the attacking

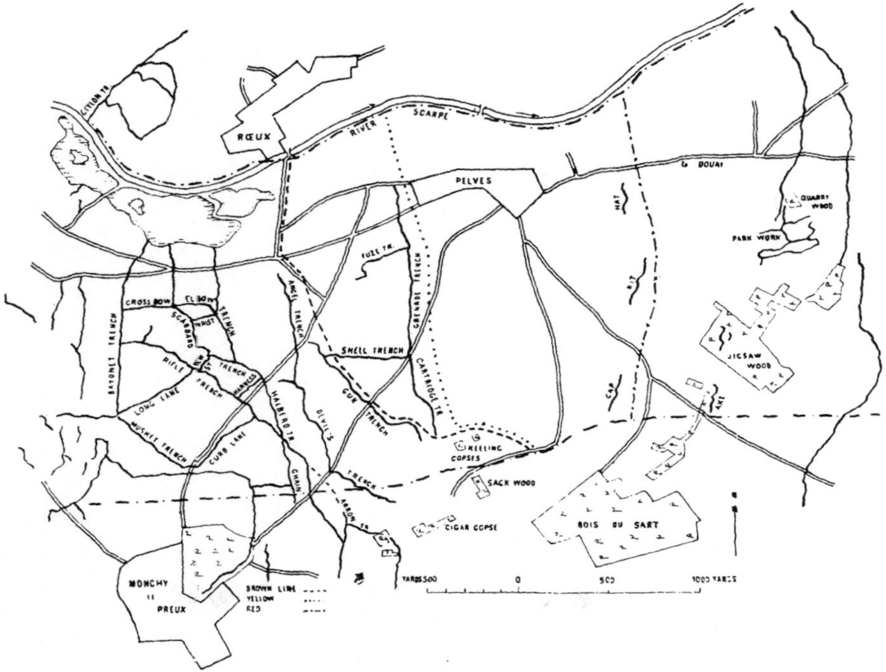

MAP No. 13. THE SCARPE

troops gaining the crest they came under a very heavy fire, both from that trench and Gun Trench.

On 14th May it was said that 100 rounds per minute fell on our front line for an hour.

On the night of the 16th the Division was relieved by the corps troops and the 29th Division (De Lisle), the 35th Brigade moving to Simencourt, the 36th to Agnez, and the 37th to Montenescourt. After resting a few days in these billets they marched to the Le Cauroy area.

The casualties from the 25th April to 18th May amounted to :—

	Killed.	Wounded.	Missing.	Total.
Officers . . .	21	87	33	141
Other ranks . .	504	2,049	827	3,380

CHAPTER XIII

THE DEFENDERS OF MONCHY-LE-PREUX
May 17th—October 19th, 1917
(*Map* 14)

THE Division, having reached the Le Cauroy area on the 24th of May, again joined the XVIIIth Corps (Maxse). It was a delightful part of the country, and as the weather was fine, all ranks thoroughly enjoyed the change from the battlefield, entering into the usual round of competitions with great spirit. The Divisional Horse Show, lasting for two days, produced some very keenly contested events, and the turn-outs of waggons, cookers, mess carts, and horses were excellent. It was during this period of rest, and after much discussion, that the Concert Troupe took the more professional title of " The Spades," in allusion to the 12th Divisional sign, the Ace of Spades.

On the 17th June the Division commenced moving back to Arras and the VIth Corps (Haldane), and on the night of the 19th–20th took over the front line, running in a semicircle about 1,000 yards east of Monchy-le-Preux, from the 3rd Division (Deverell). This division had made a successful attack on the 14th inst. and gained some ground, but the after-fighting had prevented the area being cleared, and the front line was neither continuous nor wired, the northern ends of Hook and Long Trenches being in the air. Dug-outs were conspicuous by their absence, and the cellars and ruins of Monchy could not be occupied, owing to constant attention from the German guns. A large number of dead, both men and horses, required removing, and this was one of the first duties to be carried out. Nothing of importance happened during the first few days, but it was by no means a peaceful time, as enemy aeroplanes were very active, and Hook Trench and Monchy were frequently shelled. Our artillery and machine guns also harassed the enemy every night.

On the night of the 29th June the 8th Royal Fusiliers cleared out a German post at the northern end of Hook Trench, only a few yards from our portion. This led to a counter-attack, resulting in three dead Germans being left in our hands. The bad state of the trenches, and the lack of shelter, will be gathered from our casualty list for the first ten days in the line, viz., killed, 8 officers and 54 other ranks; wounded, 15 officers, 257 other ranks—a rather heavier total than usual during the calm after a battle. On the 1st July the Division was transferred to the XVIIth Corps (Fergusson), which relieved the VIth.

A cause of great trouble in consolidating the line was the fact that due east of Monchy, towards Twin Copses, there was a belt of ground impregnated with springs, which made it impossible to maintain trenches or make dug-outs. As a consequence Hook, Hill, Dale and Shrapnel could not be continued to join up on the north. However, it was necessary to have some lateral communication in this portion of the defence, and the Royal Engineers successfully made East Reserve Trench by placing the foot-boards on piles, and using pumps to keep the water-level down.

In order to improve the situation of Long Trench, " A " Company, 7th Royal Sussex Regiment, attempted a surprise attack on a line of shell holes about 100 yards east of the northern end of Hook Trench at 2.30 a.m. on the 4th July. Owing to the vigilance of the enemy and the brightness of the night this failed.

A projected raid by the 6th Buffs on a line of shell holes opposite Tites Copse was forestalled at 5 a.m. on the 11th by a German attack on Long and Hook Trenches, which was made after a heavy bombardment by trench mortars and artillery. *Flammenwerfer* were also used, and our outposts were overwhelmed. The 6th Buffs were holding as far north as Vine and Green Lanes, and the 9th Essex in continuation. Lance-Corporal Edgington and two men, proceeding from Hook Trench up Long Trench to find out the situation, met the enemy coming in the opposite direction. Edgington at once posted Private Mapston to cover the trench with his rifle, whilst he and Private West erected a block, and this small party held the Germans back until they were joined by Second Lieutenant Stevens and two others, when further progress by the enemy was finally arrested.

The German attack on the left came against the posts of the 9th Essex, and Lance-Corporal Wall, in charge of one of these posts, taking some of his Lewis gunners, formed a block 50 yards from his gun position. He then went to the next post, where he found the men with a damaged Lewis gun. German bombers now attacked, calling on him and his party to surrender, but Corporal Wall refused, and, though wounded, regained his block with the men. The garrison at this point now consisted of Corporal Wall and sixteen men with one Lewis gun, and they maintained themselves against all attacks, only withdrawing under cover of darkness when all their ammunition was expended. Heroic resistance was also made by Second Lieutenant Capper, Corporal Perry and seven men, who were located in a sap, and drove off repeated attempts to dislodge them.

Imperial War Museum] [*Crown copyright*

MONCHY-LE-PREUX

In the northern end of Long Trench Private W. H. Prior built up ration bags as a fire screen and, being supplied with loaded rifles by Private H. Savill, fired 100 rounds, keeping the enemy back and forcing him to build a stop. The action of these two men considerably delayed the Germans and eventually permitted their own platoon to regain its front line after nightfall. Some of the enemy who obtained a footing in the Hook of Hook Trench were promptly counter-attacked, and driven out. It had been impossible to put up any wire, beyond what was rolled over the parapet, owing to the close proximity (about 100 yards) of the opposing front trenches and the fact that rifle and machine gun fire was intermittent over this ground every night.

The Germans had gained Long Trench to within 80 yards of its junction with Hook, and held a line of shell holes half-way between Long and Hook Trenches; and from the fact that an abnormal number of aeroplanes (seventeen) and observation balloons (six) were reported as active in the vicinity of the attack, and that storm troops were employed after an intense bombardment, it is evident the enemy had hoped for greater results.

It now became apparent that the German intention was to consolidate a new line connecting up the shell holes occupied on the 11th inst. and join up with Strap on the south and Devil's Trench on the north. The recapture of Long Trench being essential, it was necessary to carry out the attempt at once before the position became too strong. The attack was planned for 5 a.m. on the 15th, and was to be preceded by a hurricane bombardment of three minutes from the 18-pounders, 4·5″ howitzers, and 34,3″ Stokes mortars. Unfortunately torrential rain occurred during the night, and the attack had to be postponed. It was eventually carried out at 4.45 a.m. on the 17th inst., when the 6th Queen's and 6th Royal West Kent Regiments of the 37th Brigade attacked on the right, and the 9th Essex, of 35th Brigade, on the left. The Queen's captured the eastern extremity, and, being held up by a bombing block, rushed over the top and, enveloping it, took twelve prisoners. This assault was led by Second Lieutenant Charwood, who displayed great gallantry. The 6th Royal West Kent met with little opposition, but passed over parties of Germans who lay prone in the bottom of the trench in process of making. The consolidating troops, who were following with rifles slung, not expecting any enemy, jumped in on the top of them, and being attacked turned to with their picks and shovels and laid the enemy out.

The 9th Essex gained their line of posts, but, owing to the nature of the ground, were unable to hold them, as a commanding post in Long Trench had not been captured. All communication with the attacking force was cut off, and for the greater part of the day it was feared the attack had failed. But at 4.30 p.m. a runner, Private T. Adams of the Royal West Kent, who had taken four hours to complete his mission by crawling from shell hole to shell hole, arrived to say that three parties of Royal West Kent, under command of Captain Thomas and Lieutenant Scott-Martin, were hanging out in Long Trench. At 9.45 p.m., when it was still light enough for the troops to see the shell holes, reinforcements were pushed forward, and the portions of Long Trench still held by the enemy again attacked.

By 10.15 p.m. Long Trench, with the exception of one post, captured by the Queen's at 1 a.m., was in our hands, and on the left the Essex held posts joining up with our front line. There is little doubt that the

DEFENDERS OF MONCHY-LE-PREUX

success of the operation was due to the gallantry of Captain Thomas, Second Lieutenant Scott-Martin, and the men of the Royal West Kent under them, who held out all day in the advanced posts. Captain Thomas, with six men, held his post for seventeen hours, and Lieutenant K. R. Bull, who was one of this party, though wounded, crawled about from shell hole to shell hole, bringing food and water for this small garrison. Lieutenant Scott-Martin and fifteen other ranks held an isolated post throughout the day, and drove off repeated attacks by the enemy. The gallantry of Private Adams, who carried in the information, was of inestimable value. Mention must also be made of Private Kirkbridge, who had volunteered to take back information, but was severely wounded and later on found 80 yards from our front line. Thirty-three prisoners were captured in all.

Owing to the configuration of this debatable ground, which was at the bottom of a valley, it was now decided to consolidate the line of shell holes (to be known as Spoon Trench), and subsequently fill up Long with wire and abandon it. In order to blunt the salient that would still exist, a surprise attack on the German line due east of Hook and north of Infantry Lane was organised and carried out by the 5th Royal Berkshire Regiment at 3 p.m. on the 19th inst. However, the enemy was on the alert, and although some of the Berkshire penetrated the German trench, they were driven out again. This was the same place where a surprise attack by the 7th Royal Sussex failed on the 4th July.

Following our capture of Long Trench the enemy employed numbers of observation balloons, and his aeroplanes, flying very low over our front trenches, machine-gunned the occupants. One in particular became very familiar under the name of " Red Belly," by reason of its colour, belonging to the famous Richthofen Squadron. It came morning after morning, and many bullets were expended in attempts to bring down the pilot, who appeared to have a charmed life according to the accounts of those who held the rifles.

On the 22nd July a memorable function took place in the city of Arras, when Major-General A. B. Scott handed over to the mayor several German guns captured at the Battle of Arras, four of which had been taken by the 12th Division. A guard of honour was found by the 6th Queen's, and the divisional band played the national airs.

At 3 a.m. on the 25th inst., after a heavy trench mortar and artillery bombardment, the Germans with *flammenwerfer* attacked the 7th Sussex of the 36th Brigade, gaining the remnants of Long Trench and Spoon Trench. From now on the Germans were allowed to retain these trenches, and the Division was heartily glad to be rid of them, as they were only a source of weakness unless the whole line was to be advanced. Several times during the next two months we held them temporarily whilst carrying out raids. Our casualties for July were: killed, 10 officers and 181 other ranks; wounded and missing, 35 officers and 952 other ranks—a somewhat serious matter, as reinforcements were scarce in consequence of the main offensive at Ypres having commenced.

At 6 p.m. on the 2nd of August the Germans began a very heavy bombardment on Hook Trench, and at 9.20 p.m. assaulted. They succeeded in gaining the eastern end of Pick Avenue, but by 10 a.m. on the 3rd the 7th Norfolk (Walter) had expelled them again. The northern portion of Hook Trench was held by the 6th Royal West Kent (Alderman). A first attempt by the enemy to advance at 9 p.m. was stopped by our artillery fire; a second attempt at 9.20 p.m. reached our wire and came under heavy rifle fire, which drove them back, with the exception of one party who gained the Hook; a third effort at 10.15 p.m. was completely broken up.

While the front line was being shelled, trench mortars taking a leading part, the West Kent moved forward into the saps, which had been pushed out and wired, and thus not only escaped the shells, but effectually broke up the attacks, a method we had learnt from the successful defence of a sap by Lieutenant Capper and his party on the 11th July. The Hook remained in German possession during the 3rd, and a first attempt to regain it at 10 p.m. failed. Lieut.-Colonel Alderman then organised a bombing attack covered by an intense barrage of rifle grenades, which proved successful, but the enemy made a very determined resistance, an hour and a half being required to overcome it. This post, only about 50 yards from the German line, had been joined thereto by two new trenches, and large quantities of wire, stick bombs, and equipment were found in it. As a result of the German attack four prisoners, several dead, four machine guns and a *flammenwerfer* remained in our hands. Lieut.-Colonels Walter and Alderman had dealt with the situation with great success, and the Army Commander (Byng) said, " I consider the conduct of all ranks to be worthy of very high praise." Our trenches were badly damaged, and in some places were non-existent.

During this period of fighting the Royal Engineers and 5th Northamptonshire Regiment, assisted by working parties from the infantry, had been steadily improving the communication trenches, making dug-outs, machine gun posts, getting water pipes laid up to the reserve line, and generally bettering the conditions of trenches. A training ground had been established at

Beaurains, and there the troops, selected to take part in raids, were exercised. A carefully-made model, on a scale of 1/100, of the area of operations was erected, in order that the action of each party and of the whole operation could be explained to all concerned. Particular attention was paid to physical and bayonet exercises, so that the men should be thoroughly fit and able to carry out the special *rôle* of the raids, namely, destruction. Such operations were now on a larger scale, and guns of all calibres were concentrated for the purpose—a group of these, that were moved to any required locality, being known as " The Circus."

In the first of these " larger scale " raids, a belt of the enemy's trenches 2,000 yards long by 300 yards deep was subjected to a heavy bombardment, and then entered by strong patrols, whose duty was to kill any survivors, obtain identifications, and destroy dug-outs, etc. Owing to inclement weather on the 8th of August, a bombardment which had been postponed for twenty-four hours commenced at 6.30 a.m. on the 9th, and continued with varying intensity until 7.45 p.m., when the infantry advanced under a creeping barrage. On the right were 350 of the 7th Suffolk (Cooper), who attacked in three parties towards the Bois du Vert and the Mound. Little resistance was encountered, the enemy's trenches being much damaged, with a large number of dead lying in them, Long Trench being quite unrecognisable as such. Forward posts were established to protect the raiders at work, and the area being thoroughly searched for forty-five minutes, the troops returned to our lines. Sixty-nine prisoners and two machine guns were brought back by this battalion. Next to the Suffolk came eighty 7th East Surrey (Baldwin), also divided into three parties, who were entirely successful, and succeeded in destroying two dug-outs and bringing in about twenty prisoners and one machine gun. On their left eighty of the 6th Buffs, likewise in three groups, met with a good deal of resistance, the two right parties only managing to penetrate a short distance, and the third failing altogether. On their left the 4th Division (Lambton) co-operated, but they, too, were unable to overcome the machine gun fire, which appeared to be very cleverly masked in that area.

This was the first occasion on which small demolition parties of the Royal Engineers accompanied the raiders, and most useful they proved themselves in destroying dug-outs, a grenade dump, and machine gun emplacements. The 2″ Trench Mortars had behaved gallantly, making accurate shooting, even though frequently buried by the enemy's shell fire. The operation was very successful, as the identifications obtained were important, and the Germans suffered severely. The Commander-in-Chief sent his congratulations, and the following messages were received : From the Army Commander, "Heartiest congratulations to 12th Division on very successful operation"; from Corps Commander, "Many congratulations to you and your Division on successful work. All ranks have shown pluck and grit throughout a trying time which reflects the greatest credit on them." Our casualties consequent to this raid were : killed, 2 officers and 33 other ranks ; wounded and missing, 12 officers and 205 other ranks. The expenditure of ammunition in the divisional artillery on 8th and 9th insts. was, 18-pounder, 22,800 ; 4·5″ howitzer, 10,100 ; 2″ trench mortar, 1,358 ; Stokes' gun, 2,700 rounds.

On 19th August the Germans shelled the forward batteries, and not for the first time, very heavily, commencing at 6.45 a.m. and continuing till 12 noon. In that period it was computed 2,000 shells fell in the vicinity of the three batteries located behind a ridge south of Monchy, about 2,200 yards from the front line. " D " Battery, 63rd Brigade, had three guns knocked out, and two ammunition stores of 150 rounds each blown up, forming a huge crater, and carrying a large portion of a gun 370 yards. " A " Battery, 48th Brigade, had three guns damaged. Owing to their excellent dug-outs the gunner casualties were negligible. The close proximity of these guns to the German position had always been a great source of annoyance to them.

At 7.15 p.m. on September 2nd a raid on Strap Trench was made by 100 of the 9th Royal Fusiliers, under Captain G. A. Baudains. The chief element being surprise, there was no artillery preparation, but a box barrage was formed as the signal for the raiders to advance. The troops took thirty seconds to cross to the German line, and, the enemy being completely surprised, there was little or no opposition, only one machine gun opening fire. Two snipers were bayoneted on the way; three dug-outs were found, the occupants of two surrendering, but those of the other, refusing to do so, were bombed, and the dug-out caught fire. A machine gun was destroyed, and eighteen prisoners were taken, giving the identification of a fresh regiment in the line on its first day. Second Lieutenant R. B. McCallum was unfortunately killed as he returned, and eleven men were wounded. For his excellent leading and organisation Captain Baudains received the Military Cross.

The following message was received : " The Army Commander has the greatest pleasure in communicating the following message received from the Commander-in-Chief, and wishes to add his sincere congratulations to those who have prepared and carried out these successful enterprises.

"'The Commander-in-Chief congratulates you and your troops on the repeated successes gained in your local operations which show excellent spirit and skill. These successes help appreciably in the general plan.'"

At 2.30 on 22nd September seventy of "C" Company, 9th Essex, under Captain Brown, raided 150 yards of Spoon Trench north of Infantry Lane under the protection of a box barrage. The movement was so rapid—the enemy's front line being entered in twenty seconds—that eighteen Germans were killed, five brought back as prisoners, in the space of five minutes, and before the enemy had been able to locate the attack. Our casualty was one wounded. The Corps Commander sent his congratulations to the 9th Essex: "A plucky raid which reflects great credit on them, carried out with dash." The Army Commander remarked: "An operation which exemplifies dash and originality. A most praiseworthy enterprise, and all ranks to be commended."

On 24th September the Germans opened an artillery barrage at 4.30 a.m. on the front held by the 6th Queen's (Rolls), south of Tites Copse. The enemy appeared to have formed up in front of his wire, but any advance was completely broken up by prompt fire from the artillery, trench mortars, and machine guns, and our wire was not reached.

In each raid the artillery had rendered most efficient support, and all ranks were loud in praise of "our gunners," and it was to the regret of all that on the 28th inst. the G.O.C., R.A., Brig.-General E. H. Willis, left the Division to join the XVIIth Corps, being succeeded by Brig.-General H. M. Thomas. A week later Brig.-General A. B. E. Cator, who had commanded the 37th Infantry Brigade for one and a half years, and gained the admiration and esteem of all ranks, both in his brigade and in the Division, left to take command of the 58th Division. He was succeeded by Brig.-General Incledon Webber, Royal Irish Fusiliers.

The 7th Royal Sussex (Impey) were to have carried out a raid on the 3rd October, but early that morning an airman reported the German trenches as full of men, and that fresh wire had been put out. As a consequence the raid was cancelled and a heavy bombardment substituted. This continued from 2.30 to 6.30 p.m., and at 8 p.m. two strong patrols were sent under a protective barrage to Spoon Trench, and found it strongly held.

In the first week of October rumours as to the future of the Division became a leading topic, the only certainty being that we must either be relieved or receive strong reinforcements, though the latter, owing to the fighting at Passchendaele, was most improbable. However, one more raid was to be carried out on the 14th inst., and on a bigger scale than ever. Seven hundred and fifty infantry were to participate in the operation, and these were trained for a week over taped ground at Beaurains. There was also a large artillery concentration, which consisted of:

1	15″ howitzer.	17	60-pounders.
3	12″ howitzers.	74	18-pounders.
20	9·2″ ,,	2	9·45″ trench mortars.
27	8″ ,,	6	6″ ,, ,,
65	6″ ,,	12	2″ ,, ,,
28	4·5″ ,,		

The G.O.C., Royal Artillery, of XVIIth Corps (Willis) took command of this concentration, and the great labour in organising the tasks was most efficiently performed by him.

The operation was carried out by the 37th and 35th Infantry Brigades on similar lines to that of the 9th of August. There were three phases: first, the bombard-

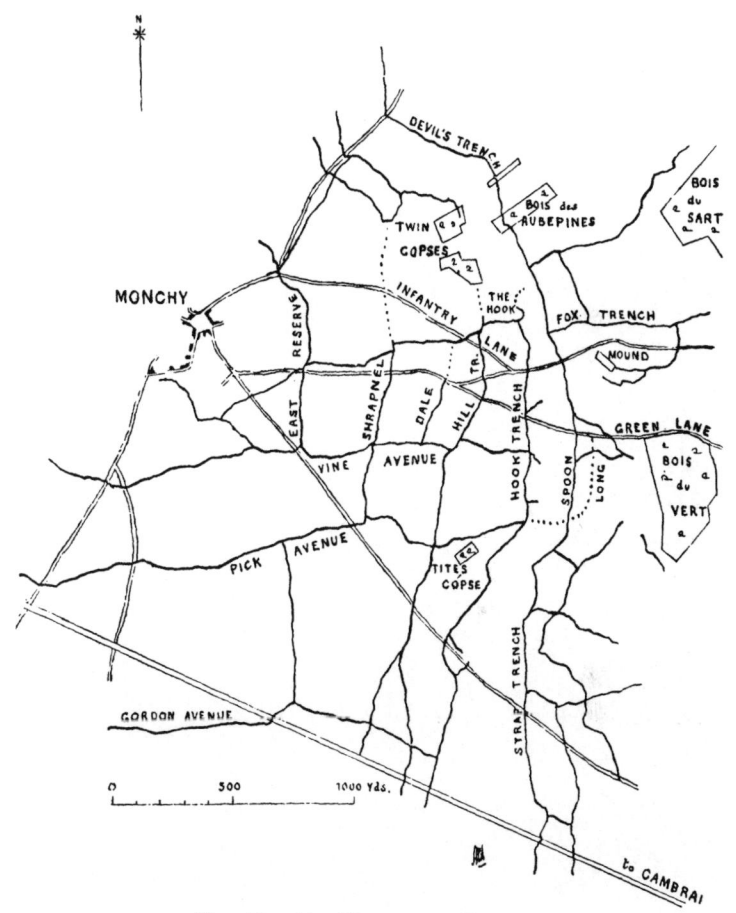

Map No. 14.   Monchy-le-Preux

ment commencing at six hours before zero ; second, the troops dribbling forward from their dug-outs to form up one and a half hours before zero ; third, the raid from zero to forty-five minutes after zero. The guns entered upon their tasks at 10.55 a.m. on 14th October, and at 4.55 p.m. the troops assaulted the German trenches. On the right the 6th Queen's (Rolls) with four parties of fifty each under Second Lieutenants C. E. St. F. Daly, J. H. Manicon, C. L. Borst, and M. Bell Smith, the whole under command of Captain J. M. Pike ; the 6th Royal West Kent (Dawson), also four parties of fifty each under Second Lieutenants G. B. Slade, R. E. Davey, J. Parminter and W. J. Elliott, the whole under Captain L. C. R. Smith. Accompanying these battalions of the 37th Brigade were twenty of the 87th Field Company, Royal Engineers, for demolition purposes, and amongst them Sapper W. J. Stainer, who was specially commended for his work on that day. On the left were 330 of the 7th Norfolk (Gethin), accompanied by fifteen of the 70th Field Company, R.E.

The German trenches were severely damaged by the fire from the guns and trench mortars, and many dead were seen lying about. There was little resistance, and the raid, proceeding according to plan, resulted in the destruction of sixteen dug-outs (two by artillery fire and fourteen by the R.E.), one *granatenwerfer*, and one machine gun and its emplacement ; also in the capture of sixty-four prisoners, including one officer, and three light machine guns, two of which were converted Lewis guns. Contributing to this success were No. 3 Special Company, R.E., which fired a thermite and smoke screen on the extremities of the attack, and the 15th and 51st Divisions, who co-operated with fire on their respective flanks. The German guns were practically silent, pointing to the good counter-battery work of our artillery; his aeroplanes were very active, however, and, flying low, machine-gunned the attackers, causing some of the casualties, which amounted to 6 officers and 17 other ranks killed, 3 officers and 144 other ranks wounded and missing. The raid was entirely successful, as a portion of the enemy's trench system had been seriously damaged and disorganised, and a considerable number of his troops killed and disabled. Congratulations were received from the Commander-in-Chief, the Army and Corps Commanders. The following remarks were made by the Army Commander on the report of the raid :

" As usual the 12th Division carried out a most successful operation.

" The plan, the preparation, the careful criticism, the arrangements for misleading the enemy reflect the greatest credit on the Divisional, Brigade, and Battalion Commanders.

" The officers, N.C.O.'s and men of these three distinguished regiments again proved their complete mastery over the enemy, and their dash and determination was again evidenced by the very satisfactory result. The Artillery, Royal Engineers, Trench Mortar Batteries, Machine Gun Companies, and all others who assisted in this enterprise deserve my very sincere praise.

" J. BYNG,
" *General.*"

From the 12th to the 16th October Major-General Clements, Colonel King, Chief Staff Officer, and Captain Boal, A.D.C., of the United States Army, were attached to the Division, and Colonel King had the opportunity of watching the raid from an excellent observation post.

On the 14th October Lieut.-Colonel F. V. Thompson, **commanding the 9th Essex Regiment**, died from wounds received in the trenches on the 7th. An officer of the Royal Engineers, he was awarded the D.S.O. for gallantry, and held the appointment of G.S.O. (3) of the Division in 1915.

On the 15th an incident occurred meriting special record. At 3.30 p.m. two snipers of the 7th Norfolks observed a wounded man in No Man's Land, about 40 yards from one of our saps, and 50 from the German line. He was crawling towards our line when, to the amazement of the snipers, he turned and began to crawl in the opposite direction, and from the manner in which he did so it seemed to them that he must be blind. Private Shave, a stretcher bearer of the same battalion, overhearing their remarks, promptly, on his own initiative, and fully aware of the risk he ran, went out from the end of the sap and succeeded in reaching the wounded man. Private Shave then attempted to get him on his back, but the man, having been wounded in the eye, was blind, and pushed away from him. The enemy, now observing them, commenced firing, and Private Shave, dragging the other man into a shell hole, remained there until another stretcher bearer, Private A. Smith, came to his assistance. Private Shave then getting the man on his back, they all regained our line in safety. It is a picture typical of the days when men thought not so much of their own lives as of the lives of others, and dared all and risked all.

On the 19th the 12th Division was relieved by the 4th, once more returning to the Le Cauroy area, reaching there by bus and lorry.

During their occupation of the Monchy sector, the Division had carried out a large number of improvements. Water was laid on to within 800 yards of the front line, Battalion Headquarters were lit by electricity, dug-outs were commodious and in plenty, kitchens were forward in the reserve line, and communication trenches were deep and well boarded. All these greatly added to the comfort of the troops, and saved them a vast amount of fatigue and carrying parties. Also, in view of the approaching winter, much labour had been expended in preparing quarters for the reserve troops, and in making artillery and transport lines.

On leaving the XVIIth Corps Lieut.-General Sir Charles Fergusson issued the following:

" G.O.C., 12TH DIVISION.

" In saying good-bye to the Division on its departure from the XVIIth Corps, I wish to express to all ranks the appreciation which we all feel for the fine soldierly spirit with which they have held the Monchy sector during the last four months.

" Whether in attack or defence, the Division has done uniformly well, and has shown qualities of tenacity and determination which has been an example to all. It has gained a great reputation which I feel sure that all ranks will endeavour to maintain.

" The XVIIth Corps will always look back with pleasure to their association with the 12th Division, and wish it all good luck and success in the future."

An order of the day was also issued by Major-General Scott, commanding the 12th Division:

" The Division has been in the trenches for eighteen weeks, and has held an important portion of the line. I desire to express my high appreciation of the manner in which all have performed their duties. The consolidation of the line and the improvement of communications have involved a great deal of hard work, and the results have been most satisfactory.

" You have had a considerable amount of fighting, repelled several attacks, and have carried out some highly successful raids. You have exhibited strong powers of endurance, and by your gallantry and determination have upheld the best traditions of the Army.

"I am glad to say that those important points of close co-operation and good feeling between the different arms are still well maintained in the Division."

CHAPTER XIV

THE BATTLE OF CAMBRAI—I. THE ATTACK

October 20th—November 26th, 1917

(*Map* 15)

THE 12th Division had by now established a record, in holding the line for eighteen weeks without relief on an active battle front, and looked forward keenly to the rest that eventually came on the 30th of October, when it was moved to the Hesdin area, with headquarters at Wail, a locality further behind the front than any to which it had previously gone to reorganise and train. We considered ourselves lucky and settled down to a real good time, with the additional interest of drilling with tanks, now greatly increased in numbers and much improved in detail. In connection with the tanks a popular idea sprang up that this new form of training would be called into use for the spring offensive of 1918, and only a few were aware that in less than three weeks a fresh effort was to be made on entirely new ground.

The weather and the state of the country in waterlogged Belgium made it impossible to proceed with the battle on that front, and as it was urgently desired to continue the offensive, a new area had to be found, suitable for the employment of a large number of tanks, and affording a reasonable chance of success with the troops available, the numbers of which were somewhat reduced, owing to the movement of two corps to Italy. The ground selected for these fresh operations was south-west of Cambrai, where the Germans were known to have weakened their forces. On the other hand, the defences in this sector were very strong, consisting of three main lines, the Hindenburg, the Hindenburg support, and Masnières-Beaurevoir lines, all heavily wired, and with concrete machine-gun emplacements. The Germans, in fact, were supposed to consider this system impregnable. It was believed, nevertheless, that the new tanks would overrun all these obstacles, and if the attack could be a surprise, that success was bound to reward our efforts. Every attempt was, therefore, made in the preparations to ensure this surprise, in which it gradually became apparent that the 12th Division was to take its share.

The villages in which the troops would have to be billeted were those blown up by the Germans during their retirement in February, 1917, and although in most cases the main walls were standing, the houses were roofless. To remedy this state of affairs the Field Companies, Royal Engineers, and the Pioneer Battalion, were sent on ahead to form shelters, and erect huts, these being most carefully camouflaged, as also were the gun positions made by the " gunners."

Meanwhile the infantry were undergoing their intensive training with tanks, learning how best to close and pass through the gaps in the wire made by them, and extend again on the other side. Fighting with tanks on a large scale being a novelty, the fear arose that our men, if lying helpless and wounded, might themselves be crushed by these monsters. In consequence, small parties of men were detailed to accompany each tank, for the purpose of removing any such wounded lying in its path.

On the 13th November, the Commander-in-Chief, accompanied by the Divisional Commander, was present at a rehearsal of an attack by the 6th Buffs and 7th

East Surrey Regiment against a trench system which had been taped out to represent their objective in the forthcoming battle, and on the 14th inst. the transport moved forward, the infantry marching to their entraining stations at Frévent and Bouquemaison, near Doullens, the succeeding day. On the 16th, Divisional Headquarters moved to Heudicourt, and the infantry, detraining at Péronne, marched to Hautallaines, Moislains, and Manancourt, joining the IIIrd Corps (Pulteney). The march was continued the next day to Fins, Sorel le Grand, and Heudecourt, and on the 18th portions of the 35th and 36th Brigades took over trenches from the 20th Division, with the exception of a screen of sentries in the front line, who were left there until the night of the 19th–20th in case of a German raid, and to guard against any chance of a man of the 12th Division being taken prisoner, and thus disclosing a movement of troops. The remainder of these two brigades proceeded to Peizières and Vaucellette Farm, the 37th Brigade remaining at Heudecourt. All movements were made after dark, that is after 4 p.m., and had to be completed before 7 a.m.

In order to ensure secrecy of the concentration of troops, the IIIrd Corps area was divided into three zones. The front, that under direct observation of hostile lookout posts; the centre, where movement and roads could be seen from observation balloons on fine days; the back, which could be observed by hostile aircraft. Movement in the open by day was also restricted as follows: in the front zone, no party was to exceed two men, and they were to move at 100 yards distance; working parties of ten were permitted to proceed to the front line along selected routes, and no horse or vehicle was allowed to enter this zone without a pass. In the central zone no party was to exceed thirty-two men on

TANK WITH 12TH DIVISION EMBLEM

foot, or sixteen mounted, and all parties were to proceed in single file along the edges of the metalling or under the trees, at intervals of 100 yards, convoys being limited to ten vehicles. In the back area men and transport were not to be in larger bodies than the equivalent of one company, and at intervals of less than 200 yards. From the fourth day before the fight, fires were restricted to one per platoon, and none were allowed at night. Thus was secrecy guarded. Stringent orders were also in existence regarding motor lights.

The attack was to be carried out by the Third Army (Byng), with the object of breaking through the enemy's line between the Canal de l'Escaut at Banteux and the Canal du Nord near Havrincourt, and to pass the cavalry through. On the south was the IIIrd Corps (Pulteney), with the 12th Division on the right, the 20th (Douglas Smith) in the centre, and the 6th (Marden) on the left, the 29th Division (De Lisle) being in reserve and destined to pass through and capture the line Masnières, Rumilly, Marcoing after the other divisions had gained their objectives. Two hundred and sixteen tanks were to operate with the IIIrd Corps, and seventy-two of these were allotted to the 12th Division.

There were two phases in the attack, namely, the capture of the blue line and of the brown line, and the special *rôle* of the 12th Division, after gaining its objective, was to form a defensive flank to the south-east, keeping in touch with the 55th Division (Jeudwine) of VIIth Corps on its right, the attack to be carried out on a 1,700-yard front by the 35th Brigade (Vincent) on the right, and the 36th (Owen) on the left. In the opening part of the first phase the German outpost system of trenches with a strong position at Sonnet Farm were to be taken. Fresh companies were then to pass through, and gaining some 1,500 yards of the Hindenburg line, establish themselves on the far side thereof. This was the blue line, an advance of 2,000 yards. After a pause of forty-eight minutes to allow the 37th Infantry Brigade and the 11th Middlesex Regiment to assemble, the attack was to be continued to the brown line, a further distance of 2,000 yards. This latter phase entailed the capture of 2,000 yards of the Hindenburg Support Trench, and the strong positions of Bleak House, Bonavis, Pam Pam Farm, Le Quennet, and Lateau Wood. As the advance proceeded the new line of defence on the flank was to be formed, but with the exception of some trenches in Lateau Wood, none of the German fire trenches faced in the required direction, thereby greatly increasing the work of consolidation. Forming this defensive flank was the most difficult portion of the 12th Division operation, and it entailed a particularly close study of maps, and most careful organisation previous to the battle.

During the night of the 19th–20th the tanks and infantry moved into the assembly positions, which had been selected at such a distance (1,000 yards) as would preclude the noise of the moving tanks being heard by the Germans. The concentration of the infantry, entailing an advance of from 6,000 to 8,000 yards across country by taped routes, was not an altogether easy problem, but it was successfully carried out, and all were ready for zero, timed at 6.20 a.m. on 20th inst. The artillery, which had been moved into position and carefully camouflaged, had not carried out registration, and it was only at zero that the guns opened fire, great credit being due to the " gunners " for the precision with which they worked out their tasks beforehand. The destruction of the enemy's wire, for the passage of the infantry, was left entirely to the tanks.

An eye-witness describes the scene as follows : " The

BARBED WIRE, HINDENBURG LINE

Imperial War Museum] [*Crown copyright*

day opened dull and overcast, not a sound could be heard. The tanks had slithered by like some huge earth monsters in the dim daylight. Behind us, men could be seen at the guns, awaiting the order to open fire, and beside us were two or three of the Signal Corps with their instruments. Everywhere men were anxiously waiting, the suspense at such moments being intense. Did the enemy know what was in store for him at daybreak ? Was he ready and prepared for this huge attack, and in quiet and confidence awaiting it ? No one on our side could answer that question. Zero was 6.20 a.m., and minutes passed like hours, and after what seemed like weeks of time our watches told us it was 6.15 a.m. Another five minutes. It was an almost breathless suspense. We watched the enemy's front line for signs of movement, the rear for flash of guns. The five minutes seemed interminable. It passed in silence. Suddenly from everywhere behind us blazed forth our artillery fire. Such a sight can never be forgotten. Down the whole front line, from Banteux as far north as the eye could see, burst British shells, thermite, shrapnel, high explosive. There was not a part of the line that seemed untouched. How any one could live under such a tornado of fire passed comprehension. Above all the noise came another familiar sound, aeroplanes, dozens of them. The morning was misty and visibility poor, and they had to fly low, so low at times it seemed as though they must strike the crest of the hill; so near the bursting shells it was marvellous how they escaped being hit. Their courage and daring were past belief. For ten minutes we stood spellbound before that wonderful sight. At 6.30 a.m., ten minutes after zero, the main tanks advanced, accompanied by the infantry, the advanced guard tanks having already gone ahead to cut lanes in the German wire. We could just see through the haze. There was no rush or excitement. It seemed impossible to believe that an attack across the open could be delivered with such deliberation. The tanks crawled 50 yards a minute, and the infantry followed leisurely in what was known as 'tank' formation. What a strangely thrilling sight it was, guns blazing away behind us, the effect of the shells visible on the white chalk trenches opposite, the air full of aeroplanes swooping down here, there, and everywhere, and the great tanks proceeding to the attack with the calm, confident infantry behind them."

In the advance of the 35th Brigade the 5th Royal Berkshire (Nichols) was on the right and the 9th Essex (La Terrière) on the left. Each battalion was accompanied by twelve tanks, but, unfortunately, nearly half of these broke down or got stuck in a sunken lane leading from Gonnelieu to Banteux. Nevertheless, the infantry, supported by the remainder, quickly gained their objective, the outpost trench system, and established themselves on an intermediary line (the black); the 5th Royal Berkshire pushing down the Banteux Spur to within 300 yards of Quarry Post, where it took up the southern end of the new line. The 7th Suffolk (Cooper) and one Company 7th Norfolk passing through, took their portion of the Hindenburg Line without much opposition, and at once organised a flank defence in continuation of the 5th Berkshire. This completed the task of the 35th Brigade. In the 36th Brigade, the 7th Royal Sussex (Impey), 9th Royal Fusiliers (Van Someran), and two companies 8th Royal Fusiliers (Elliott-Cooper), also with twelve tanks per battalion, capturing Sonnet Farm, reached the black line with little opposition. Here the second waves passing through, experienced no difficulty in taking possession

SONNET FARM

LATEAU WOOD

of the Hindenburg Trench. The blue line was thus secured up to time and in accordance with plans. The 3rd Tank Corps had swept down all obstacles, and the much-talked-of Hindenburg Trench had fallen an easy prey to our troops.

The pause of forty-eight minutes now ensued, during which time the 37th Infantry Brigade (Webber) assembled on the right, and 11th Middlesex (Wollocombe) and two companies 8th Royal Fusiliers on the left, for the further advance. On resumption of the attack the 7th East Surrey (Baldwin) rapidly gained its first objective, capturing many prisoners, amongst whom were the colonel and adjutant of a battalion; the second waves then passing through, completed the task by capturing the Hindenburg Support Line; here Second Lieutenant H. P. Wilcox, discovering a battery in position a little farther on, pressed forward and took two guns and eighty prisoners, for which act of daring he was awarded the Military Cross. The 6th Buffs (Smeltzer) carried on the attack with the 6th Royal West Kent (Alderman) on their left. Much opposition was met from Bonavis and Pam Pam Farm, but with the aid of some tanks, these were successfully rushed, and Lateau Wood became the point of resistance. After hard fighting this point came into our possession about 11 a.m. Its capture was important, as until it was taken the 29th Division could not advance on Masnières.

The 6th Royal West Kent who assisted in the fighting in Lateau Wood, met with serious opposition at Le Quennet Farm, and the battalion unfortunately sustained the loss of its brilliant commander, Major Alderman. Captain Dove, the adjutant, assuming command, eventually captured the farm, but his body of men, greatly reduced in numbers, were overpowered and he himself was taken prisoner. However, success in adjacent parts of the field compelled the Germans to withdraw, and Captain Dove escaped, bringing three Germans away as prisoners. The 6th Queen's (Rolls) had moved up to assist in the capture of Lateau Wood and now extended the line northwards, gaining touch with the 20th Division, which had been operating on the left of the 12th. Meanwhile the 11th Middlesex and two companies of 8th Royal Fusiliers, advancing on the left of the 37th Brigade, had taken their portion of the brown line, capturing 150 prisoners, including a regimental commander, six machine guns and a large dug-out replete with stores. In the dug-out there was a telephone connected with German Divisional Headquarters, where for several hours the German Staff anxiously inquired for the latest news of the battle. Having gained its portion of the brown line, the 12th Division set to work to consolidate the 5,800 yards of new line. The Division had captured 5 officers, 378 other ranks, four 15-centimetre howitzers, four 10·5" howitzers, four 7" guns, four heavy trench mortars, twenty-two machine guns and various etceteras. Our casualties were comparatively the lightest we had experienced, 144 killed, 841 wounded, 160 missing.

A thrilling episode when standing on the far-famed Hindenburg Line, not to be easily forgotten, was the sight of French civilians, who had been released from Masnières after three years' captivity with the Germans, coming down the Cambrai road singing the "Marseillaise." To the left, the cavalry were moving forward to pass through the gap, and down in the trenches were our men, squatting round fires, smoking German cigars and discussing whether Aston Villa or Tottenham Hotspur would win the next Cup final.

With eager anticipation all ranks awaited news from the other sections. Such news was good, but had the

MAP No. 15.

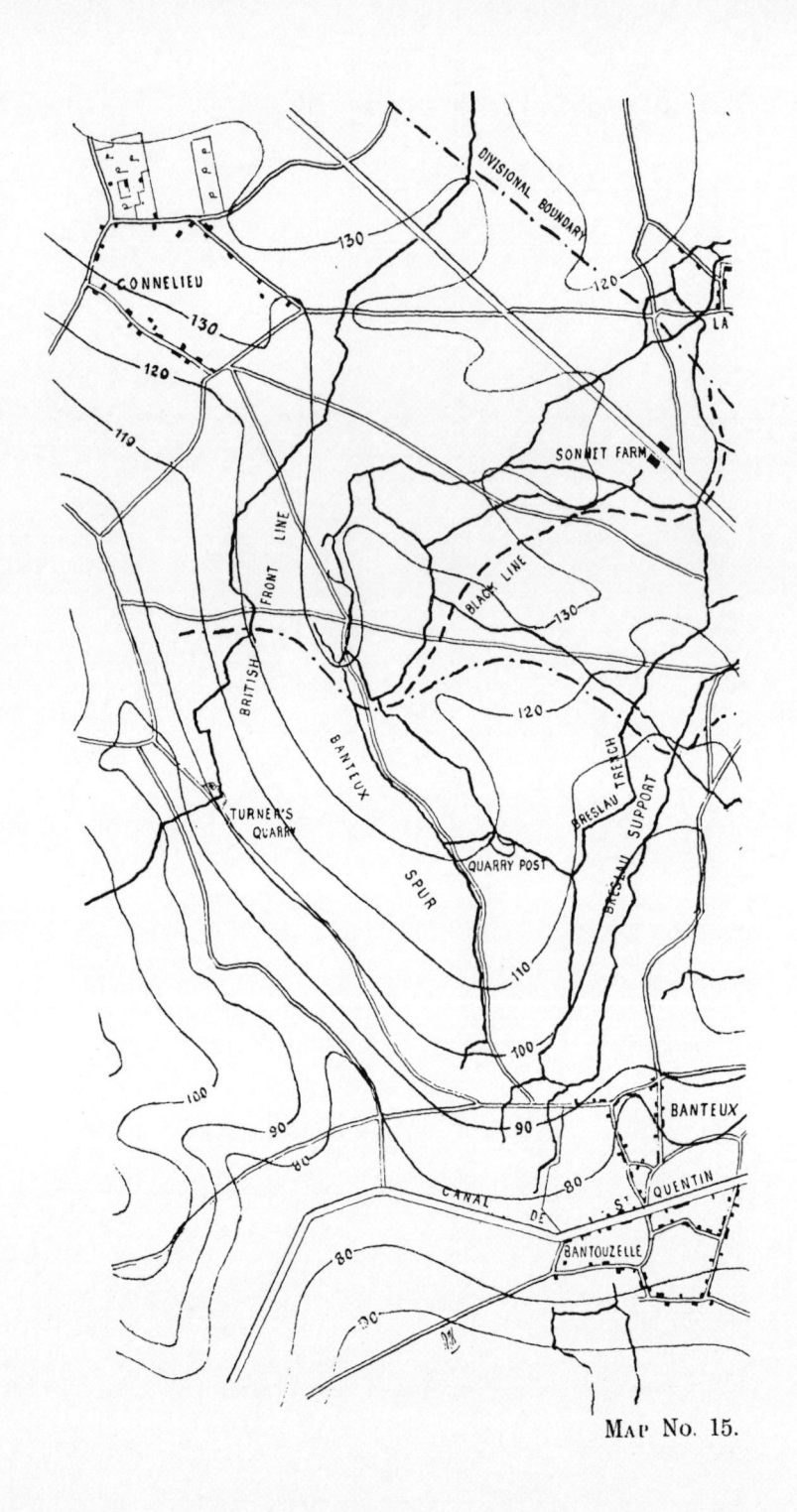

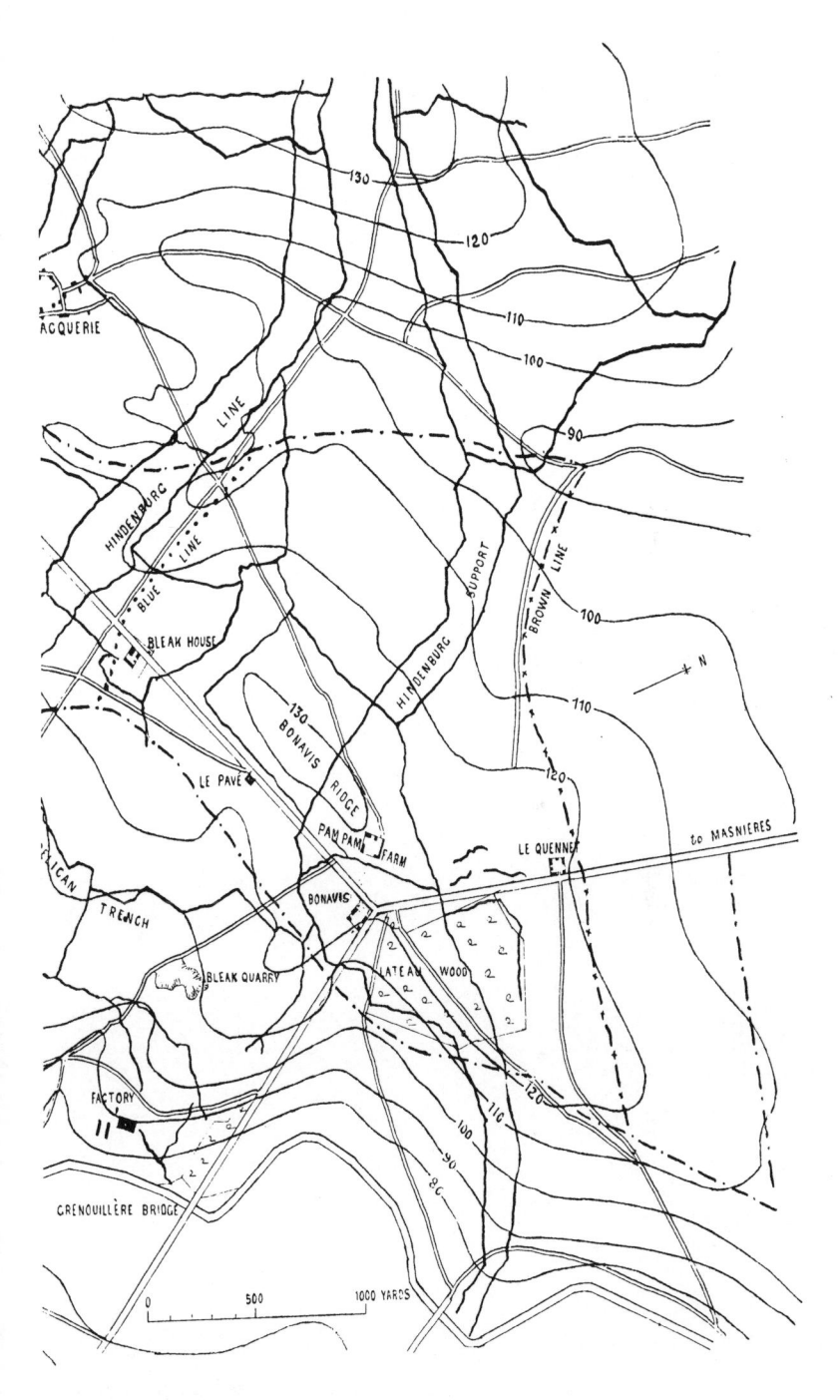

CAMBRAI, 20TH NOVEMBER, 1917

long-talked-of "break through" come at last? Unfortunately, no. However, the battle had been so far successful that the attack had been a complete surprise and the Tank Corps had justified the hopes placed in it. The Tanks from now on were the avowed friends of the infantry, who acquired a great admiration for them.

The Army Commander in writing to General Scott said : " Lateau Wood and Bonavis I look upon as being one of the finest achievements of the day. All good luck to you and that splendid Division."

For the next three days the 12th Division expended all its energies on consolidating the new line. Fortunately, the German trenches provided a large number of dug-outs, and work could be concentrated on strong points and communications. The weakness of the position was the inability to command the lower portions of the Canal Valley, either by fire or observation. To remedy this, an operation to advance the line to Quarry Post–Bleak Quarry was carried out at 8 a.m. on the 24th November by the 35th and 36th Brigades. " D " Company, 5th Royal Berkshire (Captain J. R. West), under cover of a very effective rifle grenade and light trench mortar barrage, seized Quarry Post, taking eighteen prisoners, without themselves having any casualties ; the 7th Suffolk meanwhile, moving down the Breslau and Breslau Support Trenches, threatened Quarry Post from that flank. The 8th Royal Fusiliers captured Pelican Trench and Bleak Quarry, but were driven out of the centre portion of Pelican Trench. During this operation Private J. T. Campbell greatly distinguished himself. When in command of his Lewis gun section he established his gun in advance of the trench and succeeded in breaking up the enemy's counter-attacks. He remained in position for twenty hours, and undoubtedly saved a detached party in

Bleak Quarry from being cut off; forty-five prisoners in all were taken. The 7th Royal Sussex relieved the 8th Royal Fusiliers that night, and at 7 a.m. on the 25th inst. attacked the portion of Pelican Trench still in German hands, and the trenches south of Bleak Quarry, overlooking the factory. The objectives were gained, but lost again owing to a strong counter-attack. eleven prisoners being taken by us. At 10.50 a.m. another attempt to capture the centre of Pelican Trench failed.

On the 26th inst. the divisional front was reorganised in order to institute a system of relief and give some of the battalions a rest from the trenches, which up to now had been impossible. The 6th Queen's and 11th Middlesex were consequently moved to Heudecourt as divisional reserve, and by the 27th a new trench, running due north from Turner Quarry to the old German front line, had been completed, wired and occupied, shortening the front and strengthening that portion of the line.

All this time fighting had remained fairly continuous in the northern portion of the battlefield, although comparative tranquillity was preserved in the south. But this tranquillity was shortly to be disturbed by the storm that was rapidly approaching.

CHAPTER XV

THE BATTLE OF CAMBRAI—II. THE GERMAN COUNTER-ATTACK

November 27th—December 5th, 1917

(Maps 16 and 17)

ON the 27th and 28th of November considerable movement of the Germans was observed in the vicinity of Honnecourt, opposite Villers Guislain in the 55th Division (Jeudwine) area. Owing to this apparent concentration of the enemy, and the fact that the 55th Division was holding a long front and were weak in consequence, Villers Guislain became a danger spot. On the afternoon of the 29th November the General Officers Commanding the 12th and 55th Divisions met to consider the situation. As a result reserve machine guns were placed to cover Villers Guislain; at the same time the Officers Commanding the 6th Queen's and 11th Middlesex were informed of the probabilities of an attack, and ordered to reconnoitre the ground from Vaucellette Farm to Gonnelieu as soon as possible. Warning orders were issued by the Division, and four 18-pounder batteries were directed to carry out harassing fire on Honnecourt from 5 to 7 a.m. the next morning. All were, therefore, on the alert when the German counter-attack commenced on the 30th November.

About 7 a.m. on that day reports were received of heavy shelling on the left brigade of the 55th Division. The 6th Queen's and 11th Middlesex were promptly ordered to " stand to." Knowledge of the situation, however, quickly became very obscure at Divisional

Headquarters, Brigade Headquarters losing touch with their battalions between 7 and 7.45 a.m. On a message being received from the 55th Division that the Germans were advancing from their trenches, the 6th Queen's (Rolls) were ordered to Vaucellette Farm at 8.45 a.m., and in consequence of a report that the enemy were in Villers Guislain, the 11th Middlesex (Wollocombe) was ordered to Quentin Mill at 9.15 a.m. Some 700 reinforcements, who had not joined their battalions, were organised as a provisional battalion under Major W. R. Johnson, 9th Essex, and went forward to support the Queen's at 11 a.m.

The Queen's moved at 9.5 a.m., and on reaching Vaucellette Farm, the neighbourhood of which was being heavily shelled, found it held by a small party of the Loyal North Lancashire Regiment, 55th Division. Five platoons under Captain A. L. Paish occupied the farm, and soon afterwards repulsed an advance of the enemy. Seven platoons were detailed to occupy Chapel Hill, leaving one company in support. The enemy by this time were holding the Beet Factory, Chapel Crossing, and Gauche Wood. The 11th Middlesex, moving from Heudecourt to Quentin Mill, reached the ridge half a mile north-east of Revelon about 10 a.m. Here the General Officer Commanding the 35th Infantry Brigade (Vincent) was in position with a small number of men. Under his orders the battalion took up a line astride the Revelon-Gouzeaucourt Road, and opening fire on the Germans, who were advancing up the slope, drove them back. Shortly afterwards a second attempt by the enemy was also repulsed. Touch was obtained with the Queen's at Chapel Hill, and about 11 a.m. two cavalry brigades extended the left of the Middlesex. By 1 p.m. Johnson's Provisional Battalion had taken over the defence of Vaucellette Farm and filled up a gap in the Queen's line. At this time the Northumberland Hussars (Reynolds) were sent to Vaucellette Farm to keep touch with the 55th Division on the right, and the 3rd Corps Cyclist Battalion to Revelon Farm to reinforce that part of the line. The advance of the enemy in this direction was now effectively checked. All these troops were placed under the orders of Brig.-General Vincent, who, with a few men, had been driven back from his headquarters, which were situated on the Villers Guislain-Gonnelieu Road, about 500 yards from the former village, earlier that morning, and had taken up his position on the Revelon Ridge.

It is now necessary to describe the events that took place in the early morning in the neighbourhood of Villers Guislain. The Germans commenced shelling this area at 6.40 a.m. and at 7 a.m. the fire increased considerably and a large number of gas shell necessitated the use of respirators. No information being obtainable, General Vincent despatched an officer at 7.30 a.m. to ascertain the situation. He returned in a few minutes to say the enemy was already in Villers Guislain. The alarm posts were manned at once, Captain Sievers, 9th Essex, and several of the runner and servant squad being killed. Captain Broadwood, the brigade major, returning to the brigade dug-out to destroy the papers, was taken prisoner, the two clerks with him being killed by a bomb. Meanwhile General Vincent, Major Ferguson commanding the 69th Field Company, Royal Engineers, and all the men near, withdrew to a small rise 200 yards away. Here aeroplanes attacked them, and the party withdrew to Gauche Wood, which was being heavily shelled, and passing through it took up a position on a rise on the west side. Only three or four of the original thirty men now remained. An officer of a Trench Mortar battery, a subaltern, Royal Artillery, and Lieutenant

White, brigade intelligence officer, joined the party, and and about 100 men of various units, with rifles, were collected and formed into four platoons.

The enemy were thus denied egress from the wood, but as there was no cover and the aeroplanes continued attacking, a better position was taken up on the railway embankment, 100 yards away. Here the defence became stronger, more men and rifles were collected, and Lieutenant Flowers, 5th Northamptonshire Regiment also joined with a few men. All attempts of the Germans to leave Gauche Wood on the south side were stopped. At 9 a.m. two or three battalions of the enemy were observed moving steadily down the western slopes of the Quentin Ridge on Gouzeaucourt. Having expended all their ammunition, General Vincent withdrew his force to Revelon Ridge, where he came in touch with the advancing 11th Middlesex, and found that he could replenish his ammunition from Revelon Farm. The action of this small force undoubtedly prevented an early movement of the Germans to occupy Revelon Ridge, and great credit is due to its members. It will probably be less confusing to conclude the relation of the incidents of the 30th November in this part of the battlefield, although it was not the area of the 12th Division, before entering on a description of the legitimate 12th Division fight.

Sixteen tanks having been placed at his disposal, General Vincent ordered an attack on Villers Guislain, Chapel Crossing, and Gauche Wood, in conjunction with the Guards Division attack on Gouzeaucourt at 3.10 p.m. The section of tanks detailed for Chapel Crossing, where the Germans were reported as assembling, broke down, and the Queen's did not advance in that direction. The 11th Middlesex moving with their tanks gained the Irvine Lane, and touch on their left with the Guards who had retaken Gouzeaucourt. Two cavalry divisions arrived about this period, and joining in the action the situation in this area became secure.

A line had now been established from Vaucellette Farm along Irvine Lane, with a support line through Chapel Hill, along Revelon Ridge, and then due north to west of Gouzeaucourt. A detail of units holding this line is interesting as showing the effect of a sudden break through. From right to left they were as follows : Northumberland Hussars, 12th Division Details, Cyclists, Queen's ; along front line, Northamptonshire, Cyclists, Middlesex ; along support line, Queen's, Details Royal Sussex, Royal West Kent, Machine Gun Corps, Army Troops, Royal Engineers, Motor Machine Gun Corps, Middlesex, details of 20th Division, Band of Royal Dragoons, Army Troops, Royal Engineers, Monmouthshire Pioneers, and Durham Light Infantry. At Revelon Farm the 69th Field Company, Royal Engineers, and 5th Northamptonshire formed a strong point. In addition there were a few 18-pounder guns, and one 4·5" howitzer. The fortunate presence at Heudecourt, on the morning of the 30th November, of the two infantry battalions, which formed the main portion of General Vincent's force, undoubtedly confined the German advance, and prevented the exploitation of the Fins Valley.

When the German counter-attack was launched on the 30th November, the three British Divisions affected thereby on the right, were the 55th with its long front ; the 12th on newly captured ground from 500 yards north of Turner Quarry to Lateau Wood inclusive, a front line of 4,800 yards ; and the 20th. The endeavours of the 12th Division to push forward its line so as to gain complete command of the canal valley, had been strongly opposed and only partially successful. The possession of this valley enabled the Germans to concentrate troops unseen, while owing to the contour of the ground they were largely protected from shell fire. The terrain on the west of the canal was slightly commanding, and contained several woods suitable for the concealment of troops. There had been a good deal of rain which had made consolidation difficult owing to the clayey nature of the soil. The congestion of the various divisions on the salient, formed by the success of the 20th inst., had made the allocation of Divisional Headquarters difficult, and in the case of the 12th the lines of communication ran parallel to the front line, and consequently the capture of Villers Guislain and Gouzeaucourt destroyed all the cables to the Brigade Headquarters.

The Germans commenced shelling the 12th Division front line about 6.45 a.m. on the 30th inst., a certain proportion of gas shell being used, and by 7 a.m. our guns were firing on their S.O.S. lines. On the right of the Division was the 35th Brigade with the 5th Royal Berkshire (Nicolls) and 7th Norfolk (Gielgud) in the front trenches, the 9th Essex (La Terrière) in support, and the 7th Suffolk (Henty) in reserve in the old British front line between Cheshire Quarry and Newton Post, an unsuitable position but the only place available. About 7.30 a.m. the Berkshire were attacked by a large body of the enemy and driven back to Adam Trench. Heavy bombing fights now ensued, and the Germans were bombed back to Quarry Post, but bombs running out the Berkshire were again driven back to Adam Trench, where blocks were formed and the enemy's advance stopped at about 9 a.m. Shortly after this Germans were seen on the northern end of Gonnelieu Ridge (attacking 9th Royal Fusiliers ?) and also south of Newton Post. At 12 noon it was decided to fall back on Bleak and Bleak Support Trenches. The Germans

BATTLE OF CAMBRAI—II

were now seen to be in occupation of Villers Guislain, Gonnelieu and Gouzeaucourt, and in consequence, after consultation with the officer commanding 9th Essex, these two battalions retired at 12.50 p.m. on La Vacquerie, the withdrawal being hard pressed until the Cambrai Road was crossed, when a position was taken up on Cemetery Ridge and round La Vacquerie.

The 7th Norfolk, on the left of the Berkshire, holding a position across the Hindenburg Line, were also heavily attacked, and suffering severe casualties were driven back to their support line which was reached about 7.45 a.m. Here a stand was made long enough to permit the 9th Royal Fusiliers to withdraw from Pelican Trench. The Norfolk then continued to be pressed back in conjunction with the Royal Fusiliers towards the Cambrai Road, what now remained of the Norfolk becoming incorporated with the 9th Royal Fusiliers. The Norfolk had suffered seventeen casualties in officers, amongst them Lieut.-Colonel Gielgud, and the adjutant, Captain Charlton, the only officer remaining being Second Lieutenant Maddison, recently joined.

The 9th Essex, in support on the Gonnelieu Ridge, suffered in the general shelling, and were joined at 7.30 a.m. by several of the 7th Suffolk who had been taken prisoners and escaped. A platoon of the Essex was sent forward to reinforce the Norfolk, and about 9.30 a.m. the remainder of the battalion became seriously engaged, but held its own against the enemy, who, after pushing back the Norfolk, began working round the left flank. By this time all communications were broken owing to the penetration of the Germans on the south. After consultation with the officer commanding the Royal Berkshire in Bleak Trench, these two battalions withdrew at 12.50 p.m. towards La Vacquerie, being greatly molested by low-flying aeroplanes. A position was taken up round La Vacquerie at 2 p.m. and touch was gained with the headquarters of the 36th Infantry Brigade. Later in the day the Essex was attached to the 61st Brigade of 20th Division and occupied Foster Lane.

The 7th Suffolk, in reserve, experienced a heavy bombardment, a quantity of gas shell necessitating the use of respirators. Shortly after 7 a.m. the regiment was strongly attacked from the Banteux Ravine and Mersey Street, " A " Company and Battalion Headquarters being surprised in Cheshire Quarry and taken prisoners. The other companies had some sharp fighting and suffered many casualties, the few remnants making their way back towards the Cambrai Road.

The 36th Brigade (Owen) held the centre with the 9th Royal Fusiliers (Van Someran) on the right, 8th Royal Fusiliers (Elliott-Cooper) on left, and 7th Royal Sussex (Impey) in support. This portion of the front was in the making, the Germans still retaining the centre of Pelican Trench. " C " Company, 9th Royal Fusiliers, holding the southern end of Pelican Trench, were not affected by the bombardment, the shells falling over them. Soon after 7 a.m. the Germans advanced up the spur from Banteux and commenced a bombing attack along Pelican Trench. These attacks were successfully engaged, but the enforced retirement of the Norfolk Regiment on the right entailed the withdrawal of this company. The Germans now in strength, rushing on, pressed back our troops to near the Cambrai Road. Lieut.-Colonel Van Someran, having ordered up " A " Company from reserve, counter-attacked and drove the enemy back some 200 yards, establishing blocks and taking up a position across the Hindenburg Trench, which was held until 12.30 p.m. on 1st December. Some 150 of the Norfolk were in this counter-attack, and it was during this operation that Captain Charlton, the adjutant, was killed ; " D " Company, 9th Royal Fusiliers, holding three strong points covering Bleak House, maintaining a stout resistance, were surrounded. All attempts at relief failing, these posts fell during the evening, only one man, who was afterwards killed, escaping.

" B " and " A " Companies, 8th Royal Fusiliers, were holding the northern end of Pelican Trench, when at 7.30 a.m. a heavy bombardment was placed on Bonavis Ridge. This was succeeded by a smoke barrage along the front, on the clearing of which at about 7.45 a.m. the Germans appeared in large numbers, advancing from the direction of the canal. These two companies were overpowered and the enemy, rushing forward, gained Bonavis Ridge, forced back " D " Company, which was moving up in support, and reached to within 50 yards of the reserve line, where " C " Company had taken up its position close to Battalion Headquarters. Lieut.-Colonel Elliott-Cooper, seeing the extreme danger of the situation, and judging that instant action was necessary, mounted the parapet, unarmed as he was, and calling on the officers and men of the Battalion Headquarters and " C " Company to follow him, dashed forward on the advancing enemy, driving them back some 600 yards and over the Bonavis Ridge, where the Germans rallied on reinforcing troops. Elliott-Cooper, still about 40 yards in advance of his men, was severely wounded, and realising that heavy casualties were being incurred from machine gun fire, also that his body of men were greatly outnumbered, ordered them to retire, notwithstanding the fact that he himself must be taken prisoner. This counter-attack released many of " D " Company who had been taken prisoners, and effectually stopped any serious attack by the Germans on this portion of the battlefield. The remnants of the battalion took up its position in the reserve line, and though several attempts were made by the enemy to approach this line, they were all broken up. For his very gallant act Lieut.-Colonel Elliott-Cooper was awarded the Victoria Cross.

Note.—Elliott-Cooper had already gained the D.S.O. and M.C. for gallantry. He, unfortunately, died as a prisoner of war in Germany on 11th February, 1918.

The 7th Royal Sussex who were in reserve in trenches south of La Vacquerie, moved up to the reserve line and were in position at 10 a.m., eventually having the 9th and 8th Royal Fusiliers on either flank.

The 36th Infantry Brigade Headquarters were located on the north-west side of Gonnelieu, and at 8 a.m. were ordered to collect details and defend the village, which was, however, being so heavily shelled that it was impossible to move troops to the eastern side. The 70th Field Company, Royal Engineers, were, therefore, ordered to occupy Gin Avenue, and the 5th Northamptonshire (Pioneers) Green Switch. The Germans appearing in Gonnelieu at 10.5 a.m. Brigade Headquarters moved to Farm Ravine, and later on about noon to Villers Plouich, where the 20th Division Headquarters were, and communication with 12th Division Headquarters became possible. Touch with units was maintained by runners who displayed much gallantry that day.

The 70th Field Company, Royal Engineers, and 5th Northamptonshire, held their positions until relieved by troops of other divisions, and were instrumental in preventing the enemy debouching from Gonnelieu, and also in protecting several batteries of artillery in that area.

The 37th Infantry Brigade (Incledon Webber) held

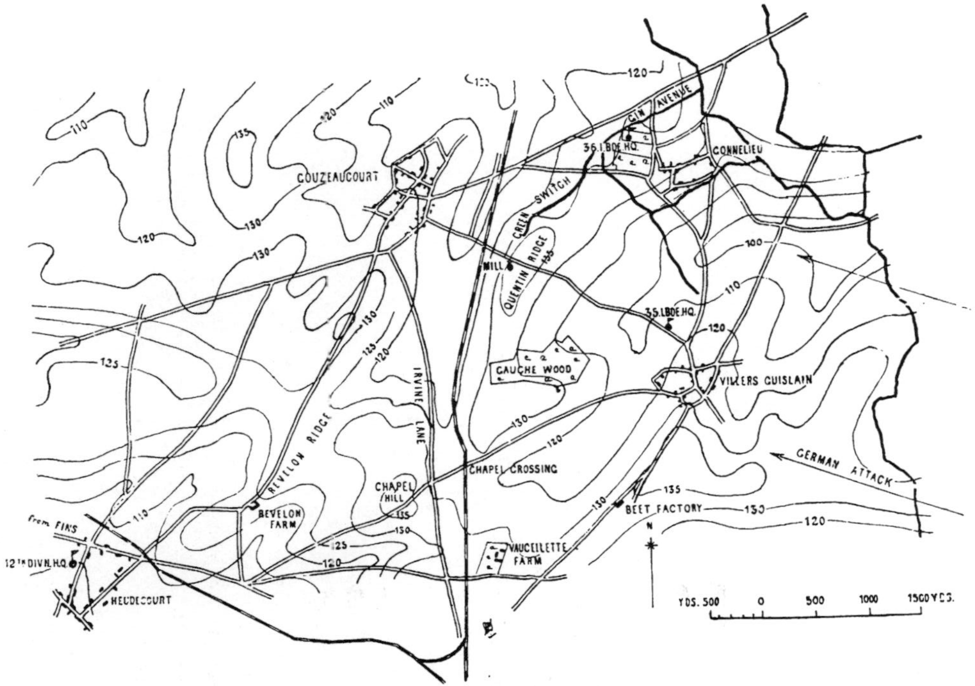

Map No. 16. Revelon Ridge

the northern section of the defence covering Bonavis and Lateau Wood, with the 20th Division on the left. Owing to the heavy casualties sustained by this brigade the records are very meagre. There was heavy shelling on Bonavis and the trenches in and around Lateau Wood, from 7 to 7.15 a.m., which broke out again half an hour afterwards on the front line, all communications being cut. The 7th East Surrey (Baldwin) on the right of this brigade, were holding the trenches covering Pam Pam and Bonavis Farms with posts well down both sides of the road from Bonavis to the canal. The Germans, who concentrated in the wood near Grenouillère Bridge, advanced there from at about 7.45 a.m., forcing these posts back on their trenches, and developing a strong attack drove the defenders across the Cambrai Road beyond Pam Pam Farm. In consequence of an appeal from Lieut.-Colonel Baldwin, Lieut.-Colonel Smeltzer, commanding the 6th Buffs (in reserve) went forward with " D " Company, and at 8.20 a.m. a combined counter attack succeeded in regaining Cable Trench, and establishing the East Surrey in that trench, and the Hindenburg Support from the Cambrai Road to the Sunken Road to the north. Eventually the Germans, coming in through Lateau Wood from the north, establishing themselves in Pam Pam Farm and attacking the East Surrey from the rear, drove them out of Cable Trench into Hindenburg Support. Here Baldwin and about forty men found themselves surrounded, and making fire steps facing in both directions held on until 1.30 p.m., when all their ammunition being expended, and only ten unwounded remaining, Lieut.-Colonel Baldwin surrendered.

The attack on the 6th Royal West Kent (Dawson), holding the southern edge of Lateau Wood, commenced at 7.30 a.m. with a bombing offensive up Hindenburg support trenches, as a result of which our men were driven along the trench. Later on, finding the enemy had entered Lateau Wood, fire was opened from the back of the trench. Only a small number of these men managed to work their way back through the wood to the Hindenburg Support where the Buffs were located. The reserve company, " D," was holding some posts north of Lateau Wood, and soon after 8 a.m. Germans were observed advancing on the wood from a northerly direction. This attack developed strongly about 8.30 a.m., and pushing back " D " Company and two platoons of the Buffs in Le Quennet Farm, the enemy gained Lateau Wood. Lieut.-Colonel Dawson, who had just recovered from his last wound, was again knocked out in this engagement.

The 6th Buffs (Smeltzer) were in reserve in the Hindenburg support trenches north of the Sunken Road. It has already been related how " D " Company went to the assistance of the East Surrey. At 8.30 a.m. " C " Company, in occupation of a communication trench north of the Sunken Road, denied the enemy any advance from the Bonavis Ridge, and " A " and " B " Companies with two machine guns in the Hindenburg Support, prevented forward movement from Le Quennet Farm. At 10.30 a.m. Germans were reported massing in La Vacquerie Valley about 1,000 yards north, and shortly after as advancing directly on the left flank of the Buffs, who were not in touch with other troops in that direction. The small remnants of the two other battalions had been absorbed into the Buffs under Lieut.-Colonel Smeltzer, who now received orders to withdraw to the reserve line. This was effected under considerable pressure from the enemy and was completed at 4 p.m., touch being obtained with the 36th Brigade on the right and the 59th Brigade (20th Division) on the left. Brigade Headquarters which had remained in the Sunken Road moved at 10.45 a.m. to the Hindenburg Line and during the night to Villers Plouich. The situation remained unchanged until the brigade handed over to the 183rd Brigade (61st Division) on the night of the 1st-2nd December.

The artillery supporting the 12th Division consisted of the Divisional Artillery, the 62nd Brigade (Wynne) and 63rd Brigade (Coates) augmented by the 169th (Pottinger) and 179th (Eley) Brigades of Army Artillery. These were formed into three groups covering the fronts of the three infantry brigades. Owing to the configuration of the ground and the fact that no other suitable site was available, it had been necessary to locate the 376th and 378th Batteries of the 169th Brigade in Villers Guislain. These two batteries were, unfortunately, overrun and captured in the German advance, but the 376th (Nicol) had been able to fire at close ranges before the *personnel* was withdrawn, the 378th (Broughton) being unable to have this satisfaction, as the enemy approached its position through the ruins of the village. Both the battery commanders were wounded. The enemy pressing on, arrived on the Quentin Ridge and in Gonnelieu, on the northern side of which village were the 377th and 379th, the two other batteries of the 169th Brigade, and to the west " C " Battery, 63rd Brigade, all three being south of the Cambrai Road. Some 500 yards north of this road being " A " and " B " Batteries, 63rd Brigade. These batteries now experienced what a gunner lives for, the opportunity of shooting at masses of infantry at close ranges with open sights. The 377th (Sutherland) and 379th (Gillespie) engaged the enemy in Gonnelieu at a range of 500 yards, but the German machine gun fire causing many casualties, forced the detachments to leave their guns and seek shelter in Gin

Avenue. Lieutenant Tuckey displayed great gallantry in attending to his brother subaltern Llewellyn, who was wounded, and bringing him in under heavy fire.

Meanwhile " C " Battery, 63rd Brigade (Belcher) was heavily engaged. This battery had commenced firing at 5 a.m., being one of the four batteries carrying out harassing fire on Honnecourt. On receiving a report at 8.45 a.m. that the Germans were just south of Gonnelieu, two guns were moved to cover Quentin Ridge. Though at this time the battery was under shell fire few casualties were incurred until 10.30 a.m., when the number increased owing to machine guns. Five minutes later the enemy appeared in rear of the battery crossing the Quentin Ridge from the direction of Gouzeaucourt, when Lieutenant Wallace turned round a gun and firing at a range of 600 yards drove him back over the ridge. The battery was now heavily attacked by rifle and machine gun fire, and casualties became severe, five out of six senior non-commissioned officers being incapacitated, and Major Belcher falling mortally wounded shortly after, Lieutenant Wallace assumed command. Soon only sufficient men remained to keep two guns in action, these being fired on various objectives at ranges of 100 to 500 yards. On one occasion a party of Germans appearing at the corner of Gonnelieu Cemetery were fired into at 100 yards and disappeared. Men continued to fall, and fire from these two guns was only maintained by manning each in turn. About noon infantry reinforcements reached Gin Avenue, and as only five men remained with the battery, which was getting no objectives to shoot at and only suffering casualties from snipers, Lieutenant Wallace, having cleared his wounded, decided to withdraw the gallant remnant. The battery had inflicted heavy casualties and prevented the enemy crossing the Cambrai Road. For this gallant action

Lieutenant Wallace was awarded the Victoria Cross, and Sergeant W. Howard, Bombardier W. Coyles, Gunners F. C. Gould, J. W. Mantle and A. Burgess, the five survivors, Distinguished Conduct Medals. The guns remained in No Man's Land for several days, being eventually recovered by the 9th Division.

" A " Battery (Kindersley) and " B " Battery (Woodward) 63rd Brigade, each brought three guns into action in the open, supporting " C " Battery and being instrumental in denying the enemy the Cambrai Road, and in inflicting punishment on him in the vicinity of Gonnelieu and the Quentin Ridge. These batteries were withdrawn to the vicinity of Beaucamp about 3 p.m. The 62nd Brigade, R.F.A. (Wynne), supporting the 36th Infantry Brigade, were in the neighbourhood of La Vacquerie and experienced anxious moments, but the batteries were all safely withdrawn to fresh positions. " A " Battery (Captain Mackenzie) and " D " (Ormsby) moved about 1.30 p.m. to near Villers Plouich ; " B " Battery (Stamper) first moved to Cemetery Ridge about 1 p.m., engaging the enemy on Gonnelieu Ridge, and to Beaucamp half an hour afterwards. " C " Battery (Captain Roney Dougal) was forced, by machine gun fire, to leave the guns temporarily about 1 p.m., but on arrival of the limbers at 4 p.m. the battery withdrew to Beaucamp.

The 179th Brigade (Eley), supporting the 37th Infantry Brigade, were to the east of La Vacquerie, and consisted of the 383rd, 462nd, 463rd, and 464th Batteries. These had remained in action all day, and at dusk found themselves close to the line being held by the infantry. It had been decided to withdraw the guns at night, but owing to messages miscarrying and misdirected orderlies, the teams with the limbers did not arrive. However, Captain Witham, commanding the

463rd Battery, assisted by Lieutenant S. B. Kekewick and twenty-two men, manhandled his guns to La Vacquerie, a distance of 600 yards, completing the work between 7 p.m. and midnight, and the teams arriving later the guns were moved, and in action at Beaucamp at 10 a.m. on 1st December. It had been a trying time for the artillery, as all communications were destroyed early in the day, information had been very vague, withdrawing guns in close proximity to the enemy was difficult, and the supply of ammunition was not the least of the troubles. All batteries had run guns out of their positions and brought them into action in the open.

For the rest of the Division it was likewise a hard day, every one, from the infantry brigade commanders down to the clerks and servants, taking a hand in the battle. On the disappearance of daylight matters quieted down and the situation became known. The Division was holding its reserve line covering La Vacquerie, with a forward position across the Hindenburg Line south-west of Bleak House. Elements of the Division were in Foster Lane and Green Switch. On the south, from Vaucellette Farm along Irvine Lane to within 1,000 yards of Gouzeaucourt, 12th Division troops predominated.

On the 1st December the Germans renewing the attack, the 9th Essex in Foster Lane, attached to the 61st Infantry Brigade, came under heavy shell fire at 9.30 a.m., resulting in the enemy obtaining a footing in the trench, from which he was ejected by bombing shortly afterwards. An intense bombardment between 12.30 and 1 p.m., followed by a bombing attack, was directed on the 9th Royal Fusiliers, who were holding the advanced position across the Cambrai Road, and running short of grenades, the battalion was forced

MAP No. 17. CAMBRAI,

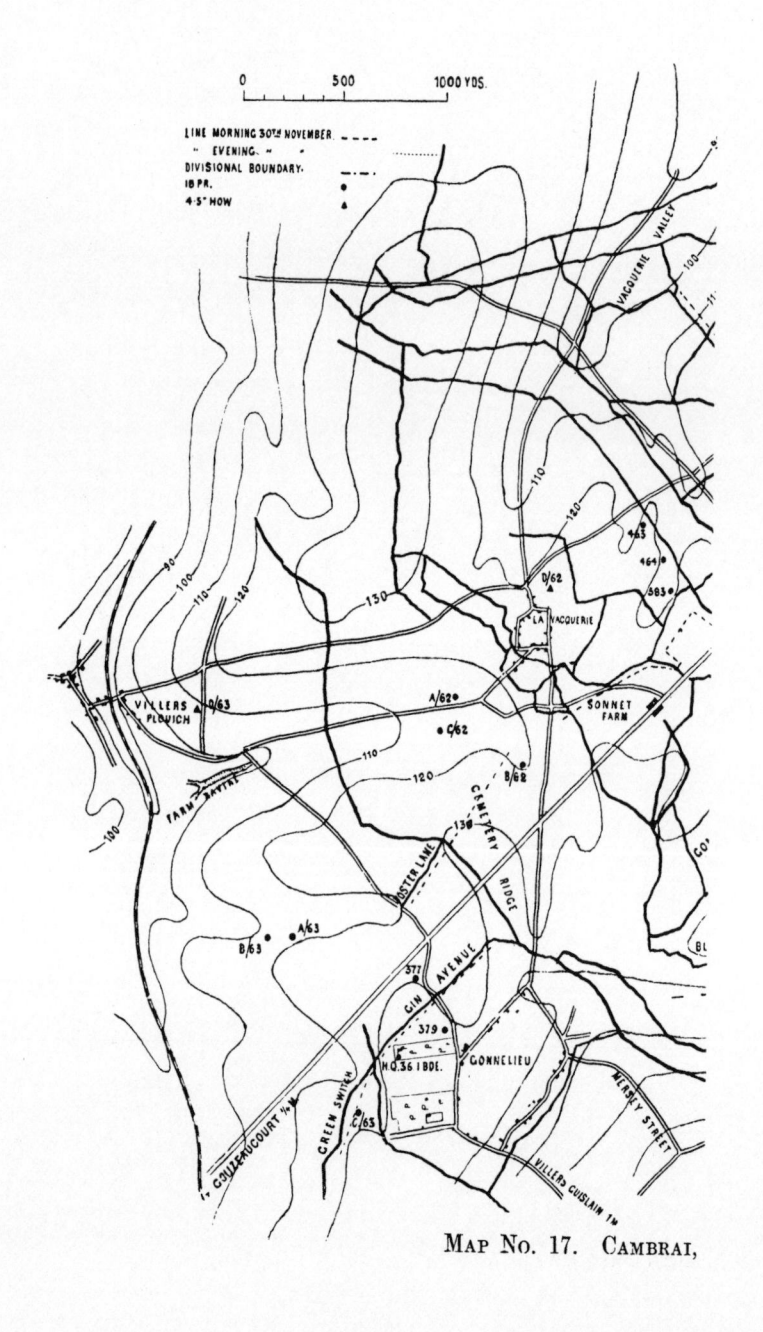

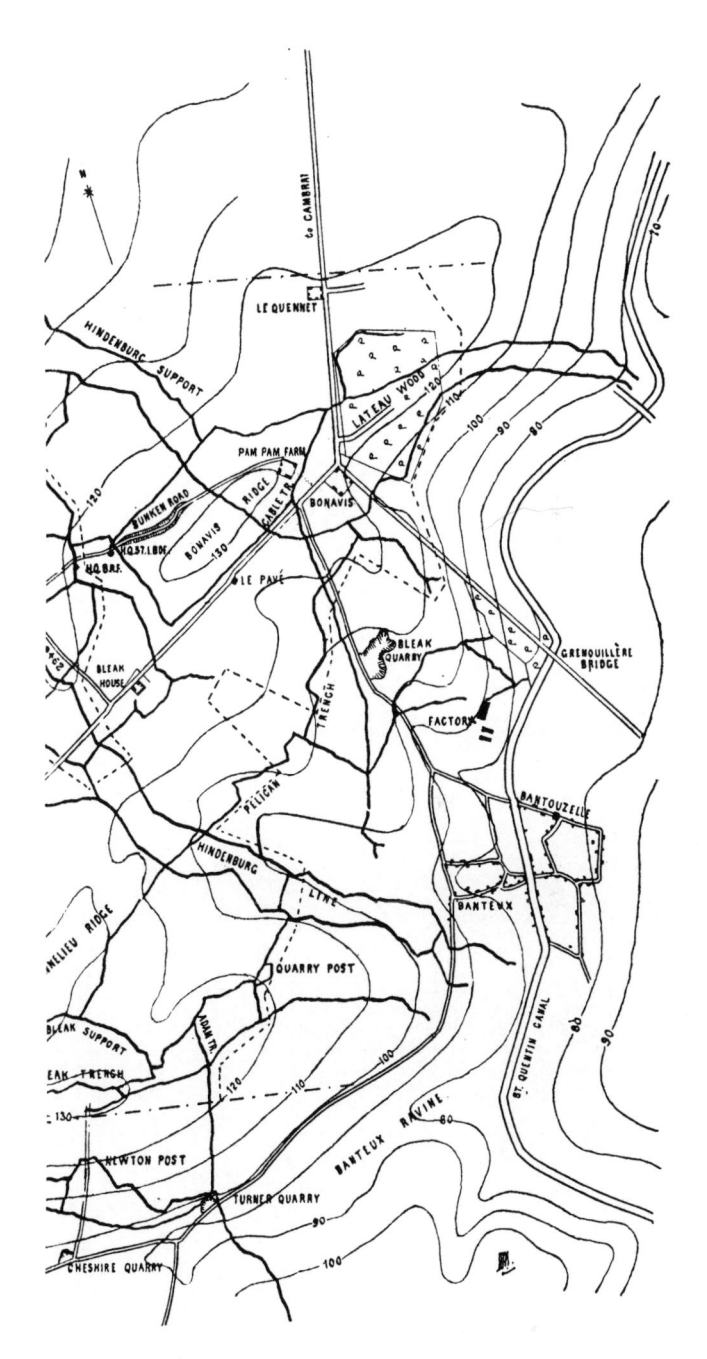

30TH NOVEMBER, 1917

back to a position 50 yards north of the road. Here all further efforts, seven in number, of the Germans against the 36th Infantry Brigade to cross the Cambrai Road failed, and the line held by this brigade and the 37th was handed over that night to the 61st Division.

As a brief summary of this battle it would appear that on the 30th of November the Germans launched two main attacks on the eastern side at 7 a.m., one from Bantouzelle, the other from Crèvecœur, with the object of gaining Bonavis Ridge and Lateau Wood respectively, a third attack from Grenouillère Bridge, being dependent on their success, took place somewhat later. A striking feature throughout the operations was the large number of low-flying aeroplanes firing machine guns, employed by the Germans to support their attacks and harass our troops.

The troops on the Revelon Ridge and its neighbourhood having been relieved on the night of the 3rd–4th, the Division, after assembling at Heudecourt, marched on the 4th and 5th of December towards Albert. On the 7th inst. the 35th, 36th, and 37th Infantry Brigades, entraining at Aveluy, Dernancourt and Albert respectively, eventually reached the villages round Aire, where Divisional Headquarters opened on the 8th December, joining the XVth Corps (Du Cane), and the First Army (Horne).

At the time of the German counter-attack on the 30th of November the infantry battalions were very short of men, reinforcements not having reached them. The casualties incurred on that day, 164 officers and 3,362 other ranks, represented well over 50 per cent. of the actual strength.

In writing to the General Officer Commanding the 12th Division, the Army Commander, General Sir Julian Byng, wrote as follows : " I wish to express to you and your Division how much I have appreciated the work done by them whilst forming part of the Third Army. During their long period in the line, and in the attack on the Hindenburg Line, and finally in the successful repulse of the German counter-stroke, the Division has fully lived up to its splendid reputation."

In publishing the above, Major-General Scott desired " to add his thanks to all concerned in maintaining this high record. The events of the 30th November, 1917, called for the highest soldier-like qualities under very trying circumstances. The counter-attack was carried out by a large number of the enemy, and although pushed back the Division can be justly proud of the fighting spirit it displayed."

CHAPTER XVI

OUR THIRD WINTER

December, 1917—March 24th, 1918

(*Map* 18)

ON arrival at Aire, the troops were billeted in that town, and at Thiennes and Berguette. The losses from the fighting near Cambrai had left the battalions very weak, but reinforcements soon commenced to arrive, and their organisation and training was taken in hand at once. For the third successive year the Division was fortunate in spending Christmas out of the line, though some of the troops did move towards the front line area on Christmas Day. The Christmas of 1916 had been very enjoyable, but this one was even better. It was a good rest area, and the reaction after the severe fighting at Cambrai probably made the festivities more appreciated. Divisional Headquarters entertained the children of Aire to a Christmas tree, cinema, and juggling performance, and in the brigade areas the *Entente Cordiale* was likewise well maintained.

The Divisional Artillery, which had been left behind at Cambrai, arrived on New Year's Day, 1918, having had a hard march owing to snow and the slippery state of the roads, and on the 5th January the Division moved nearer to the front, headquarters being at Merville. Although battalions were still very short of men, they were once more ready to take their place in the line, and on the 13th inst. the 36th and 37th Brigades relieved the 38th Division (Blackader) on the Fleurbaix sector, Divisional Headquarters moving to Croix du Bac, with the 35th Brigade in reserve. The Portuguese held the line on our right, and a post well-named " International," was garrisoned by both British and Portuguese. On the left was the 57th Division (Barnes), holding Armentières. These three divisions formed the XVth Corps. It was a quiet sector, nothing having occurred there since September, 1915, but in common with the remainder of the front it assumed a more lively aspect from the commencement of the year. The front line trenches, situated in very low lying ground, marshy at this time of the year, were mostly derelict and suffering from old age. As a consequence they were held by posts, the support line being the one of resistance.

With the defection of Russia and the consequent massing of German troops on the Western Front, it was certain the enemy would launch an attack at an early date in 1918. It was necessary to be prepared along the whole front, and this area being particularly weak, strenuous work now commenced to rectify that state of affairs. Several new series of trenches with switches were dug, reaching as far back as the western bank of the river Lys, concrete machine-gun emplacements were built, and miles of wire put up. Unfortunately at a later date, 11th April, this was of little avail, as the Germans broke through on the right, and though the position held out for a short time, it was eventually enveloped, and the troops had to be withdrawn. This is somewhat foretelling events, however, and when it did occur the Division was far away at Albert.

At 8.15 p.m. on the 29th January a party of about twenty-five Germans succeeded in getting behind one of the 36th Brigade posts, but a relief party, arriving opportunely, drove them off, taking two prisoners who provided a useful identification. On the 4th of February, after a five minutes' bombardment, the Germans attacked another post of the same brigade at 5.35 a.m., and succeeded in killing two and wounding two of the garrison, also unfortunately taking prisoners three signallers and a stretcher-bearer who were in a shelter. At 2 a.m. the next morning, we retaliated with a raid by " A " Company, 9th Essex, under Lieutenant S. A. Warner, resulting in the capture of four prisoners and a machine gun, and the killing of two more, without any casualties. On the 17th inst. the 6th Royal West Kent surrounded three supposed strong points but found them unoccupied, and were themselves attacked the following night, suffering four casualties. Owing to the fact that both opponents were holding a front line of posts, patrolling was incessant during the hours of darkness, leading to frequent small attacks on the posts, which were easy of approach unless they happened to be well guarded by the watercourses abounding in this area. In addition to these attacks, enemy aeroplanes became busy in dropping literature, apparently for the consumption of the French civilians, by means of small parachute balloons.

After the campaign of 1917 the question of man power became more serious than ever, and as it was evident the existing battalions could not be kept up to strength, it was decided to reduce each infantry brigade by one battalion. Though a necessity, it was an unfortunate one, as by this reduction many greatly distinguished battalions disappeared. This alteration was carried out early in February, the 36th Infantry Brigade losing the 8th Royal Fusiliers, famous for their fighting at the Craters, Ovillers, and Cambrai, and the 11th Middlesex, and receiving the 5th Royal Berkshire from the 35th Brigade ; the 37th Infantry Brigade losing the 7th East Surrey, a consistently hard-fighting battalion.

Early in March the Division lost a most valuable Staff Officer in Lieut.-Colonel E. H. Collen, A.A. and Q.M.G., who was transferred to the Staff School at Cambridge. He had held his appointment since October, 1915, and much of the success of the Division and comfort of all ranks was due to his ability in organisation and his untiring zeal and personal supervision.

March opened with additional activity on both sides. It was obvious that the great German offensive could not be delayed much longer. American troops were beginning to arrive in France, and it was generally believed that the offensive would materialise before they could be ready to take their place in the front line. The enemy's artillery fire increased considerably, roads and back areas were heavily shelled, bridges across the River Lys were registered, Fleurbaix underwent a heavy gas shelling, and Estaires, La Gorgue, Merville, Bailleul, amongst others, received a quota of shell. Meanwhile our various new lines of trenches and concrete emplacements were rapidly nearing completion, and raids continued to be recorded.

After a careful reconnaissance over a difficult piece of ground by Second Lieutenant Knights, Captain Nash and thirty men of " C " Company, 7th Norfolk, carrying out a raid, on the 1st March, killed ten of the enemy and took one prisoner. On the 8th inst. an operation by the 7th Royal Sussex resulted in several Germans being killed and two taken prisoners, at a time when identifications were urgently needed. This success was greatly due to Second Lieutenant R. F. Clements, who had constantly patrolled the ground previously. On the 9th, 200 of the 6th Royal West Kent raiding at 5.30 a.m., reached as far as the German support line, killing about thirty of the enemy, and capturing nine

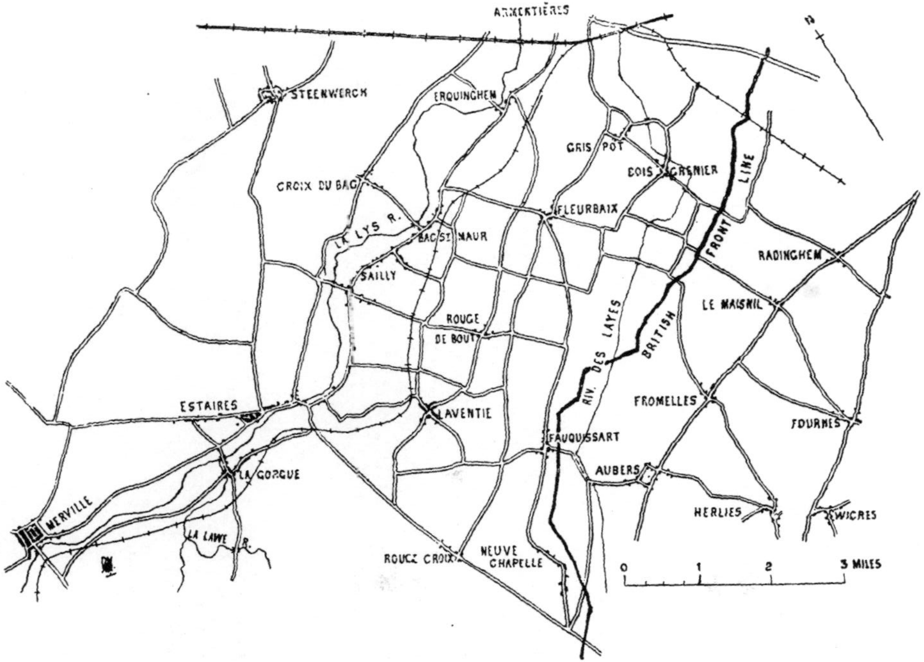

Map No. 18. Fleurbaix

prisoners and a machine gun, Sergeant James Sutton being chiefly instrumental in the matter. Next day information was received that four fresh German divisions were in the line opposite Neuve Chapelle and Bois Grenier, suggesting an early offensive on the enemy's part. As a consequence the artillery was reinforced, the emergency bridges over the River Lys placed in position, and all unnecessary *personnel* moved to the western bank of that river. At 5 a.m. on the 11th the 6th Royal West Kent had two posts raided after heavy shelling, one man being killed, an officer and twelve men wounded, and two taken prisoners, a machine gun and one prisoner being left in our hands. The following night the enemy paid attention to the Portuguese on our right, but returned to us on the evening of the 12th, when after a heavy bombardment on the greater portion of the 35th Brigade area, he advanced at 11.30 p.m. with two strong parties of about 100 each. These attacked a post held by two N.C.O.'s and ten privates of the 9th Essex, with a Lewis gun under Corporal Carlton. The Germans were driven off, leaving three dead, and the garrison sustained no casualties. In the neighbourhood, however, we had two killed and twenty-five wounded.

On the 15th inst. the Portuguese reported that their wire was cut and that there were gaps in the German wire, and on the 17th enemy observation balloons were much in evidence. Everything again pointed to an early offensive, but nevertheless the night of the 18th–19th was to be a record of raids. The 7th Suffolk of 35th Brigade, and 6th Queen's of 37th Brigade, had been detailed to carry out an operation. At 8.30 p.m. the former made a silent raid, but finding the enemy's trenches unoccupied, returned to our lines. At 9 p.m. the Germans attacked a post of the 7th Norfolk, but failed to get in and were counter-attacked by a support party which captured a prisoner. At 10.10 p.m. the enemy raided two posts held by the 6th Buffs, but were driven off. At 11 p.m. he entered our line between two posts held by the 6th Royal West Kent and was immediately ejected. At the same time he attacked the front of the 37th Brigade. The right of this was repulsed, but the left came in contact with the 6th Queen's, who were waiting in No Man's Land to raid at 11.10 p.m. The Queen's at once attacked, driving the Germans back and capturing four prisoners. At 3.20 a.m. on the 19th, a post of the 9th Essex was heavily bombarded, suffering ten casualties out of a garrison of thirteen. Private S. Nightingale, though only a young soldier, took command and, with the assistance of the two others, repulsed all attempts to capture the post. At the same time an adjacent post was rushed, and Sergeant Pollington dragged off the parapet and taken prisoner. However, on his way with a guard of two men, Sergeant Pollington suddenly hit one across the face with his steel helmet, and knocking the other down with his fist, escaped.

Whilst searching the ground next morning a German was captured, who was clearly out of luck. Managing to escape from the prisoner of war camp at St. Omer, he had reached our front line posts and most certainly would have got free, but for the incessant raids.

In the general turmoil of this night the Division had gained two identifications and lost none. Congratulatory messages were received from the Army and Corps Commanders, and on the two following nights the 57th Division relieving the 12th, the infantry marched to Estaires and its neighbourhood, headquarters returning to Merville, and reaching there at midday on the 21st inst., in confident expectation of a period of rest.

But it was not to be. Early that morning the line from Laventie to Armentières was heavily gas shelled, and the towns and back areas also received attention, evidently to suggest an attack in this locality, and prevent any withdrawal of troops to the south, where the long-expected German offensive had broken out. On the 22nd warning orders were received, and it appeared that the Fifth and Third Armies were falling back everywhere. On the 24th inst. the Division, minus its artillery, concentrated in the Busnes area, and thence moved by motor that night to the vicinity of Albert.

CHAPTER XVII

STEMMING THE TIDE

March 25th—April 12th, 1918

(*Maps* 19 *and* 20)

ON the morning of the 25th March the 12th Division, less artillery and transport, after travelling all night, arrived between 8.30 a.m. and 10 a.m. at Senlis, Warloy and Bouzincourt, headquarters being at Senlis, and joined the VIIth Corps (Congreve), Third Army (Byng). A small amount of transport had been collected from various sources, till our own should arrive. The Fifth and Third Armies were still falling back and information was vague.

At 4.30 p.m. the 36th and 37th Brigades, with the 35th in support, moved forward to occupy the line Montauban-Bazentin-le-Grand, and gain touch with the Vth Corps on the left, Divisional Headquarters moving to Méaulte. At 5.30 p.m., however, the 37th Brigade, which was leading, was ordered to Contalmaison, the 36th and 35th being intercepted by a Staff Officer of the 35th Division (Franks) who was in possession of a VIIth Corps order directing these two brigades to proceed to Montauban and Maricourt respectively, and support the 35th Division. On nearing Carnoy at 8 p.m. the 35th Brigade (Vincent) was met by a Staff Officer of the 9th Division (Blacklock) who stated that that division was conducting operations at Maricourt. Passing through Maricourt, which was in flames, General Vincent reached the 9th Division Headquarters, where he learnt that fresh orders had been issued, and he was to return to Albert at once and report again to the 12th Division Headquarters which had returned to Senlis. This was carried out, the brigade reaching Albert about 12.30 a.m. on the 26th, having marched fifteen miles with packs. After resting for a few hours the troops took up their position covering the approaches to Albert and their portion of the west bank of the Ancre.

The 36th Brigade (Wollocombe) was moving *viâ* Mametz and Carnoy on Montauban, and Lieut.-Colonel Wollocombe went forward to gain touch with the brigade of the 35th Division he had been ordered to support, when a Staff Officer of the 12th Division, overtaking the brigade, gave orders to halt and sent forward to recall Lieut.-Colonel Wollocombe, who returned at 11 p.m. The brigade eventually returned *viâ* Albert, and by 4.30 a.m. on the 26th had taken up a position on the west of the Ancre river in accordance with fresh orders.

The leading troops of the 37th Brigade (Incledon Webber) arrived at La Boisselle at 6.15 p.m., and found the advanced headquarters of the 47th Division (Gorringe) established there. General Gorringe, explaining the situation, ordered the 37th Brigade to counter-attack Pozières and establish communication between the 47th and the 63rd Division (Lawrie) on the left. At 8.45 p.m. the 6th Queen's and 6th Royal West Kent were astride the Albert-Bapaume Road, ready to carry out this operation, which was then cancelled and fresh orders issued for a line of outposts to be taken up through Ovillers. However, at 9.15 p.m. General Webber ordered a company of Royal West Kent to patrol in the direction of Pozières and form a covering party, whilst preparations were made for the destruction of an ammunition dump situated there. Pozières was found unoccupied, and the dump was successfully destroyed. The 37th Brigade, which had taken up the line through Ovillers, then covered the withdrawal of the 47th Division over the Ancre, and commencing its own retirement at 4.30 a.m. on 26th, arrived at the Aveluy Bridge. Here General Webber found the 36th Brigade in position, and completing the crossing of his own troops by 7 a.m., took his place on the left of the 12th Division line.

On the dispersal of the infantry brigades to the 35th and 47th Divisions, the advanced headquarters returned to Senlis, the Division being transferred to the Vth Corps (E. Fanshawe). At 11.35 p.m. orders were received to take up a line covering Albert (the right connecting with the VIIth Corps on the Bray-Albert Road) along the western bank of the River Ancre to Hamel inclusive. This was the line taken up by the brigades during the night and early hours of the morning of the 26th, and great credit was due to the several staffs and commanders for the successful manner in which, under the circumstances, it was accomplished. The position was about 9,000 yards in length and divided into three almost equal sectors. The 35th Brigade held the right with the 7th Suffolk (Cooper) covering Albert, the 7th Norfolk (Rees) along the railway embankment, to Aveluy Bridge, and the 9th Essex (La Terrière) in support; the 36th Brigade in centre, with the 9th Royal Fusiliers (Van Someran) in touch with the Norfolk, the 7th Royal Sussex (Impey) on left, and 5th Royal Berkshire (Nicolls) in reserve at Martinsart; the 37th Brigade on the left with 6th Royal West Kent (Dawson) and 6th Queen's (Whetham) holding as far as Hamel inclusive, and the 6th Buffs (Smeltzer) in reserve at Mesnil. Two companies of the Machine Gun Battalion (Oakley) were attached to the 35th, and one company each to the 36th and 37th Brigades. There were no trenches, and so the natural line of resistance for the greater portion of the front became the railway embankment, wherever it was suitable.

The lack of entrenching tools was now severely felt, as any scraps of old trenches still in existence were quite useless. The Division had no hand or rifle grenades, no Verey lights or means of communicating S.O.S. signals, and there was no defensive wire. In this condition the German attack was awaited. The position ran along the bed of the valley entirely commanded by the high ground on the east, and though the River Ancre ran in front, it was not really impassable, and none of the bridges had been destroyed or prepared for destruction, and attempts to rectify this were too late. On the Division front the morning passed quietly, the greatest difficulty being to get in touch with troops on the right flank, as the VIIth Corps could not be found on the Bray Road, nor the 1st Cavalry Division reported in the same direction. Eventually touch was gained with the 27th Brigade of the 9th Division on the Albert-Amiens railway line. On the left we were in touch with the 2nd Division (Pereira). The situation on that flank was, however, very unsatisfactory, as bodies of Germans had reached Colincamps. Later in the day these were driven back by the New Zealand Division (Russell) and some " Whippets," a light form of tank, with improved turning powers and greater speed than the older and heavier ones.

The divisional artillery not having arrived, the 35th, 36th and 37th Infantry Brigades were supported by the artillery of the 17th, 47th, and 63rd Divisions respectively.

Soon after midday on the 26th the Germans were observed advancing into the Ancre Valley all along the opposite slopes, and notwithstanding our artillery fire pressed steadily onwards, taking advantage of our old system of trenches. The enemy were also seen in large numbers to the south of Albert moving on Méaulte and Dernancourt, thus showing we had no troops on the Bray-Albert Road. At 5.50 p.m. the 35th Brigade reporting further large bodies of Germans moving on Albert, the 5th Northamptonshire (Trent) was placed at the disposal of the G.O.C. of that brigade. At 7 p.m. Albert was reported full of Germans, the Suffolk having fallen back to the railway line, and a company of Northamptonshire was sent up in support.

Note.—The River Ancre ran under the town and formed no obstacle in Albert itself, which unless properly prepared for defence and with many more troops than were now available, could not be held against such an advance as the one under consideration.

At 12.15 a.m., 27th inst., the Suffolk position in the railway cutting becoming untenable owing to enfilade machine gun fire, a new position was taken up on a bank about 300 yards in rear. The Norfolk on the left reporting between 7.30 and 9 p.m. that the Germans were across the river, and although counter-attacks had been launched, the battalion was hard pressed, one company each of 9th Essex and 5th Northamptonshire were sent up in support.

On the 36th Brigade front the Aveluy Bridge was held by the 9th Royal Fusiliers, and two determined attempts by the Germans to cross the river during the night were repulsed.

To the north, although the New Zealand Division had restored the line early on the afternoon of the 26th, the enemy was still well across the Ancre, and large numbers of them were reported between Grandcourt and Beaumont Hamel, covered by artillery which constantly molested the left of the 37th Brigade, seriously threaten-

MAP No. 19.

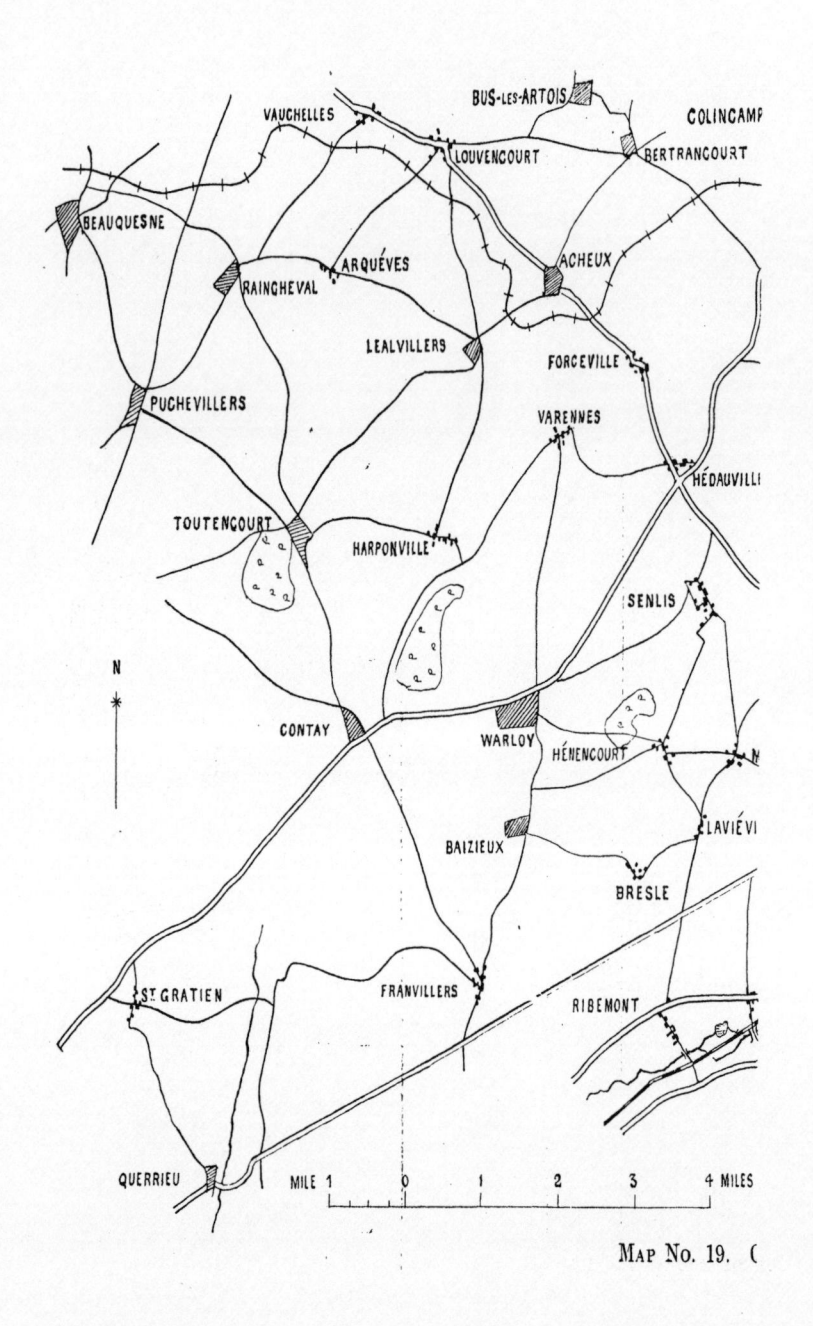

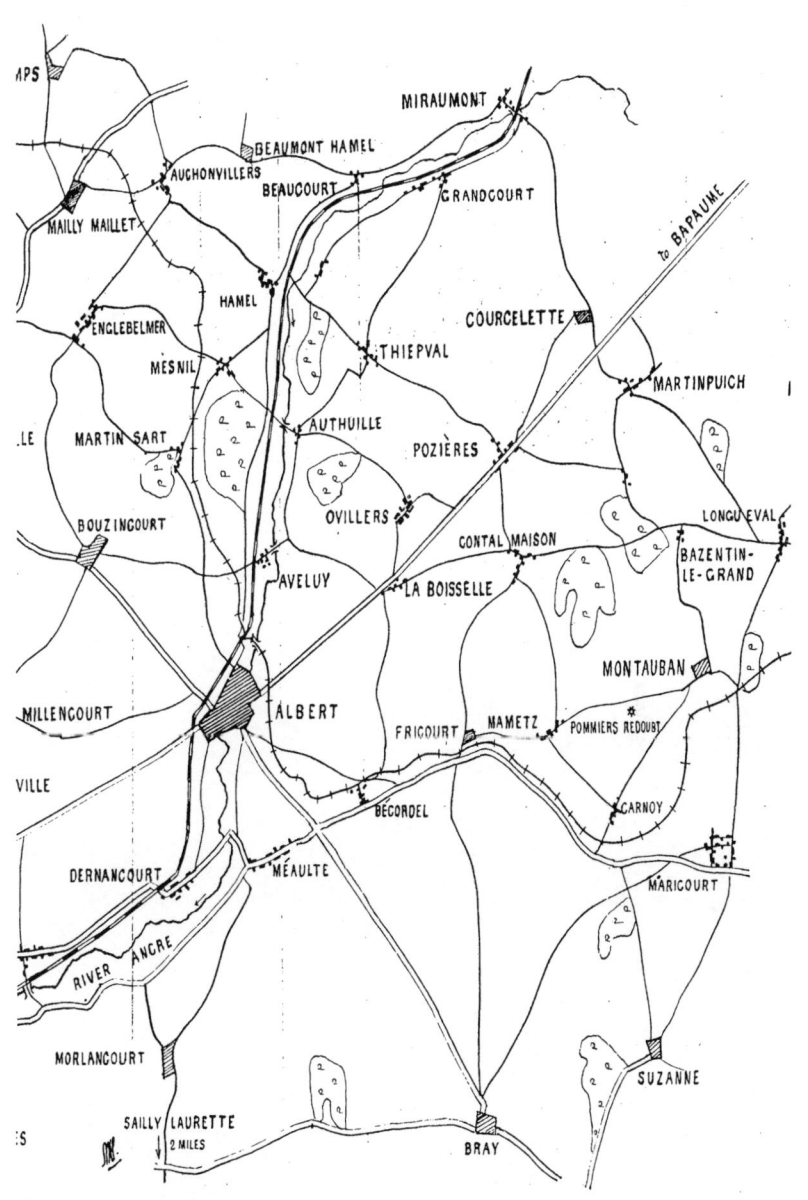

COUNTRY ROUND ALBERT

ing that flank, which as a consequence was reinforced by a company of the Buffs. At 9 p.m. the enemy attacked this portion of the line, held by the 6th Queen's, and some of the 188th Brigade of 63rd Division in process of relief. This attack was repulsed, six prisoners and one machine gun remaining in our hands, fifteen also being killed. At 11.30 p.m. heavy rifle fire in the direction of Mesnil was heard at Brigade Headquarters at Martinsart, and a German patrol was reported on the Mesnil-Martinsart Road. The G.O.C. 188th Brigade, also in Martinsart, placed his troops at the disposal of the G.O.C. 37th Brigade, and the Anson Battalion was ordered to counter-attack and reoccupy Mesnil. This counter-attack was launched at 12.30 a.m., 27th inst., and mixed fighting ensued in which two companies of the Buffs and some Royal West Kent took part. Our lines were cleared of the enemy, who left many dead and a number of prisoners behind; eight machine guns were claimed by the Anson Battalion, and four by units of the 37th Brigade.

At 11 p.m. Lieut.-Colonel Smeltzer with the headquarter company of the Buffs at Mesnil Station receiving a report that " B " Company, holding a post in Aveluy Wood was heavily attacked and surrounded, sent up his support company, which, capturing a machine gun on its way, arrived at " B " Company's post to find it intact with twenty to thirty Germans lying dead round it. The post also had seven prisoners. Meanwhile a lively fusillade started at Mesnil Station between the Anson Battalion and the Buffs; fortunately the mistake was soon discovered. It would appear that the Germans, having attacked " B " Company post, passed on, becoming engaged in the counter-attack from Martinsart. Mesnil itself had never been out of our hands.

No further movements were made by the enemy during the remainder of the night of the 26th, activity recommencing at 7.30 a.m. on the 27th when the 1st Artists Rifles and 10th Bedfordshire, belonging to the 190th Brigade, 63rd Division, attempted to retake the railway line south-west of Albert, but, owing to heavy casualties from machine gun fire from the houses on the outskirts of the town, this attack failed. An attempt by the enemy to debouch from Albert at 8 a.m. was frustrated. The left company of the Suffolk suffered heavily from shell fire, but " A " Company, 9th Essex (Second Lieutenant Comber) in support, firing some 15,000 rounds of small arms ammunition, strewed the ground in front of them to within 20 yards with German dead. At 10 a.m. a second attack developed, our artillery firing on the vicinity of the railway station and towards Aveluy, stopped the main portion of it, but the enemy succeeded in getting machine guns into position on both flanks of the 7th Norfolk on the railway, thus enfilading the battalion and causing it to withdraw, first to the road close by, and subsequently to a position about 1,000 yards up the slope. During this retirement Second Lieutenant Blackwell and Company Sergt.-Major Hoare, with a company of the 5th Northamptonshire, which was in support, behaved with great gallantry, the former unfortunately being killed ; " D " Company, Machine Gun Battalion, under Major W. Chalmers, found itself 100 yards in front of the infantry line, and holding their post, inflicted heavy losses on the advancing enemy ; Lieut.-Colonel Rees, with about forty men, also counter-attacked successfully at a critical moment.

On the 36th Brigade front attempts to cross the river early in the morning and again at 8 a.m. had been repulsed, but when the Norfolk fell back at the later

AVELUY BRIDGE

attack, the right flank of the 9th Fusiliers was driven back to its support line. This advance of the enemy cut off a platoon of " A " Company under Captain Baudains, which was on the far side of the Aveluy Bridge. A counter-attack by the reserve company " D " to re-establish the front failed, as also an attack on Aveluy by a company of the 5th Royal Berkshire at 11 a.m. Meanwhile Captain Baudains, realising the situation, decided to cut his way back to his battalion, and leading his troops he succeeded in getting through. The left of the Royal Fusiliers and the Sussex still held their original line.

At 5 p.m., preceded by an intense bombardment of ten minutes, the Germans, again attacking in force from the south-east and south assisted by low-flying aeroplanes, overpowered our outposts and front line, fighting taking place as far back as the reserve line on the right and the support line on the left. The enemy drove in a wedge between the two companies of the Sussex, but his further progress was held up by the Battalion Headquarters under Lieut.-Colonel Impey. The line was now reorganised, the 5th Royal Berkshire taking up a position on the right of the 9th Royal Fusiliers, south of Martinsart Wood and in touch with the 5th Northamptonshire, who had come to the assistance of the Norfolk ; the Sussex in Aveluy Wood having two companies facing south and two east, the Germans being in the south-east corner of the wood.

The 37th Brigade had prevented several attempts to cross the river early in the morning of the 27th inst., but Hamel being continuously and heavily shelled, the troops withdrew from the village at 1.15 p.m., covering the approaches thereto by Lewis guns. The Germans had been observed massing at Beaucourt, and an attack from the north at 5.45 p.m. was beaten off. A further concentration of the enemy in the direction of Thiepval resulted in another attack about 6.30 p.m., in which the right of the 6th Royal West Kent was forced to evacuate the railway line. In this area the remainder of the night passed quietly, but late in the evening immediately preceding the relief of the 35th Brigade by the 17th Division, the 7th Norfolk were again attacked, losing a small portion of ground, and Lieut.-Colonel Rees, who had been wounded, was taken prisoner. Two companies of the 5th Northamptonshire, moving up in support, assisted in maintaining the remainder of the position. On relief the 35th Brigade moved to Hénencourt, the 7th Norfolk having lost 19 officers and 284 other ranks, and the 7th Suffolk 12 officers and 243 other ranks, which, at this period of reduced numbers, represented a very large percentage.

At 9 a.m. on the 28th inst., a strong attack from the direction of Aveluy, was completely repulsed by the 5th Royal Berkshire and 9th Royal Fusiliers in co-operation with artillery and machine guns, and such heavy casualties were inflicted that the enemy were observed during the remainder of the day carrying his wounded across the river and up the slopes towards La Boisselle. The 7th Sussex holding the south side of the wood, were successful in beating off an attack there, but on the east side of Aveluy Wood another company of the Sussex and the 6th Royal West Kent lost some portions of the line, which was re-established later in the day by a counter-attack. The 6th Queen's on the left underwent a heavy shelling during the afternoon, and although there was a considerable movement of the enemy in that direction, no action materialised. During the night of the 28th–29th the 37th Brigade was relieved by two brigades of the 2nd Division, and the 37th Brigade itself took over the right half of the 36th Brigade front. No attacks developed on the 29th, and that night the 47th Division, relieving the 36th and 37th Brigades, these troops marched to Warloy.

The 12th Division, having made an obstinate resistance to the six enemy divisions opposing it, had been instrumental in bringing the great German advance to a halt in this area. It had suffered 1,634 casualties and captured thirteen prisoners and four machine guns.

A day or two to clean themselves and get a few hours unmolested sleep, was greatly appreciated by the troops before returning to the front on the night of the 2nd April, when the 35th Brigade on the right, the 36th (Owen) on the left, and 37th in reserve, relieved the 17th Division in the right sector of the corps front due west of Albert. The 4th Australian Division was on our right, and the 47th on our left. This sector was about 4,000 yards long, and we were supported by the 78th and 79th Brigades, Royal Field Artillery, of 63rd Division, and the 34th Army Field Artillery Brigade and 89th Heavy Artillery Brigade; advanced Divisional Headquarters were at Warloy. The 4th Australian Division was attacked unsuccessfully twice on the 3rd inst., no action developing on our front. However, at about 1 p.m. on the next day, after twenty minutes' intense artillery and trench mortar fire, the Germans advancing in two waves, attempted to rush the trenches of the Suffolk and Essex, but beyond gaining a small post held by the Suffolk were beaten off, the Lewis guns of the 5th Royal Berkshire on the left greatly assisting in this success. Later in the day, Captain Crandon and " D " Company, 7th Suffolk, retook the post lost by the battalion.

During the night a warning message was received, emanating from the French General Headquarters, that the enemy would probably attack on the 5th inst. This proved correct, as at 7 a.m. the next morning the whole divisional front was shelled by guns of all calibres ; at the same time our batteries and the back areas received gas shell in addition, the bombardment spreading to right and left. The first attack at 7.30 a.m. was repulsed, but during a second at 9.30 a.m., after heavy fighting, the Germans succeeded in gaining a footing in the Berkshire position, from which they were ejected by a successful counter-attack delivered by the 9th Royal Fusiliers. The 35th Brigade, on the right, repelled all attacks, but the left of the Australian Division being driven back slightly, the right of the 35th Brigade conformed in the night. During these operations the so-called corps line, which had come into existence since the line of the Ancre held, was occupied by the Divisional Field Companies, Royal Engineers, the 5th Northamptonshire, and one and a half companies of the Machine Gun Battalion, under the command of Lieut.-Colonel Trent. The fighting on this day had been very severe and casualties were heavy, but the Germans could not get free of Albert, which now systematically received its full share of gas shell and harassing fire.

During that night and the following morning the situation remained quiet. About 5 p.m. on the 6th inst. an attack on the 9th Essex was repulsed except at the Quarry, which had resisted an earlier attack at 10 a.m., but now had to be evacuated by its small garrison under Second Lieutenant C. S. James, who was found wounded in the thigh, in a shell hole, about four hours afterwards. Later in the day an outburst of artillery fire was answered by our guns, and no infantry action took place. On the 7th inst. the 12th Division Artillery arrived and took over our protection ; the 37th Brigade relieved the 36th, and the 5th Northamptonshire was attached to the 35th Brigade, which was very weak.

Infantry activity on the enemy's part now ceased,

MAP No. 20.

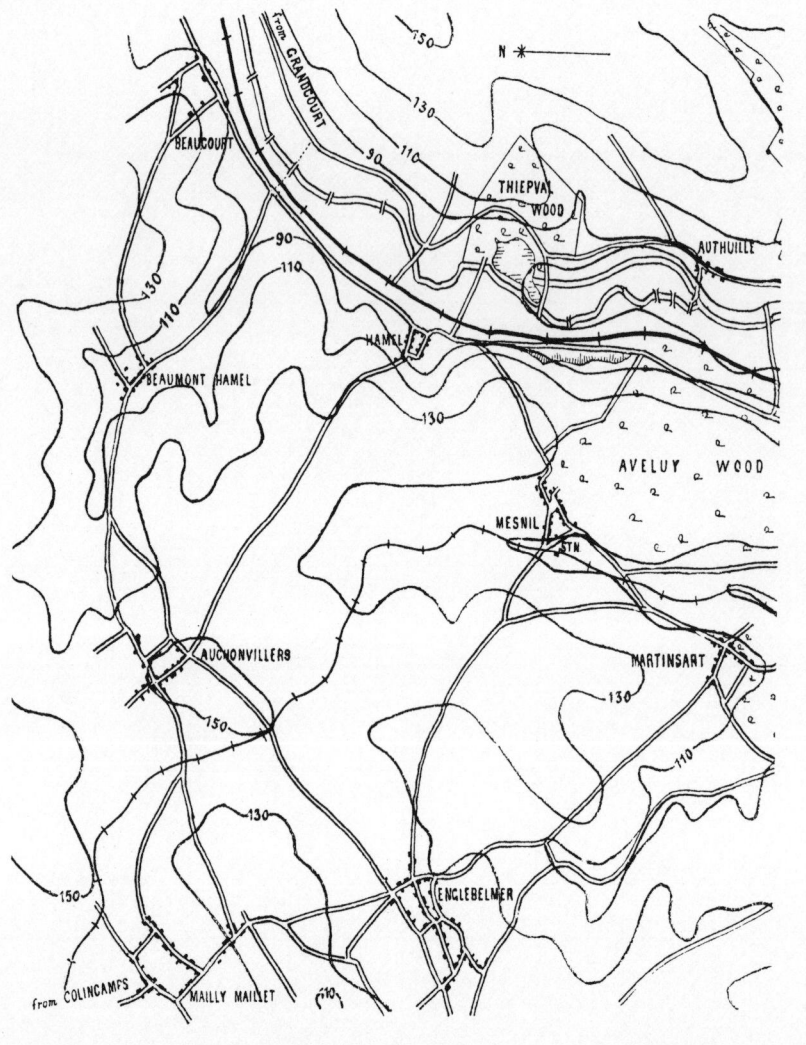

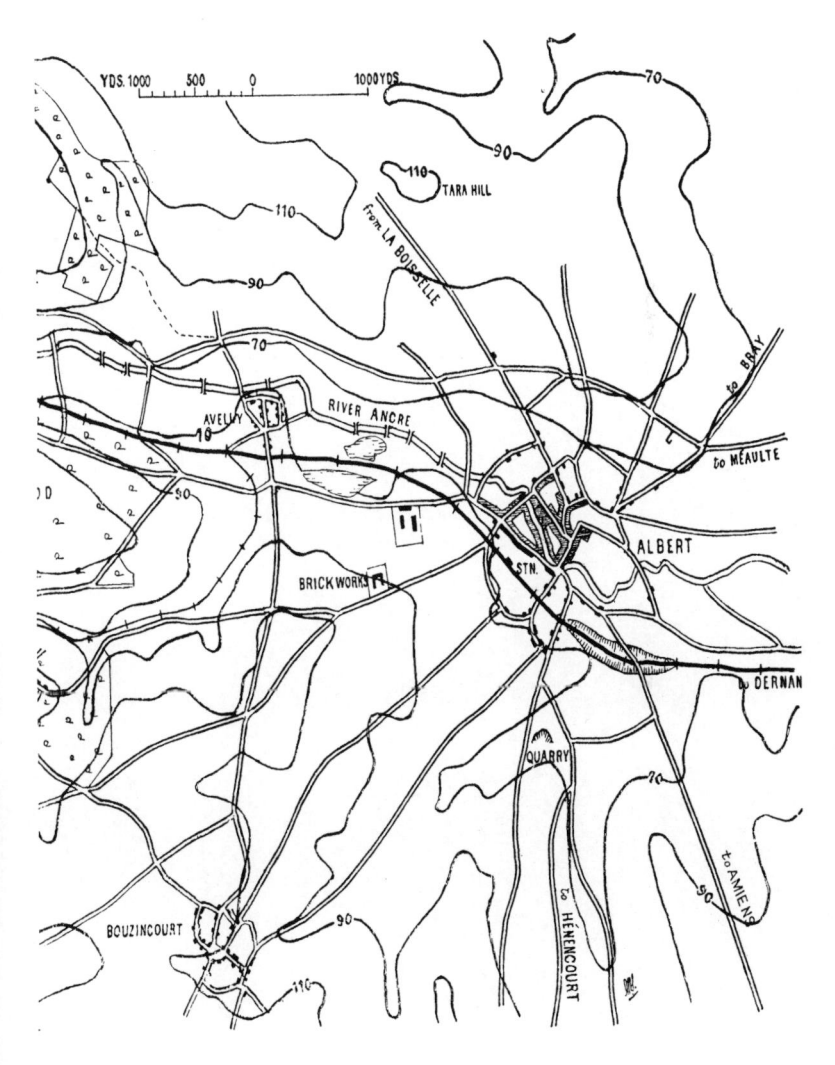

Albert, March, 1918

although a considerable amount of shelling, with a large percentage of gas projectiles, continued, and on the 8th inst. a good many of the Signal Company, Royal Engineers, became casualties therefrom. During the shelling and for a suitable period after, gas masks were worn, but later on, rain causing the gas to rise again, the men became affected before realising the reason. Rain and an attempt at frost had made the trench conditions bad, brigade reliefs becoming frequent in consequence. On the nights of the 11th and 12th the 38th Division relieved the 12th, which marched back to the Toutencourt area, headquarters being at that village. For this period of eight days the losses had amounted to 1,285.

It may not be out of place to record here the words of a contemporary historian referring to the deeds of the 12th Division during the period from 25th to 29th March. " The whole of the Twelfth Division was now rested for a time, but they withdrew from their line in glory, for it is no exaggeration to say that they had fought the Germans to an absolute standstill." *

* " The British Campaign in France and Flanders, January to July, 1918." Arthur Conan Doyle.

CHAPTER XVIII

BACKS TO THE WALL
April 13th—August 2nd, 1918
(*Maps* 19 *and* 20)

THE 12th Division was by this time greatly reduced in numbers, and although reinforcements commenced to arrive, training on an extensive scale could not be carried out, owing to the fact that very large working parties were required daily for employment on the rear defensive lines. In view of a further offensive by the Germans, the rapid completion of these lines was most important, as no organised system of trenches existed in this area. Nevertheless, training was pushed on, and the attachment of some officers and non-commissioned officers from the army school enabled special instruction to be given, mainly in musketry.

The capture by the Germans of Fleurbaix and Merville in the north had so far affected the 12th Division that some of the battalions lost the stores that had been deposited in that area on leaving for the south on the 25th March. During this period of rest the 1st/1st Cambridgeshire Regiment (Lieut.-Colonel Saint, D.S.O.) joined the 35th Infantry Brigade and absorbed the remnants of the 7th Suffolk Regiment.

Rumours of renewed offensives by the enemy, entailing the occupation of the new defences, had passed without materialising, and on the 23rd April the Division again moved forward, relieving the New Zealand Division on that portion of the line covering

Mailly Maillet and Auchonvillers, the 36th Brigade taking over the right and the 35th Brigade the left, being supported by the 93rd, 232nd and 315th Army Field Artillery Brigades.

On the 26th April the Division had to say farewell to Major-General A. B. Scott, who had been appointed to a command in India. General Scott had commanded the 12th Division for over two and a half years of its service in France, and had won the esteem and regard of all ranks by his constant courtesy and kindness, as well as the admiration of all for his leadership and soldierly character.

Before leaving the Division he issued the following order :

" In relinquishing command of the 12th (Eastern) Division I once more desire to express my high appreciation of the fighting qualities of the Division. I also wish to thank all those who, by carrying out their duties efficiently, have aided the Division in reaching the high standard it has attained. The mutual confidence between all branches has greatly assisted to this end, and made the task of commanding an easy one. To my staff and all those in command I express my deepest gratitude for their assistance.

" There is no better command than that of a division in the field, and I thoroughly appreciate the honour I have had in commanding the 12th Division for over two and a half years. To leave it is a great wrench and I feel it very much, but, you may be assured, my thoughts will always be with you and I shall continue to watch carefully for your doings. Under all circumstances be as you always have been, cheerful and confident. To you all good-bye and the best of luck.

" 25th April."

Major-General H. W. Higginson succeeded to the command of the Division. General Higginson arrived in France in March, 1915, as Brigade-Major of the 143rd Infantry Brigade, 48th Division. Later on he commanded the 2nd Battalion Royal Dublin Fusiliers, and for two years the 53rd Infantry Brigade, 18th Division, from which appointment he was now transferred.

Artillery and trench mortar activity was, at this time, the predominating feature on both sides, our concentrations dealing chiefly with Beaumont Hamel, Beaucourt and the bridges over the River Ancre. The enemy shelled Auchonvillers, Mailly Maillet and Englebelmer systematically, and the villages in rear with long-range guns. It was not exactly a "healthy" sector, and a senior "gunner" considered the German artillery was never better nor more effective than at this time.

Auchonvillers, close to the front, was naturally a point to which relieving troops and supplies proceeded immediately it was dusk, that is about 7 p.m. at the end of April. The Germans, well aware of this, were in the habit of bringing down two-minute artillery "crashes" on the village at irregular intervals for several hours. As a consequence, the endeavours to escape the shelling caused the officer in charge of the troops or ration party going up to the front some anxious moments. It is not surprising that a daily toll was exacted from such parties, when a typical day, the 29th April, is taken as an example. On that evening the Germans fired their crashes at 7.10, 7.25, 7.40 and 8 p.m. followed by nine salvos in all parts of the village at 9.15 p.m.

The casualties for April amounted to 1,437.

Early in May three patrol actions against our posts were repulsed, and on each occasion a prisoner was left in our hands, Sergeant Cox, " A " Company, 6th Buffs

[Swaine

COLONEL (TEMP. MAJOR-GENERAL) H. W. HIGGINSON,
C.B., D.S.O., A.D.C.

being commended for gallantry during one of these raids. Lewis guns were now attached to all horse transport to deal with low-flying aeroplanes operating against it.

On 11th May two enemy patrols, approaching our lines, entered a sap held by the 5th Royal Berkshire. Hand to hand fighting ensued, and the enemy attempting to drag one of our men over the parapet, Sergeant F. Varney at once attacked with bombs, and wounding two of them forced them to withdraw. Sergeant Varney, accompanied by Private Bushell, then proceeded into No Man's Land and captured a wounded man, who proved to be an officer, thereby gaining a useful identification. Sergeant Varney was awarded the Distinguished Conduct Medal and Private Bushell the Military Medal for their bravery on this occasion.

At 10 p.m. on the 16th May four groups, of one officer and twenty-four men each, of " D " Company, the 6th Buffs, under command of Captain McCallum, raided the German trenches west of Beaumont Hamel with a view to examining the crater situated there. Having overcome two listening posts with garrisons of five men each, who refused to surrender, the front trench was entered and three dug-outs bombed. A bombing fight commenced on the east of the crater and the garrison of about ten men was driven back. There being no signs of fresh mining the parties withdrew, having captured three prisoners and accounted for twenty-eight more of the enemy. The Buffs lost three killed, and one officer and fourteen other ranks wounded. The raid was well executed and ably supported by the artillery, trench mortars, and machine guns.

Increased activity was shown by the enemy's aeroplanes both by day and in night bombing, Auchonvillers receiving twenty bombs on the 22nd inst. On the

24th inst. a raid on a large scale was carried out by the 5th Royal Berkshire (Nicolls) in conjunction with the Anson Battalion of the 63rd Division (Lawrie) on the right. The German trenches were to be exploited in depth, " A " and " B " Companies under Captain J. N. Gregory operating on the right, and " C " and " D " Companies under Captain G. E. Collins on the left. The leading companies, " A " and " C," were to occupy the German front line and consolidate it sufficiently to cover the final withdrawal, whilst the following companies, " B " and " D " were to pass through to the support trenches and thoroughly search them. The operation, which had been carefully rehearsed, proved very successful, eight prisoners and five machine guns being captured, and estimated casualties of fifty inflicted on the enemy. Our losses were thirteen other ranks killed, four officers and seventy other ranks wounded, and seven other ranks missing. Congratulations were received from the Army and Corps Commanders.

In this raid Corporal J. J. Sargeant displayed conspicuous bravery in dealing with dug-outs, from which the enemy made a stout resistance, and Lance-Corporal C. Gale distinguished himself in capturing a machine gun.

On the 25th inst. the Division, on being relieved by the 17th (Robertson), moved to the Puchevillers-Beauquesne area with headquarters at Raincheval. During this relief a medical officer of the United States Army, attached to the 9th Essex, displayed great self-sacrifice. A heavy bombardment of gas shell on the Auchonvillers-Mailly Maillet Road necessitated the wearing of gas masks. Owing to the number of casualties Lieutenant McCarthy found he could not deal satisfactorily with the cases whilst wearing his mask. As a consequence he removed it, and remaining in the gas area for three hours, succeeded in evacuating all the cases, but was himself so badly gassed that he had to be taken to hospital.

On the 4th June the Division was transferred to the XXIInd Corps (Godley), in reserve to the French Army. The troops remained in their locations, officers of the Divisional and Infantry Brigade staffs and battalions reconnoitring the ground south of Amiens in view of possible operations in that area. No action materialised, and on the 16th inst. the Division was transferred back to the Vth Corps (Shute), and on the 18th relieved the 35th Division (Marindin) on the Bouzincourt sector, the chief features of which were the Bouzincourt Spur and the high ground between Aveluy and Mesnil, mostly covered by the Aveluy Wood. The 36th Brigade were on the right and the 37th on the left, the ground being familiar to both, having been held by them in the German attack in March and April.

In the early hours of the 20th inst., from midnight to 2.50 a.m., a heavy bombardment was placed on the southern portion of Aveluy Wood, trench mortars and machine guns also co-operating. At 2.50 a.m. four patrols of the 6th Buffs proceeded towards the German trenches, but failed to reach them owing to the enemy's fire, which apparently came from advanced posts that had escaped the bombardment. They were compelled to retire to our lines without having carried out their object.

On the 23rd June the 35th Brigade relieved the 37th, and four officers and twelve non-commissioned officers of the 106th American Regiment, arriving for four days' training, joined this brigade in the trenches.

An operation was now planned to gain the remaining high ground of the Bouzincourt Spur. The attack was to be made by the 37th Brigade in conjunction with the

18th Division (Lee) on the right, and the troops were specially trained for the purpose. The principle of the operation was to assault, and hold, what was practically the German front line, other troops passing through to gain the support line, and hold that long enough to enable the front line to be consolidated, when the advanced troops would withdraw. Careful preparations were made as to communications, and materials for consolidation were collected in convenient centres. The artillery concentration consisted of eighty-two 18-pounders, eighty medium and heavy howitzers, twenty-two 4·5″ howitzers, ten 6″ trench mortars, thirty-six Stokes Mortars, and 116 machine guns. Zero hour was 9.35 p.m. on 30th June, and the withdrawal of the advanced troops was to commence at 2.10 a.m. on the 1st July. The advance was made under a creeping barrage, the 6th Queen's attacking on the right and the 6th Royal West Kent on the left.

The guns opened fire at zero, and after three minutes' bombardment of the front line, the troops assaulted, and experiencing little trouble from the enemy's wire, which had been cut the previous night, captured the first objective. The enemy's artillery fire opened at five minutes past zero, falling chiefly on the right of the divisional front. Considerable opposition was met with from the support line, mainly on the right, but about 11.10 p.m. this was also gained, the Royal West Kent having captured twenty-two prisoners and three machine guns. At first, touch was not obtained with the 18th Division on the right, but a small party of Germans, holding out there, were bombed by the 6th Queen's, and touch acquired at 7.30 a.m. on 1st July. During the night a weak counter-attack was repulsed.

At 8 p.m. on the 1st the enemy delivered a strong counter-attack, which was repulsed by the Royal West

Kent, but by 10 p.m. the Queen's had been driven back to our own lines. " A " Company, however, again attacking at 11.35 p.m. regained the German front line. This battalion was relieved by the 6th Buffs at 5 a.m. on the 2nd. At 9.30 p.m. that evening the Germans again attacked under cover of an intense bombardment, and succeeded in driving back the 18th Division and the Royal West Kent, the Buffs maintaining their position, from which they withdrew at 6.30 a.m. on the 3rd inst. In the enemy attack on one of our bombing blocks, Lieutenant E. A. Dudeney distinguished himself by maintaining his post single-handed, after his party had all become casualties. Second Lieutenant Hobbs and his group of men likewise distinguished themselves in covering the withdrawal. The operation resulted in the capture of twenty-five prisoners and six machine guns, and 170 Germans were computed to have been killed. Our casualties were heavy, fifty-six killed, 483 wounded and forty-one missing. The Corps Commander (Shute), in sympathising with the Division in its heavy casualties, and failure to hold the captured position, congratulated the troops on their gallantry.

The next few days passed quietly, but, unfortunately, on the 5th inst. the Division sustained a great loss in the death of Lieut.-Colonel Bovet, D.S.O., who was mortally wounded near Bouzincourt on his way back from the trenches. Lieut.-Colonel Bovet had held the appointment of Commanding Royal Engineer for nearly two years, and had served with distinction, showing great zeal and ability in all his duties. He was succeeded by Lieut.-Colonel A. T. Shakespear, D.S.O., M.C.

On the 10th July the Division was relieved, and joining the XXIInd Corps on the 12th inst., proceeded to the area south of Amiens. It was placed at the disposal of General Debeney, commanding the First French Army, and was detailed as a reserve to the IXth French Corps (Garnier du Plessis), or XXXIst French Corps (Toulorge). A mobile detachment was formed of four lorries manned by Lewis and machine guns, under the command of Major C. O. Skey, 9th Royal Fusiliers, its *rôle* being to reinforce any portion of the line required. These precautions for defence were not called into use, however, as on the 18th inst. the Allied Commander (Maréchal Foch) commenced his counter-attack on the Chateau Thierry front.

On the 20th July the Divisional Artillery (Thomas) moved to the IXth French Corps area, and was detailed to support the attack of the 66th Division de Chasseurs in the vicinity of Moreuil, by forming a smoke screen on the flank. The batteries, in billets at Lœuilly, were to occupy positions at Remiencourt, some fourteen miles away over a very hilly road. Time was limited, but all difficulties were overcome, and with the assistance of the Divisional Ammunition Column, the guns were got into position and the necessary dumps of ammunition formed during the nights of the 20th–21st and 21st–22nd July. As secrecy was important, no registration by the guns was permitted, the positions being resected and fire lines laid out from maps supplied by the French artillery. The attack was delivered on the 23rd inst., the smoke screen being very successful. The French, who did not possess this form of shell, were very pleased with the effect.

On the night of the 24th inst. the artillery returned to Lœuilly, and on the 26th, at a parade of the artillery, Général de Division Brissaud Desmaillet, commanding the 66th Division de Chasseurs, accompanied by Major-General Higginson, made a complimentary speech and presented the Croix de Guerre to Majors Roney-Dougal, Stamper, Munro, Campbell, Captain Johnson, and four non-commissioned officers. The 6th Buffs provided the guard of honour for the occasion.

On the 31st July the artillery came into action east of Gentelles Wood, covering the 2nd Australian Division (Rosenthal), and on the 7th August took up positions near Villers-Bretonneux in support of the Canadian Corps (Currie) in its attack on the 8th August, remaining with that corps until the 25th, when it rejoined the 12th Division near Mametz. Letters of appreciation for their gallant services were received from the First French Army (Debeney) and the Fourth British Army (Rawlinson).

Meanwhile the infantry brigades were reorganising and training, and on the 30th July they entrained for Vignacourt, Canaples, and Pernois. The Division now joined the IIIrd Corps (Butler), relieving the 58th Division (Ramsay) in the centre sector of the corps front on the night of the 2nd–3rd August.

CHAPTER XIX

THE ADVANCE TO VICTORY

Phase I—August 3rd—30th, 1918

(*Maps* 19 *and* 21)

WE are now to enter on a new phase of the fighting. The tedious trench warfare was rapidly coming to an end, and henceforth the allied troops were to pursue a defeated enemy across the ground he had so completely dominated for nearly four years. In the hard struggle ahead, ending with the Armistice, the 12th Division was once more to take a brilliant part.

The Allied success having straightened the line between Rheims and Soissons, plans were made to capture the salient towards Amiens. The attack was to be carried out on the 8th August by the First French Army, and the Fourth British Army (Rawlinson), consisting of the IIIrd, the Australian and Canadian Corps, with the Cavalry Corps in reserve, between Ribecourt and Albert.

The IIIrd Corps (12th, 18th, 47th, and 58th Divisions) was on the left, the 12th Division being astride the River Ancre. Four hundred and fifty-six tanks, ninety-six being "Whippets," took part in this action on the Fourth Army front. The operations of the 8th August originally only included the two right divisions (18th and 58th) of the IIIrd Corps (Butler), but the Germans, commencing to evacuate the left bank of the Ancre, were in process of withdrawing from Dernancourt, and consequently the 35th Brigade (Vincent), on the right, became involved.

On the 6th August the Germans, capturing some of the positions of the 18th Division, the 36th Brigade (Owen) was sent to its support. During the night of the 7th inst. the enemy carried out a heavy bombardment with gas shell, greatly interfering with the movement of the 35th Brigade to its assembly positions, and causing several casualties, amongst whom, unfortunately, was the commander, Brig.-General Vincent, who had to be removed to a field ambulance. Brig.-General A. T. Beckwith, C.M.G., D.S.O., assumed command of the brigade temporarily.

The main offensive of the 8th August commenced at 4.20 a.m., although that of the 35th Brigade was two hours later. The 1st/1st Cambridgeshire Regiment (Saint) was on the right, the 7th Norfolk (Scarlett) in the centre, and the 9th Essex (Green) on the left, with the 6th Queen's (Whetham) (37th Brigade) in support, and 5th Northamptonshire (Trent) in reserve. The morning opened with the usual low-hanging Somme mist, and this mist, accentuated by a smoke screen, added to the difficulty of maintaining direction; one result being that the tank of a neighbouring division, losing itself, came to the assistance of the 35th Brigade.

The Norfolk and Essex achieved their objectives, consolidating a new line from the western outskirts of Morlancourt to the Ancre, patrols reaching the high ground to the east. The left company of the Cambridgeshire also gained its position, but the right failed to get forward owing to the heavy fire from the Sailly Laurette-Morlancourt Road, which had held up, as well, the 18th Division. Eventually the battalion was driven back to its starting line. The attack, with the co-operation of artillery and a tank, and in conjunction with the 18th Division, was renewed at 12.15 p.m. "C" Company (Hollis) and "D" Company (Wallis), consisting of about 200 all told, making a determined assault, carried all their objectives, taking 316 prisoners, fourteen machine guns, and ten trench mortars, thirty dead being found in addition. No small share of this success was due to Lieut.-Colonel Saint for his resolution and leadership.

An interesting point in this action was, that whilst the 35th Infantry Brigade was attacking, another brigade of the Division, the 37th, was coming out of the line on the right bank of the Ancre, having been relieved by an American battalion attached to the 47th Division (Gorringe).

At 8.35 p.m. on the 8th orders were received for a renewal of the attack at 4.30 a.m. on the 9th, the 37th Brigade being detailed to assemble in rear of the 35th, in readiness to pass through and carry on the offensive. At midnight the operation was postponed to 5.30 a.m., and at 1.45 a.m. on the 9th there was a second postponement to 5.30 p.m.

The 37th Brigade (Webber) had taken up its position before the latest orders reached it, and the 6th Buffs (Smeltzer), attacking at 5.30 a.m., without artillery support, succeeded in penetrating the enemy's position and capturing a machine gun, ten trench mortars and some prisoners. On receiving the fresh orders Lieut.-Colonel Smeltzer went forward, stopped the attack, and withdrew his troops to the assembly point.

The 6th Queen's were in the centre, and the 6th Royal West Kent (Dawson) on the left, when at 5.30 p.m. the attack, assisted by tanks and under a creeping barrage, was renewed. The 6th Buffs, on the right, starting again south of Morlancourt, met with severe opposition, a field gun firing over open sights causing considerable casualties, and holding up the advance. Thereupon Privates K. Caldwell and R. H. Wallace, going forward with the Lewis gun, by skilful manœuvring succeeded in inflicting such heavy casualties on the gun team as to place it out of action, and so enable the company to proceed to its final objective. The remaining companies, assisted by tanks, gradually overcame the opposition, and the battalion took up its position east of Morlancourt, having captured 350 prisoners and two anti-tank guns.

The 6th Queen's, attacking to the north of Morlancourt, were held up by a strong point, when Captain A. L. Paish, seeing a tank a few hundred yards away, crossed the zone of the German machine-gun fire, and obtained the assistance of the tank, which, destroying the strong point, permitted the battalion to complete its task. Several prisoners, including a battalion commander, and five machine guns were taken.

The 6th Royal West Kent, making a brilliant advance, gained their objectives, securing forty prisoners, fifteen machine guns, and four trench mortars. It was, however, met by considerable opposition from machine guns skilfully concealed in the cornfields. Sergeant Harris, " C " Company, on his own initiative and singlehanded, rushed one of these positions, killing seven men, and capturing the gun. Shortly afterwards he captured a second position, but, unfortunately, in attempting such gallantry a third time, he was killed. For his valour and inspiriting example to all ranks he was posthumously awarded the Victoria Cross. The attack of this battalion was marked by the composure and bravery of its gallant commander, Lieut.-Colonel Dawson, who led his men into action on horseback, thereby setting an example of courage and calmness.

The attack had been very successful, and the 12th

Machine Gun Battalion (Oakley), from positions in the railway embankment north of Dernancourt, had rendered valuable assistance.

On the completion of the 37th Brigade task, the 1st/1st Cambridgeshire, assisted by tanks, was ordered to clear the village of Morlancourt. Notwithstanding the fact that the advance of the 37th Brigade had practically isolated it, considerable opposition was still met with from machine gun positions. This battalion, attacking with gallantry and determination, finished its task, capturing seventy-seven prisoners, nineteen machine guns, and four trench mortars on its way to join up with the battalions of the 37th Brigade. For his distinguished conduct on this day, Sergt.-Major Betts received the Military Cross, one of his actions being to capture, single-handed, a nest of four machine guns and thirty men.

Continuing the attack at 6 p.m. on the 10th August the 37th Brigade, with the 6th Buffs on the right, 9th Essex (Green) (attached from 35th Brigade) in the centre, and 6th Queen's on the left, supported by tanks, gained the old front line of the Amiens defences, the Buffs claiming to have captured a battery of 4·2" howitzers. During the night the line was consolidated, the 108th Regiment of the United States Army taking part in this work.

The 36th Brigade on leaving the Division on the 6th inst. detailed the 5th Royal Berkshire to the 58th Division, with which formation that battalion operated on the 18th Division flank. The 9th Royal Fusiliers and 7th Royal Sussex were attached to the 18th Division, and assisted in the attacks on the 8th and 9th instants, several of the non-commissioned officers and men distinguishing themselves during the action. A strong point south of Morlancourt was giving trouble, when Sergeant Barton, with Lance-Corporal Flack and Privates Leavers and Parker, of the Royal Fusiliers, creeping forward through the corn, arrived close to the post, and rushed it. After a stiff fight the garrison, of an officer and thirty men with three machine guns, surrendered. This brigade rejoined the 12th Division on the 10th August.

On the 12th August H.M. the King visited the IIIrd Corps, six officers and 100 other ranks from each Division in the corps being paraded for His Majesty's inspection at Querrieu Chateau.

At 4.55 a.m. on the 13th inst. the 36th Brigade attacked the position on Hill 105. The right company of the 7th Royal Sussex (Thompson) capturing 300 yards of the trenches, took a few prisoners, eight machine guns and two trench mortars, but the centre and left companies, encountering heavy fire and being counter-attacked, were eventually driven back to their starting line. The Royal Fusiliers gained their objectives, the trenches on the left.

The operations of the two armies had pushed back the Montdidier salient, and Amiens was again free from German menace. The 12th Division, acting on the extreme left of this movement, had advanced some 3,000 yards, including the capture of Morlancourt. In this situation the offensive of the Fourth Army paused, and preparations were now made for gaining the high ground east of the Bray-Méaulte Road.

At 4.45 a.m. on the 22nd the Fourth Army offensive recommenced: on the right the 35th Brigade (Beckwith), with 1st/1st Cambridgeshire and 7th Norfolk leading, the 9th Essex and 6th Buffs (37th Brigade) in support; on the left the 36th Brigade (Owen), the 9th Royal Fusiliers with 7th Royal Sussex in support, and 5th Royal Berkshire. The advance was accompanied by tanks and under cover of a creeping barrage. The Cambridgeshire and Norfolk suffered from gas shell in their assembly positions, but overcoming a strong resistance, established themselves in their objective by 6.40 a.m., having advanced some 2,500 yards. The Essex and Buffs then passed through. The former battalion was unable to get on, owing to the machine gun and trench mortar fire, directed on the crest of the ridge over which it had to pass, and eventually an enemy counter-attack at 2 p.m. drove this battalion to the western side of the Bray-Méaulte Road, to which place the 6th Royal West Kent were sent as a reinforcement. The Buffs were entirely successful, advancing a further 2,500 yards.

The 9th Royal Fusiliers having gained the first 2,400 yards, the 7th Royal Sussex passed through and, driving the enemy from position to position, reached the sand pit on the Bray-Méaulte Road, where Sergeant Trevor, entering a large dug-out, emerged with thirty prisoners. The battalion, pushing on, arrived at its goal about 10 a.m., having completed another 2,500 yards. This was the first occasion, in the history of the 12th Division, that conditions had approximated to " open " warfare, and although unaccustomed to such conditions, much initiative was shown by all concerned.

To the 5th Royal Berkshire was allotted the capture of Méaulte. Assisted by three tanks, one of which passed up and down the main street, whilst the two others moved on either side of the village, the battalion overcame all resistance, capturing twenty machine guns.

Except on the right, where the adjoining division was also held up, the Division had advanced 5,000 yards, taking nine officers and 470 men as prisoners, with many machine guns.

During the afternoon of the 23rd orders were received

for a moonlight attack at 1 a.m. on 24th inst. to capture the high ground, from which the Germans stopped the advance of the Essex on the 22nd. The left flank of the Division was also to be extended beyond the village of Bécordel, to gain touch with the 18th Division. The attack of the 6th Royal West Kent and 6th Queen's on the right failed, but that of the 7th Royal Sussex, in capturing the village of Bécordel, and gaining touch with the 18th Division beyond, was successful. At 1.30 p.m. a second attempt was made on the right, assisted by three Whippets, of which two were knocked out, and the guns of the third jammed. This also failed. Later on the 47th Division having worked forward on the right, and the 36th Brigade on the left, the position became outflanked, and at 6 p.m. the enemy withdrew, the 37th Brigade moving forward at once.

The advance was renewed at 2.30 a.m. on the 25th, the 6th Buffs and 6th Queen's on the right, and 9th Royal Fusiliers on the left. A thick fog made it impossible to see more than 50 yards, but practically no opposition was met, as the enemy were in retirement, and an advance of 3,000 yards was completed at 7.15 a.m., without any casualties. It was now open warfare, battalions moving in extended order, while the fog brought the compass, so long put aside, into use.

The 35th Brigade now formed the advanced guard of the Division, being covered by the XXIInd Corps cavalry, which was directed on the high ground between Carnoy and Montauban. Having overcome slight opposition in Mametz, and a few isolated strong points, one near Pommiers Redoubt, the Division took up a position on the Carnoy Ridge, with patrols pushed forward in touch with the 58th Division on the right and the 18th on the left.

The enemy held strong positions half-way between

Montauban and Mametz and at the craters a little to the south, and all attempts to push on towards these were repulsed. In view of this resistance it was decided that a definite attack, supported by artillery, should be made. Besides clearing the high ground towards Montauban, the advance was to be carried east to the Maricourt-Bernafay Wood road. At 4 a.m. on the 26th the 36th Brigade attacked with 5th Royal Berkshire and 7th Royal Sussex. The Berkshire, moving through Carnoy, met with heavy artillery and machine gun fire, and suffering many casualties only a small number reached the trenches on the forward slope, these being counter-attacked and cut off by the Germans about 9 a.m.

The Sussex made small progress, and much bombing took place round the craters, in which the Cambridgeshire likewise became involved. By midday the 18th Division had advanced on our left, and later on reached the western outskirts of Montauban, but no further progress was recorded by the 12th Division.

In continuing the next day the 37th Brigade was first to gain the line of the Maricourt-Bernafay Wood road, and then that of Hardecourt-Maltzhorn Farm. The 18th Division, on the left, was moving by the north of Montauban, Bernafay and Trônes Woods, with a view of attacking these latter from the north. Opposition to the 37th Brigade was expected from the Briqueterie.

The operation began at 4.55 a.m. on the 27th. The 6th Buffs on the right, and 6th Royal West Kent on the left, met with much opposition, and all attempts to advance came under heavy fire from the heights of Maltzhorn Farm Ridge, Favière Wood, and the Briqueterie. During the morning artillery brought fire to bear on these points, and the Buffs filtrated into Favière Wood. Meanwhile, the 18th Division had

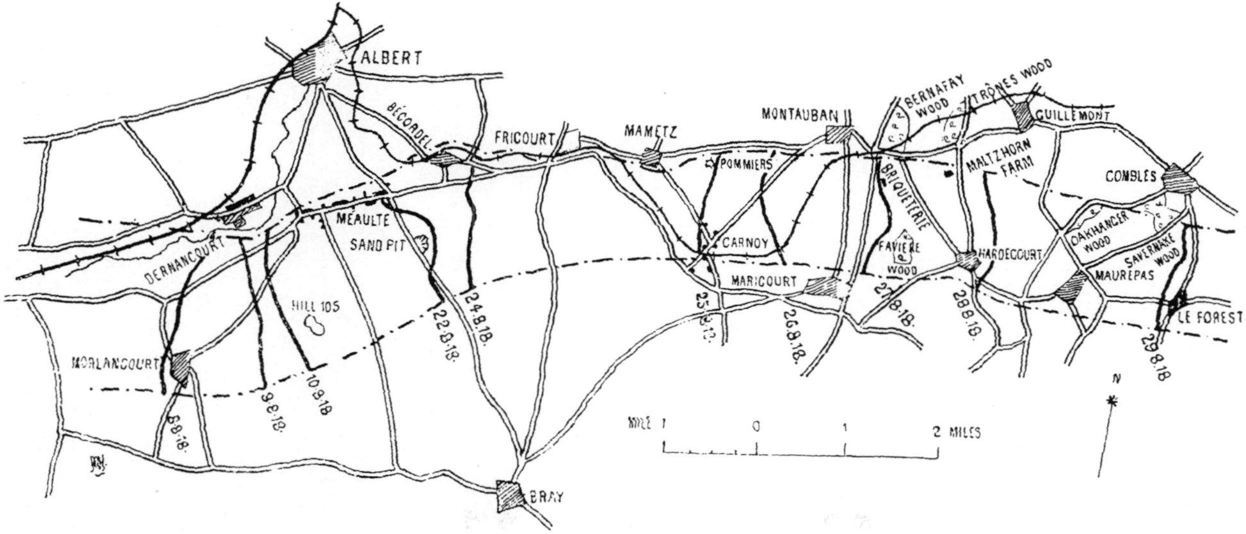

MAP No. 21. MORLANCOURT

successfully repulsed a counter-attack between 9 and 11 a.m., and in the afternoon took Bernafay and Trônes Woods, on the capture of which the Royal West Kent secured the Briqueterie. The position was then consolidated. Two ·77" guns and many machine guns were amongst the day's spoil.

On the 28th inst. the attack was renewed by the 9th Royal Fusiliers on the right, and 1st/1st Cambridgeshire and 9th Essex of 35th Brigade on the left, the objective still being the line Hardecourt-Maltzhorn Farm. The Royal Fusiliers having skilfully cleared Favière Wood, moved forward and occupied Hardecourt. The action of this battalion was particularly creditable on this day. It had just received 350 recruits whose ages varied from eighteen and a half to nineteen and a half. It was their first week in France, and they behaved with great gallantry, more especially as they were opposed to the German Fusilier Guards. They captured many prisoners and sixteen machine guns, and received the special congratulations of the Corps Commander. The 35th Brigade secured the Maltzhorn Farm Ridge and over 100 prisoners by 7 a.m., Captain Hollis again distinguishing himself by overcoming points of resistance.

During the afternoon the Germans shelled our new positions heavily, and unfortunately Lieut.-Colonel Saint, commanding the 1st/1st Cambridgeshire Regiment, was mortally wounded. He arrived in France with the battalion in February, 1915, as a company commander, and obtained command of the battalion in September, 1917. His record was a distinguished one. He was succeeded by Major M. C. Clayton.

By 10 p.m. the enemy's artillery and machine gun fire had died down, and soon after it became evident that a further withdrawal was taking place, and the 37th Brigade was ordered to form the advanced guard next day. After daylight on the 29th, it was discovered that the Germans had retired, and touch was lost. Patrols were at once sent forward, but the enemy was moving so rapidly, that it was impossible for the units of the 37th Brigade to get up in time to pass through the other brigades, which had pushed forward their patrols early in the morning. The 9th Royal Fusiliers were on the outskirts of Maurepas at 12.30 p.m., before orders reached them that the 37th Brigade was to pass through. Essex patrols also had reached Oakhanger Wood.

At 1.30 p.m. the 37th Brigade passed through, the Buffs on right, Queen's on left, and Royal West Kent in support. The Buffs moved through Maurepas, and again employing their filtration method, penetrated to the rear of a German company without observation, and cut off and captured two officers and sixty men. Lieutenant S. H. S. Marchant displayed commendable initiative in the reconnaissance and leadership of this capture. Considerable opposition was met with from the direction of Le Forest, and it was clear that resistance was stiffening. Therefore, according to orders, consolidation was commenced, and endeavours made to gain touch on the flanks. This was somewhat difficult on the right, but eventually patrols came in contact with the Australian Division to the south. The 6th Buffs were always proud to recall the conversation of that evening, when the Corps rang up to ask why the 12th Division were not in position, and had not got into touch with the division on its right. The delight of the battalion can be imagined when the Corps was informed that the 6th Buffs had failed to secure touch with the division on the right (who were 2,000 yards in rear), but had gained touch with the Australian Division on the right again.

The 6th Queen's had progressed equally well on the left, but on reaching the top of the Maurepas Ridge, strong opposition was encountered from Savernake Wood. A line was therefore taken up. The Division was relieved by the 47th Division passing through it at 6 a.m. on the 30th August.

The 12th Division had been fighting since the beginning of August, and had made a continuous advance from Morlancourt to Le Forest, a distance of 15,000 yards. The 35th Brigade moved to the Briqueterie, the 36th to Carnoy, and the 37th to Favière Wood, where they were re-equipped, re-organised, and reinforced.

CHAPTER XX

THE ADVANCE TO VICTORY

Phase II—September, 1918.

(*Maps 22 and 23*)

THE German retirement had been pressed all along the front, and at the end of August the enemy was rapidly falling back on the Hindenburg Line, in which he still maintained great faith, and where he hoped to hold up the Allies for another winter. In order to get well established in this line the enemy fought many actions to delay our advance, and the Division speedily found itself moved to the front again.

On the night of the 4th-5th September the 35th and 36th Brigades relieved the 18th Division, taking over a line of outposts running along the southern and eastern boundaries of Riverside Wood, on the east of the Canal du Nord, and just south of Manancourt. Owing to the exceptional darkness of the night, and the fact that small isolated groups of the enemy still remained in the wood, relief was somewhat difficult.

In view of an approaching attack on Nurlu, the task allotted to the 12th Division, the question of communications became important, and great credit is due to the Royal Engineer Signal Company for its work in this direction. Corporal S. Tuffil and Lance-Corporal J. R. Kenyon, of this company, worked continuously for twenty-two hours to complete the task, gas masks being worn for eight hours of this period, owing to the fact that the lines ran through a wooded valley heavily shelled with gas.

At 6.45 a.m. on the 5th September the Division attacked ; the 36th Brigade on the right with the 7th Royal Sussex and 9th Royal Fusiliers leading, and the 5th Royal Berkshire in reserve ; the 35th Brigade on the left with the 7th Norfolk and 9th Essex in front, and the 1st/1st Cambridgeshire (Clayton) in reserve.

The Sussex, unable to gain its objective owing to undestroyed wire, was compelled to dig in in front of it, but later on some of them, filtering through a gap, succeeded in reaching the trench system west of Nurlu, where they established themselves. In a similar manner the Royal Fusiliers were forced to dig in.

The Norfolk were also brought to a standstill by broad belts of wire. However, Private Johnson, under heavy fire, crawled forward and, cutting a lane, enabled a platoon to get through and capture twenty prisoners and five machine guns. The Cambridgeshire carried on the attack. " B " Company, struggling forward under Lieutenant Nock, reached to within 100 yards of Nurlu village, where the machine gun fire became so severe that all were killed or wounded. " A " Company and " D " Company reaching the ridge, consolidated there. The Essex established itself in the enemy's front line, but could not advance therefrom.

A second attack at 7 p.m. failed to make any progress, and after dark the Germans, making a strong bombing counter-stroke, drove the Essex out of the trench it had gained. The 35th Brigade, having been ordered to regain this ground, assaulted at 8 a.m. the next morning with the 5th Royal Berkshire on the right, the 1st/1st Cambridgeshire in the centre, and the 9th Essex on the left. In spite of formidable wire and strong resistance the position was carried, and the whole of Nurlu village fell into our hands. Four guns were captured, and an officer and forty men of the 6th Cavalry

Division taken prisoners. These men had been railed down from the Ypres salient the night before. The Corps Commander, Lieut.-General Sir A. Godley, sent the following message :
" Many congratulations on your occupation of the Nurlu Ridge. The advance of the troops yesterday after the heavy gas shelling, and their progress both yesterday and to-day in overcoming the stubborn hostile resistance, merits high praise."

With the capture of Nurlu the enemy retreated in haste, pursued for several kilometres by our troops, who reached the line Lieramont Cemetery-Sorel Wood in the afternoon, touch being gained with the 47th Division on the right and the 21st (D. Campbell) on the left.

During this day a valuable piece of engineer work was completed by the 87th Field Company, Royal Engineers, and a company of the 5th Northamptonshire Regiment, under the direction of Major R. W. Brims, R.E. A 45-foot span bridge was thrown over the Canal du Nord in seven hours, strong enough to take heavy traffic, and greatly facilitating the advance of the artillery, whose co-operation aided the success of the day.

At 8 a.m. on the 7th inst. the advance was continued by the 37th Brigade with the object of gaining a line east of Epéhy and Peizières. The 6th Buffs, on the right, were held up very early in the movement by fire from the high ground west of Guyencourt and from Saulcourt Wood. However, Major Kindersley, commanding " A " Battery, 63rd Brigade, who was in the front line, directed the fire of his battery with such success that the battalion was able to advance, and Guyencourt was occupied at 10.10 a.m. The pursuit was then continued, until, heavy machine gun fire from the Epéhy-Peizières position making further progress impossible, the troops dug in.

The 6th Royal West Kent reached the valley between Guyencourt and Heudecourt at 9.30 a.m., and from there the advance of this battalion was so rapid that the enemy, unable to occupy a prepared position, were forced back to Jacqvenne Copse. These two battalions had advanced 4,000 yards, and now consolidated a line about 1,000 yards west of Epéhy and Peizières, both of which were strongly held.

The Division was relieved by the 58th at 7.30 a.m. on the 8th, and the following order was issued by Major-General Higginson:

"I wish to convey to all ranks of the 12th Division my high appreciation of the great services they have rendered during the past month, and of the gallantry and soldierly qualities they have shown in the many actions in which the Division has taken part. In the initial attack on the 8th August as well as on several occasions the Division went into action at very short notice.

"The energy and determination shown by officers, warrant officers, N.C.O.'s and men have on many occasions enabled us to overcome great difficulties and to gain a great victory over the enemy.

"Since the 8th August the Division has delivered no less than seventeen attacks and advanced a distance of seventeen miles.

"The captures amount to :

PRISONERS.

Officers	17
Other ranks	1,010

who have passed through the divisional cage.

"In addition a large number captured by the Division have proceeded through other cages.

Guns	17
Machine guns	194
Trench mortars	102

"The present lull in operations is only temporary, and I have the utmost confidence that the Division will continue to show the same splendid fighting qualities in the future which it has done in the past. We have many hard battles still before us, but final victory is already assured. I request that commanding officers will ensure that my personal thanks are conveyed to all ranks under their command for the great services they have rendered to our King and Empire."

The Division now had a short respite in the vicinity of Manancourt, with headquarters in Vaux Wood. This gave it the opportunity to reorganise, and rehearse for its next task, the capture of Epéhy, which had become a very strong outpost of the Hindenburg Line, to which the Germans had now succeeded in retiring.

The attack on Epéhy was to take place on the 18th September, the 18th Division operating on the right, and the 58th against Peizières on the left.

The 12th Division was disposed as follows: on the right, the 7th Royal Sussex and 9th Royal Fusiliers, of the 36th Brigade, their objective being the Malassise Farm area; on the left, the 7th Norfolk and 9th Essex with two tanks, and two companies of the 1st/1st Cambridgeshire (35th Brigade) for the capture of Epéhy. The 37th Brigade, with the 5th Royal Berkshire (36th Brigade), were in support east of Guyencourt, their *rôle* being to pass through, and pushing on take Little Priel Farm and Kildare Post, two miles east of Epéhy.

Notwithstanding a heavy fall of rain from midnight, and a considerable amount of harassing fire and gas shelling, the troops were in position to time. The 36th Brigade, clearing the line of railway, pushed on into the system of trenches beyond, the Sussex taking Ridge Reserve, and the Fusiliers reaching the western outskirts of Malassise Farm, which was stoutly defended

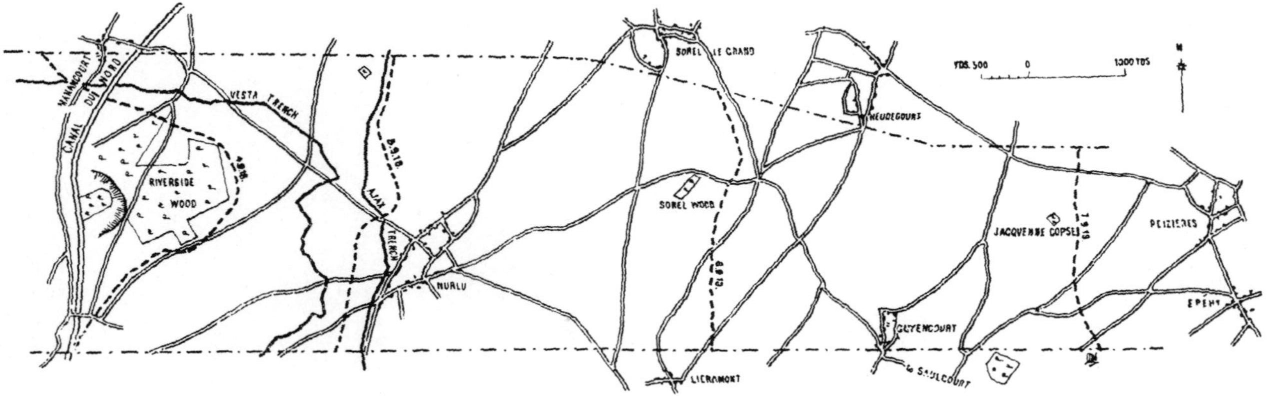

MAP No. 22. NURLU.

and defied capture. Some of the latter battalion also worked along Deelish Trench and established a post towards Old Copse.

After heavy fighting the Norfolk and Essex gained the southern end of Epéhy, but that portion known as Fisher's Keep held out. The Cambridgeshire (Clayton) was then ordered to make a fresh advance through the village, the 58th Division being asked to co-operate by moving down from Peizières. The battalion suffered heavily, as many of the enemy were still amongst the ruins, and "A" Company lost all its officers; Sergeant R. C. Reeves taking command of the remnants of this company, succeeded in passing through. "C" and "D" Companies also reached the other side, taking prisoners on the way. This operation, completed about 9 a.m., enabled the Norfolk and Essex to reach Prince Reserve.

Throughout the afternoon the Germans continued to hold the northern end of Epéhy, and it was only at 5.30 p.m. that they were observed retiring to the northeast, although Fisher's Keep did not surrender finally until 7.45 p.m. The Essex, pushing down Chestnut Avenue, established a block 250 yards from Prince Reserve. The casualties in the 35th Brigade having been very severe, three companies of the 5th Royal Berkshire and two companies of the 5th Northamptonshire were placed under the orders of this brigade.

At 6.15 p.m. the Berkshire captured the trenches between Tétard Wood and Chestnut Avenue.

At 11 a.m. on the 19th inst. the 37th Brigade, passing through the 36th, carried on the advance, the enemy's artillery fire being particularly heavy in the vicinity of Tétard Wood and Malassise Farm. The 6th Buffs pushing on gained Old Copse. The 6th Queen's found some difficulty with the wire round Malassise Farm, but eventually overcoming that and the opposition, captured the farm and advanced a further 500 yards to the east. In the 35th Brigade the 1st/1st Cambridgeshire and two companies 5th Northamptonshire, attacking Ockenden and Room Trenches, were held up by wire and forced to dig in some 150 yards short of their objective. During the afternoon, Major Stamper (" B " Battery, 62nd Brigade), who was with the Cambridgeshire Headquarters in Prince Reserve, directed the fire of his battery with such success that the enemy was driven out and the trenches were rushed. Some spirited hand-to-hand fighting took place with the Germans, who had withdrawn to the long grass in rear during the shelling.

During the night of the 19th–20th the divisional boundary was extended to the right as far as the road from Ronssoy to Vendhuile.

In the area now reached, the enemy had numerous posts, well entrenched, well wired, and strongly held by riflemen and machine guns.

On the 20th inst. attempts by the 6th Royal West Kent to gain Bird Trench, and by the 6th Queen's to gain Horse Post and No. 12 Copse, having failed, it was decided to make an attack in strength on the 21st, the 18th Division operating on the right.

Zero was fixed at 5.40 a.m., and at that hour the 6th Royal West Kent, advancing with Little Priel Farm as its objective, was held up by Braeton and Heythorp Posts. Bombing attack followed bombing attack, and five times did this battalion attempt to gain Braeton Post. The men were weary and depressed at failure, when at this critical stage Lieut.-Colonel Dawson, one of the great leaders of every fight of the Division, came up, and calling on Lieutenant Berger and four or five men, put such enthusiasm into this small body that the post was rushed, and the enemy driven out in confusion.

The 36th Brigade, on the left, had as objectives Cruciform Post and Cottesmore Trench. Heavy fire was encountered from Little Priel Farm, and after heroic fighting the 9th Royal Fusiliers and the 7th Royal Sussex gained Mule Trench, but could not proceed further. The 9th Royal Fusiliers suffered very heavily, ten out of thirteen officers and 270 other ranks being casualties. By 10 p.m. the Royal West Kent had extended their success at Braeton Post along Bird Trench, joining up with the Royal Fusiliers at St. Patrick's Avenue.

The 5th Royal Berkshire, having assembled in Bird and Mule Trenches, advanced at midnight to capture Little Priel Farm. The conditions were favourable. It was a bright moonlight night, and the Germans had been considerably shaken by the many attacks during the day. In excellent spirits, and full of determination, the Berkshire made a brilliant bayonet charge, resulting in heavy fighting in and around Heythorp Post and Hoythorp Trench. All resistance was overcome, and within an hour Little Priel Farm was captured. One officer and eighteen men were taken prisoners, fifty dead counted about the position, and forty machine guns found in the ruins of the farm. In fact, to describe it as a post "bristling" with machine guns would be no exaggeration.

On the night of the 23rd-24th the 36th Brigade, relieving the 175th Brigade of 58th Division, extended the divisional front to the north, to include Dados Lane.

On the 24th inst., after a heavy bombardment, commencing at 11 a.m., the enemy attacked from Kildare Avenue, supported by low-flying aeroplanes. He gained a footing at the eastern end of Dados Lane and Dados

Loop, capturing a few of the Royal Fusiliers, who had taken over during the night.

The Dados Loop position was one of peculiar strength. It was situated on the crest of one of the many spurs leading down to the Escaut River, and possessed command in several directions, especially over the Escaut Valley. The Germans evidently attached great importance to it, and for several days it became the scene of fierce fighting, attack and counter-attack following each other without intermission.

During the afternoon of the 24th, constant endeavours by the Royal Fusiliers to regain this lost trench failed, and a further attempt at 10 p.m. by the Royal Berkshire met with no success.

At 5.15 a.m. on the 25th a German attack on Braeton Post was repulsed, greatly due to the fact that Sergeant Levins, of the 9th Essex, moving along the parapet, fired his Lewis gun from his hip, and inflicted many casualties on the enemy. During this night projectors were used for firing gas into the next enemy positions that had to be overcome. At 3 a.m. on the 26th the Royal Berkshire made some progress against the enemy in Dados Loop, but were driven back again at 6.10 a.m. Bomb fighting went on all day without any definite change in the situation.

Orders were now received for the assault to be made by the Third and Fourth Armies on the Hindenburg Line on the 27th September. The *rôle* of the 12th Division was to secure the vantage points up to the canal, and protect the left flank of the 27th Division, United States Army, which was operating on the right. Accordingly, on the 27th, the Knoll having been captured by the American Division, patrols were pushed forward, but, Lark Post and the Quarries being strongly held, no further progress could be made.

MALASSISE FARM

LITTLE PRIEL FARM

On the same day the 6th Queen's gained an initial success in Dados Loop, but were driven back by a strong counter-attack, in which the enemy used hand gas grenades. At a second attempt at 9.30 a.m., however, a slight advance was maintained, and a block established in Stone Lane.

At 5.50 a.m. on the 29th inst. the main attack was renewed. "A" and "C" Companies, 6th Buffs, on the right, attacked the Quarries, a position of some natural strength. Lieutenant Fiske, finding his company held back by two enemy machine guns, went round to the flank, rushed the guns, and bombed and killed the teams, thus enabling his men to advance. On capturing the Quarries these two companies took 150 prisoners and many machine guns. The success was greatly due to Lieut.-Colonel Smeltzer, who directed the attack from his observation post at Braeton Post, where he had with him an artillery and a machine gun company officer, who were able to bring the fire of their respective arms on any required points. Later on the battalion occupied Lark Trench and Tino Trench, gaining touch with the 18th Division on the right.

The 6th Royal West Kent, on the left, advancing on Swallow and Catelet Trenches, met with strong opposition, and were badly enfiladed from that portion of Dados Loop still in German hands. Catelet Trench was taken, and an enemy counter-attack on it at 3.20 p.m. from the Catelet Valley easily repulsed. At dawn on the 30th the battalion assaulted Dados Loop and was repulsed, but Lieut.-Colonel Dawson, with his usual gallantry and determination, kept a continuous pressure on the position, and during the afternoon finally cleared it. Immediately Dados Loop fell, the advance was pushed on vigorously, Stone Lane, Stone Trench and Kildare Avenue on the left being cleared of the enemy, and Bird Cage and Bird Post, on the right, occupied. Later on patrols reached Ossus Wood to the north, occupied Below Trench, and finally arrived on the canal bank.

On the right of the Brigade the 6th Buffs, co-operating with the 18th Division, reached the western outskirts of Vendhuile, where it was suddenly attacked by an American tank, which caused some confusion. Company Sergt.-Major J. Smith, however, rushed up and, beating on the front plate with his rifle, attracted the attention of the crew, who stopped firing. The further advance presenting no difficulty, the canal bank was reached at 11 p.m.

During the night the Division was relieved. It had been heavily engaged for twelve consecutive days, and had become so reduced in numbers as to be unfit for active operations until reinforced. For this purpose, therefore, it was withdrawn from the battle front.

All ranks by their gallantry, zeal and determination in face of every difficulty, had nobly borne their part in the triumph of the British Army over a formidable enemy: the infantry by their dash and bull-dog tenacity, the Royal Artillery by its close co-operation with the infantry, the Royal Engineers and Pioneers by their skill and application, and the administrative services by their care and forethought.

Since the 8th August an advance of twenty-six miles, from Morlancourt to the Escaut Canal, had been made, and many prisoners taken. In addition 22 guns, 320 machine guns, 72 trench mortars, and 11 *minenwerfer* had been captured. On the other side of the register, we had suffered heavy casualties : 80 officers and 769 other ranks being killed ; 204 officers and 4,466 other ranks wounded ; 6 officers and 704 other ranks missing, a total of 6,229.

MAP NO. 23. ÉPÉHY

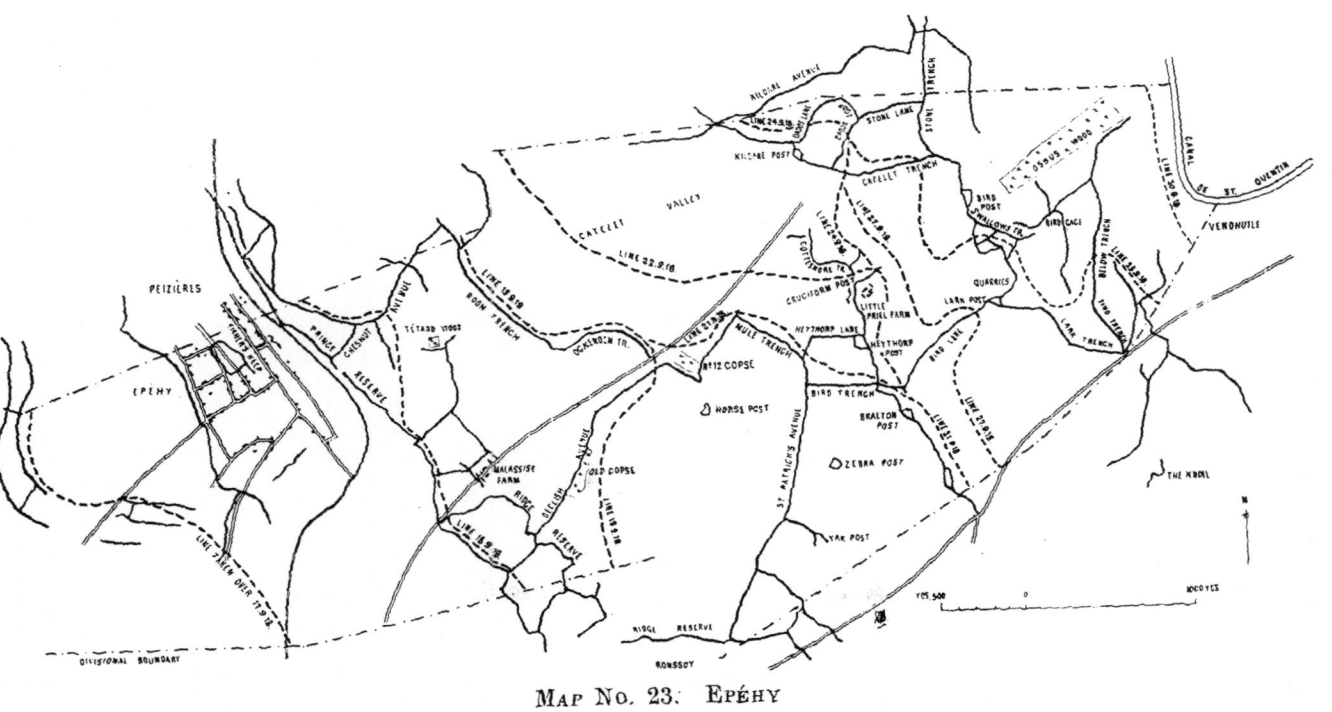

During the advance from Morlancourt, the Division had been supported by the 25th Divisional Artillery (Brig.-General K. J. Kincaid Smith), and all appreciated the gallant and efficient manner in which these batteries had co-operated in the many hard-fought actions.

On leaving the IIIrd Corps and the Fourth Army the following were received :

" It is with the greatest regret that I bid *au revoir* to the 12th Division.

" During the brief period the Division has been with the IIIrd Corps, it has not only fought with gallantry and determination, but also with that spirit of mutual co-operation and comradeship which ensures success.

" I wish also to convey my personal thanks to General Higginson, the Staff, and all ranks of the 12th Division for their loyal support and for the manner in which they have always ' played up.' I trust that it may be my good fortune, at no distant date, to have the Division in my command again in further victorious operations.

(*Signed*) " R. BUTLER, *Lieut.-General,*
" Commanding IIIrd Corps.
" 30th September, 1918."

" Orders have been received for the transfer of the 12th Division to another part of the battle front, and before it leaves the Fourth Army I desire to express to all ranks my appreciation of the prominent part it has played during the recent fighting, and my admiration of its gallantry and fighting spirit.

" After two and a half months' strenuous operations and a great deal of heavy fighting, the Division has maintained a really high standard of discipline and efficiency, of which all ranks may justly feel proud.

"Throughout the advance, and in spite of hard marching with few opportunities for rest, all ranks have invariably responded to the call of duty and have exhibited a degree of endurance and tenacity which has been admirable.

"A long list of successes, including Morlancourt, Carnoy, Maricourt, Hardecourt, Maurepas and Nurlu, culminating in the capture of the strongly-fortified village of Epéhy, constitutes a record which has seldom been equalled, and I wish to convey to every officer, N.C.O. and man of the 12th Division my gratitude for the magnificent example they have set, and my warmest thanks for the invaluable services they have rendered.

"I wish all ranks every good fortune in the future, and trust that at some future time I may again find the 12th Division under my command.

(*Signed*) "H. RAWLINSON, *General*,
"Commanding Fourth Army.

"2nd October, 1918."

CHAPTER XXI

THE ADVANCE TO VICTORY

PHASE III—October 1st—November 11th, 1918

(*Maps* 24, 25, *and* 26)

ON leaving the battle front on the canal at Vendhuile, the Division moved on the 1st of October by bus to the Proyart area, and on the 2nd entrained for Savy, Acq, and Aubigny. The Division now joined the VIIIth Corps (Hunter-Weston) of the First Army (Horne), which was operating in the Vimy sector, and on the 3rd inst. orders were received to relieve the 20th Division (Carey). This relief commencing on the 5th, was completed during the night of 6th–7th.

The front to be held by the 12th Division was from Oppy to Eleu dit Leauvette on the Canal de Lens, and being 11,000 yards in extent, all three infantry brigades were up in the line, and disposed as follows: Right, 35th Brigade, 7th Norfolk, 1st/1st Cambridgeshire, with 9th Essex in reserve; centre, 36th Brigade, 9th Royal Fusiliers, 7th Royal Sussex, with 5th Royal Berkshire in reserve; left, 37th Brigade, 6th Buffs, 6th Queen's, with 6th Royal West Kent in reserve.

The 20th Division had reported the enemy as holding his front with outposts, and also that there were indications of the withdrawal of his guns. As a consequence, the troops were ordered to be especially active in patrolling, and prepared to follow up any retirement at once.

Immediately the relief was completed the patrols of the 36th Brigade, discovering that the enemy was withdrawing, pushed forward and occupied Acheville Trench and the village of Méricourt without opposition. The remainder of the Division also advanced. On the 7th inst. further progress was made to the Fresnes-Rouvroy line.

Early on the 10th the 35th Brigade (Vincent) was established in Bois Bernard, and reaching Drocourt, the 7th Norfolk cleared that village, and drove off a party of the enemy which was endeavouring to blow up the railway bridge. The brigade then occupied the Quéant-Drocourt line. On the same day the 9th Royal Fusiliers, holding the line west of Rouvroy, were attacked and driven back some 300 yards. A counter-attack by " A " Company, under Captain Duff, re-established the line, capturing one machine gun, Private E. Stephenson displaying great courage and initiative during the operations. Later on, patrols finding Rouvroy unoccupied, the battalion moved to its eastern outskirts. In addition, the 36th Brigade took possession of the large railway centre of Mabel Corons, 1,000 yards east of Méricourt. In the 37th Brigade the 6th Royal West Kent reached the important coal mining centre of Billy-Montigny, finding no enemy there; the 6th Queen's after slight opposition took possession of Noyelles.

By the evening of the 10th October, therefore, Acheville, Bois Bernard and the ridge south of it, Rouvroy, Drocourt, Méricourt, Avion, Sallaumines (with its important hill), Noyelles and Billy-Montigny had fallen into our hands.

On the 11th inst. " B " and " D " Companies, 9th Royal Fusiliers, meeting with no opposition, reached the Quéant-Drocourt line, and the Queen's, seizing position after position, occupied Fouquières late in the afternoon, and also finding the Quéant-Drocourt position unheld, moved up to it and to the village of

Montigny. By that evening the whole of the Division was in the Quéant-Drocourt line.

The advance having assumed the characteristics of "open" warfare, the troops moved in accordance. Telephonic communication became almost impossible, owing to the rapidity of the movements, and visual signalling had to be depended upon. The enemy evacuated position after position, not even venturing to hold this much-vaunted Quéant-Drocourt line.

The 58th Division (Ramsay) taking over a portion of our front on the left, permitted the 37th Brigade to be placed in reserve. Orders were now received to push on to the Canal de la Haute Deule, make good the crossings, and seize the railway 1,000 yards to the east of it.

On the 12th the 35th Brigade met with little resistance until reaching Courcelles, where the 9th Essex, after a good deal of street fighting, captured the village, Sergeant Baum receiving special mention for bravery in leading his platoon. Patrols then went forward to the canal bank, but an attempt to gain a crossing at the railway bridge was strongly opposed and progress stayed. The enemy were also found in strength at Auby, where the 1st/1st Cambridgeshire came to a standstill.

Resuming its advance on the 12th the 9th Royal Fusiliers occupied Henin Liétard, and late in the day reached Basse Noyelles, and Noyelles Godault, at which latter village much opposition was met. This, however, was overcome by Lieutenant H. J. Ellard, who skilfully led his men through the village to the eastern outskirts, so ensuring its capture. On the following day the battalion, continuing against stiffening resistance, reached the banks of the canal and secured the railway crossing at Pont à Sault. The 9th Royal Fusiliers, having led the advance for seven days, was relieved by the 7th Royal Sussex.

It was now decided to make an organised attack on Auby, in conjunction with the 8th Division (Heneker) on the right. Attacking at 5.15 a.m. on the 14th inst., "A" and "D" Companies, 1st/1st Cambridgeshire, reached the light railway on the western extremities. Here "C" and "B" Companies, passing through, gained the eastern outskirts of the village on the banks of the canal, where they encountered heavy machine-gun fire from a wood on the other side. At 11 a.m. the Germans, strongly reinforced in the southern end of the village, drove the two companies back to the light railway line. Meanwhile the 8th Division had been held up at the Cemetery on the south side, and the 7th Norfolk were sent up to secure the gap between it and the Cambridgeshire. In this street fighting a great deal depended on the leadership of the non-commissioned ranks, and particular mention must be made of Company Sergt.-Major W. C. Parry, who took command of a platoon when the officer was wounded, and later on of a second platoon when its officer fell, eventually leading half the company successfully through the village. Sergeant C. W. Clarke and Lance-Corporal Sammons also distinguished themselves in clearing a portion of the village. No further advance was made during the day. One officer and fifty-eight men had been captured in addition to several machine guns.

The enemy's artillery now increased in activity, and it appeared as if he would hold a position on the east bank of the canal, which was distinctly favourable for a rearguard action, owing to its command and strength, both natural and artificial. Our positions in Dourges, Noyelles Godault, Courcelles, Fosse 4 and Fosse 7, where some batteries had come into action, were all fairly heavily shelled.

There was no change in the situation on the 15th,

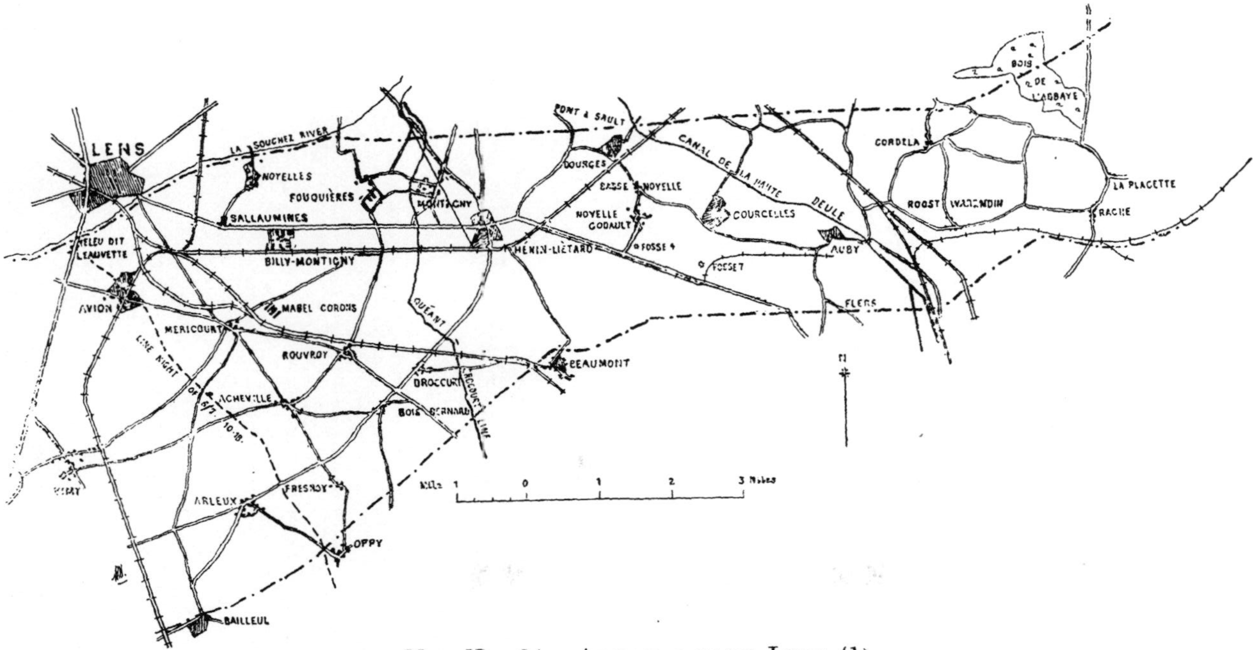

MAP No. 24. ADVANCE FROM LENS (1)

though two attempts by the 35th Brigade to establish posts on the canal bank east of Courcelles had at first succeeded. Lieutenant H. G. Thomas, 69th Field Company, Royal Engineers, crawling forward 400 yards in front of our outposts, reached the tow path, and made a reconnaissance for the construction of a bridge.

This, however, was not acted on, as during the night the 7th Royal Sussex, on the left, succeeded in gaining a crossing by means of a small floating bridge, composed of trench boards fastened on cork, constructed by the Royal Engineers. Having secured the crossing, the whole battalion was moved over, and patrols hurrying forward reached the village of Cordela. Here there were no signs of Germans, and the troops received a most enthusiastic reception from the inhabitants.

The enemy, finding his flank threatened by the crossing of the 7th Royal Sussex, evacuated Auby and the whole of the canal bank. The Norfolk, following on at once, cleared the village of Auby, crossed the canal, and took up an outpost line 2,000 yards to the east of it, near Roost Warendin. This village was found to be full of civilians, who gave the battalion a glad welcome.

The presence of the French in the villages showed that the retreat of the Germans was now something more than a withdrawal. Previously demolitions had been systematic, and civilians had been compelled to evacuate their homes as the enemy retired. Now there was evidently no time for this, undamaged villages were found by our troops, and the enthusiasm of the inhabitants, after four years of enemy occupation, can be better imagined than described. The French Tricolour was everywhere displayed, and decorated villages waited to acclaim their deliverers. Where the flags came from nobody seemed to know, though it was suggested that the Germans, with an eye to business, had themselves provided them. Gratitude was shown in many ways, in one village a special dinner being given to a Battalion Headquarters, and it was only at the end of the meal that the lucky participants discovered the fatted calf to have been the mayor's pet dog. A medical officer described this period as "*café*, cognac, and cisses."

On the 18th October the 37th Brigade having relieved the 36th, the 6th Royal West Kent took over from the Royal Sussex, and continued the advance. On reaching La Placette, on the Douai-Orchies Road, German cavalry patrols were encountered, and one of these, charging a patrol of the West Kent, was driven off, leaving one dead and three wounded in our hands. Proceeding along the main road to Orchies, Flines was occupied. On the left the 7th Norfolk, advanced guard to the 35th Brigade, passing through Bois l'Abbaye and Boujon, in the outskirts of which Lieut.-Colonel Scarlett and his orderly captured four prisoners and a machine gun, eventually reached La Pieterie. Contact was gained with rearguards of the enemy at Crupez, Sauvagerie and Hem.

On the 19th the 6th Buffs and 9th Essex led their brigades. The enemy everywhere retiring before the advance, the village of Beuvry and the town of Orchies were occupied. At the former village a pathetic incident occurred. A French veteran of 1870, who had strongly resented four years of German domination in his home, prepared to greet the advancing Allies with a present of vegetables from his garden. Whilst collecting them he came between two opposing patrols, and received a wound to which he succumbed. The old chap declared that he was proud to die. It was fitting, he considered, only having been wounded in 1870, that he should have the opportunity to die for his country in 1918.

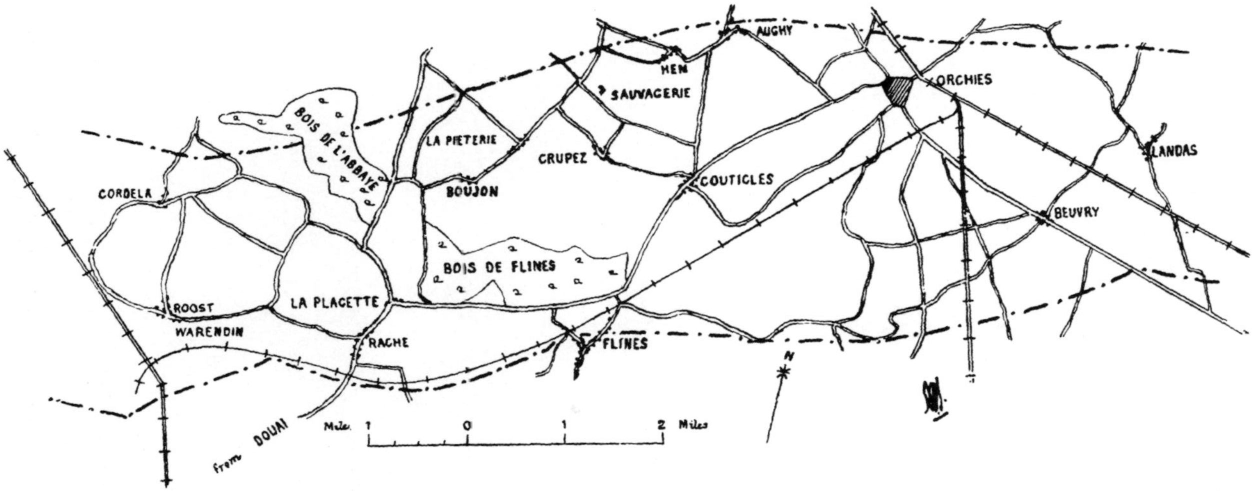

MAP No. 25. ADVANCE FROM LENS (2)

On the 20th the 6th Queen's, passing through the southern outskirts of Landas, met with slight opposition from scattered hamlets at Petite Rue, and reached the Rosult-Saméon Road. Meanwhile the 1st/1st Cambridgeshire, on emerging from Landas, came under a certain amount of fire from a position to the west of Saméon. " D " Company (Harding Newman) and " A " Company (Lieutenant Hardman) working to the right and left of the village respectively, captured it without loss, taking seven prisoners and three machine guns.

On the following day the 6th Queen's, passing through Rosult and Lecelles, reached the St. Amand-Maulde Road. The 7th Norfolk, on clearing Saméon, encountered some opposition on the extreme left from the direction of Choques, but also reached the St. Amand-Maulde Road.

On the 22nd inst. the 6th Royal West Kent, taking up the advance of the 37th Brigade, arrived on the bank of the River Scarpe, and two platoons, crossing at St. Amand, which had been occupied by the 8th Division, took up a position on the eastern side. Small rafts were then made by lashing planks and three barrels together. With these the river, which was 80 feet wide, was crossed, two more platoons being got over that day, and the remainder of the battalion during the night. It was then discovered that the area from the Scarpe to the Canal de l'Escaut, 2,000 yards to the east, was flooded.

The 36th Brigade having relieved the 35th, the 9th Royal Fusiliers took up the duties of advanced guard. Strong opposition was encountered at Le Maroc, from Fort de Maulde, a strong bastion between Le Maroc and the town of Maulde, and also from Mont de la Justice, east of the St. Amand-Maulde Road. An endeavour to turn these positions from Flagnies was not successful, and further progress was stopped; touch, however, was obtained with the 58th Division on the left. On the 23rd this battalion still tried to reach the river bank. One platoon of "D" Company posted itself in Flagnies, and one of "C" Company under Captain Baudains worked forward as far as Thun, establishing itself on the Décours river, a small tributary of the Scarpe, and only a few hundred yards from it. A platoon of "A" under Captain Duff took up a position in Le Maroc. Opposition was strengthening, and these small bodies only maintained themselves with difficulty, the battalion at this time holding 4,000 yards with a strength of about 400.

On this day the Division sustained an irreparable loss. Whilst reconnoitring for the site of a temporary bridge Lieut.-Colonel Dawson was wounded for the seventh time. Unfortunately on this occasion his wound proved fatal. Thus as it turned out, on practically the last day his battalion was in action, this fearless and intrepid commander fell gloriously for his King and Country. His record was unique, and the whole Division mourned the loss of such a gallant soldier.*

The 6th Buffs, having crossed the Scarpe at St. Amand on the previous day, took over the advanced guard from the West Kent on the 24th inst., and moving along the banks of the Traitoire river, a small tributary on the east of the Scarpe, reached Cubray and Haute Rive. From the latter small parties with Lewis guns were sent forward towards Buridon, a few hundred

* *Note.*—Lieutenant-Colonel W. R. A. Dawson received his commission in June, 1914, in the 1st Battalion, the Queen's Own (Royal West Kent Regiment). He was posted to the 6th Battalion on its formation, and served continuously with it until his death. He was promoted temporary captain in March, 1915, temporary major in August, 1916, and appointed to command in December, 1916. He was awarded the D.S.O. in April, 1916, a bar in August, 1917, a second bar in March, 1918, and a third bar for his gallantry and leadership during this last phase. He was promoted brevet-major in 1918, and mentioned in despatches several times.

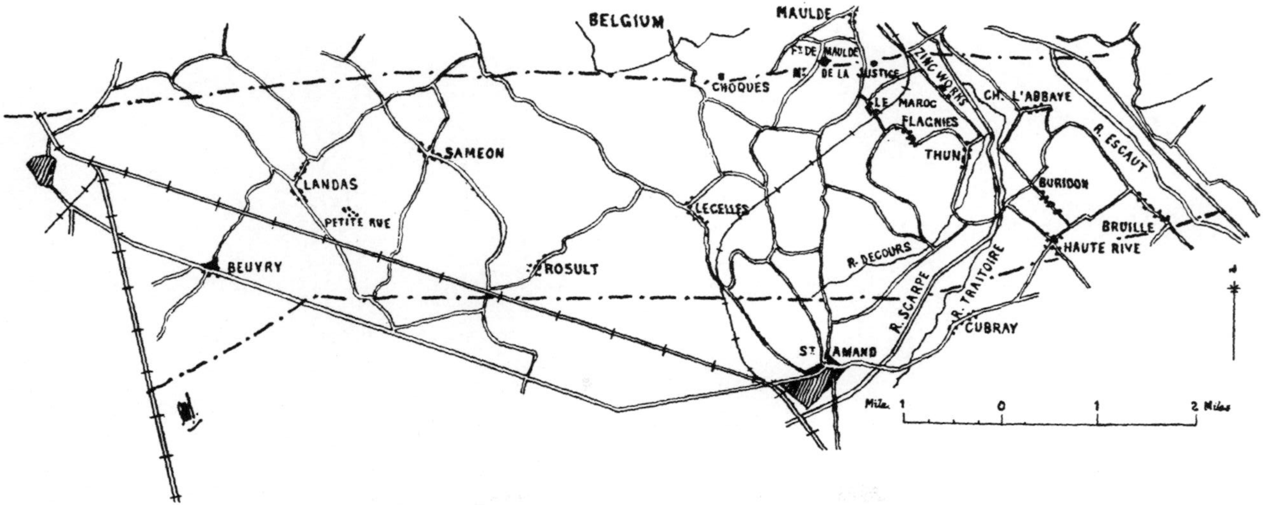

MAP No. 26. ADVANCE FROM LENS (3)

yards away, in which one or two houses were occupied, and Lewis guns skilfully placed to give covering fire to the battalion when it attacked. Sergeant R. H. Pennel did especially good service in this manner, when the village was eventually rushed and captured.

The 9th Royal Fusiliers were unable to make any progress on the 24th inst.

Having decided to make a dash for Bruille, a large village on the bank of the Canal de l'Escaut, Lieut.-Colonel Smeltzer advanced the 6th Buffs at 9 a.m. on the 25th inst. without any artillery preparation. His attack being quiet and unexpected, the enemy was caught unawares, and the village captured with little loss. Great credit is due for this masterly stroke, which turned the German position between the two rivers, and caused the opposition on the left to be withdrawn.

The Royal Fusiliers finding Mont de la Justice unoccupied by the enemy, a platoon was sent there early on the 26th inst., on which day also the battalion advanced to the Zinc Works, establishing posts along the canal, and later on moving to the Scarpe. The 7th Royal Sussex, having passed through the Royal Fusiliers, crossed the river early in the morning, and attempted to occupy Château l'Abbaye, but owing to the inundated state of the country, this was unsuccessful, unlocated machine guns sweeping all those approaches to the village that were not inundated. Later in the day General Higginson locating these positions, artillery was brought to bear on them, with the result that Château l'Abbaye was taken by the Sussex during the night.

On the 27th inst. the 36th Brigade took over the whole of the divisional front, and on the 28th attempted to establish a bridgehead over the Canal de l'Escaut in co-operation with the 8th Division on the right. The attempt was strongly opposed by the enemy, and was not a complete success, though later in the day, under cover of the machine guns, the 87th Field Company, Royal Engineers, and " A " Company, the Queen's, succeeded in constructing a cork bridge.

On the 29th October the 156th Brigade of the 52nd Division (Marshall) relieved the 36th, and the 12th Division, which had been continuously in action since the 8th August, was withdrawn for a short period of rest.

During this advance the Field Companies, Royal Engineers, and the 5th Northamptonshire Regiment (Pioneers) earned a deep debt of gratitude from the Division. Repairing roads, removing obstacles, and making bridges were arduous tasks, and on many occasions carried out under heavy fire. These, however, were vital to the maintenance of supplies. They also hunted for " booby traps," the old and favourite pastime of the Germans, and how successful they were will be gathered from the fact that 150 were discovered in three days in October, in Méricourt and Billy-Montigny.

Although quite unforeseen at the time, this actually closed the active share of the 12th Division in the war. The Central Powers now rapidly disintegrating, the Armistice was signed on the 11th of November.

CHAPTER XXII

FAREWELL TO THE 12TH

THE terms of the Armistice having been agreed to, troops were detailed for the occupation of the Rhineland Bridgeheads. The 12th Division not being amongst this number, thoughts naturally turned to home and the prospects of taking up the old employments. Much had to be done, however, before the demobilisation of the vast Army that Great Britain had organised could be carried out.

The Division was moved to the Masny-Auberchicourt-Somain-Erre area, east of Douai, headquarters being at Masny. It was a mining district, and had suffered considerably during the German retreat. The accommodation, poor at the best of times, had become very indifferent. However, the troops set to work to improve matters.

The war and its prodigal expenditure having ceased, our main object became "salvage," always an unpopular occupation, and at times a dangerous one, owing to the large amount of shells and explosives which had to be handled. Unfortunately two fatal accidents occurred by which one officer and several men lost their lives. Under the prevailing conditions, nevertheless, it was only natural that recreation and competitions of every description should take a prominent place, and the Pioneer Battalion (5th Northamptonshire Regiment) made an excellent racecourse on which two most successful meetings were held. The Association Football Tournament for Major-General Scott's cup was won by the 9th Essex Regiment, who beat the 5th Royal Berkshire Regiment by 3 to 1, and the 9th Royal Fusiliers won Major-General Higginson's cup for the cross-country race.

In addition to the above there were boxing, Rugby football, and various competitions. The " Spades " maintained their reputation and popularity by playing nightly to crowded houses, and the Divisional Band gave some excellent performances.

In this manner the winter was passed, all awaiting the acceptance of the Peace terms, and anticipating their return home.

On the 4th of February, 1919, His Royal Highness the Prince of Wales spent two days with the Division, during which time he presented Colours to the Infantry Service Battalions.

The parades were held as follows :

10.30 a.m. at Erre, the 36th Infantry Brigade: 9th Battalion the Royal Fusiliers (City of London Regiment), Lieut.-Colonel W. V. L. Van Someren, D.S.O., M.C. ; 7th Battalion the Royal Sussex Regiment, Lieut.-Colonel A. L. Thompson, D.S.O. ; and 5th Battalion Princess Charlotte of Wales's (Royal Berkshire Regiment), Lieut.-Colonel H. T. Goodland, D.S.O., under command of Brig.-General C. S. Owen, C.M.G., D.S.O.

11.45 a.m. at Somain, the 35th Infantry Brigade : 7th Battalion the Norfolk Regiment, Lieut.-Colonel H. A. Scarlett, D.S.O. ; 9th Battalion the Essex Regiment, Lieut.-Colonel H. M. B. de Sales La Terriere, M.C. ; the 1st/1st the Cambridgeshire Regiment, Lieut.-Colonel M. C. Clayton, D.S.O., with the Colours presented to it by His Majesty King Edward VII. in 1908, under command of Brig.-General B. Vincent, C.M.G. Also on this parade was the 5th Battalion the Northamptonshire Regiment, Lieut.-Colonel G. A. Trent, C.M.G.

2.30 p.m. at Auberchicourt, the 37th Infantry Brigade: 6th Battalion the Queen's (Royal West Surrey Regiment), Major D. Mann, M.C.; 6th Battalion the Buffs (East Kent Regiment), Lieut.-Colonel A. S. Smeltzer, D.S.O., M.C.; and 6th Battalion the Queen's Own (Royal West Kent Regiment), Lieut.-Colonel H. Peploe, D.S.O., under command of Brig.-General A. B. Incledon-Webber, C.M.G., D.S.O.

The ceremony was identical on each occasion. The senior chaplain of the Division, the Rev. H. P. Berkeley, M.C., having consecrated the Colour, the senior major of the battalion presented it to His Royal Highness, who then handed it to the Senior Lieutenant, who received it kneeling.

His Royal Highness addressed the battalions in the following words :

"It gives me very great pleasure to be here to-day and to have the honour to present the King's Colours to the battalions before me.

"You were raised in August, 1914, and came out to France in the 12th Division in May, 1915.

"Since that date, in addition to much hard fighting in minor engagements and long periods of strenuous work in the trenches, you have taken a conspicuous part in the following battles :

"Loos, Hohenzollern Craters, Somme 1916, Arras, Cambrai, Somme 1918, Epéhy, and the German retreat to the Scheldt, which culminated in the final victory of our arms.

"I know full well that these Colours will always be honoured and cherished by you and that you will worthily uphold in the future, as you have always done in the past, the glorious traditions of the regiments to which you belong.

"These Colours are emblems of the heroic deeds which

have been performed by your battalions. I now entrust them to you, confident that you will guard them as worthy successors of those gallant soldiers who have so gloriously fallen in the service of their King and Country."

On the 3rd March the 6th Battalion Royal West Kent Regiment proceeded to the Rhine, and joined the 34th Division, afterwards called the Eastern Division.

Field-Marshal Sir Douglas Haig visited the headquarters at Masny on the 13th March to say good-bye and express his thanks for the part the Division had taken in the war.

On the 16th March Major-General H. W. Higginson, C.B., D.S.O., received orders to take up an appointment in the Army of Occupation. He had been a great personality in the Division, a brave leader of men whom all ranks had learned to admire for his soldierlike qualities. His farewell order of the day ran as follows :

" On relinquishing command of the 12th Division I wish to express to all ranks of every unit and department my deep sense of gratitude for their unfailing support, loyalty and comradeship during the past eleven months, during which it has been my privilege to have the proud honour of being its commander.

" The months of May, June, and July, 1918, were ones of constant vigilance and hard work in the trenches owing to the expected renewal of the German offensive. During this period the Division distinguished itself in several successful raids which were on a considerable scale.

" On the 8th August, 1918, you attacked with the rest of the Fourth Army, and during a period of constant hard fighting and attacking almost daily you drove the enemy from position to position to Vendhuile, which you reached on the 30th September, a distance of twenty-six miles from your position on the 8th August.

"You were then transferred to the First Army and went into the line near Lens on the 6th October.

"The following day the enemy was in retreat in front of you, and you drove him back in daily encounters until you reached the line of the River Escaut, a distance of thirty-two miles from your starting line, on the 27th October, and were relieved there on the 29th.

"This is the record of the six months preceding the Armistice.

"Previous to this the Division played a prominent part in many famous battles. Its achievements at Loos, the Somme, Arras, and Cambrai were worthy of its best traditions.

"Between May, 1915, when the Division first landed in France, and the 11th November, 1918, the Division lost 2,105 officers and 46,038 other ranks in action. This testifies that your laurels have not been lightly earned and to the gallantry and devotion to duty shown by you who have survived the great ordeal, and by those brave comrades who have given their lives for our King and Country, and who by their sacrifice have won immortal fame.

"In a few weeks the Division will have ceased to exist, but wherever our fortunes may lead us in the future we shall all remember with pride the days when we fought in the 12th Division, and will retain the spirit of comradeship and loyalty to each other which has carried us to victory in this Great War.

"I wish you all good luck and God-speed."

Demobilisation proceeding steadily, the Division melted away. There was no triumphant home-coming, no public welcome—the Divisions of the New Army simply disappeared. They had finished their task.

Nevertheless, in countless English homes, memories of their heroism will be for ever gratefully preserved, and may future generations of the Home and Eastern Counties continue to be inspired by the example of those who fought, who died, who conquered, in the ranks of the 12th Division.

APPENDICES

APPENDIX I

TERMS OF ARMISTICE WITH GERMANY.

Signed at 5 a.m. on 11th November, 1918.

A.—CLAUSES RELATING TO WESTERN FRONT.

1. Cessation of operations by land and in the air six hours after the signature of the Armistice, viz., at 11 a.m.
2. Immediate evacuation of invaded countries—Belgium, France, Alsace-Lorraine, Luxemburg—so ordered as to be completed within fourteen days from the signature of the Armistice.

German troops which have not left the above-mentioned territories within the period fixed will become prisoners of war.

Occupation by the Allied and United States forces jointly will keep pace with evacuation in these areas.

All movements of evacuation and occupation will be regulated in accordance with a Note.

3. Repatriation, beginning at once, to be completed within fourteen days, of all inhabitants of the countries above enumerated (including hostages, persons under trial, or convicted).
4. Surrender in good condition by the German Armies of the following equipment :—

    5,000 guns (2,500 heavy, 2,500 field).
    30,000 machine guns.
    3,000 *minenwerfer*.
    2,000 aeroplanes (fighters, bombers—firstly D.7's—and night-bombing machines).

The above to be delivered *in situ* to the Allied and United States troops in accordance with detailed conditions laid down in the Note.

5. Evacuation by the German Armies of the countries on the left bank of the Rhine. These countries on the left bank of the Rhine shall be administered by the local authorities under the control of the Allied and United States Armies of Occupation.

The occupation of these territories will be carried out by Allied and United States garrisons holding the principal crossings of the Rhine (Mayence, Coblentz, Cologne), together with bridgeheads at these points of a thirty-kilometre (about nineteen miles) radius on the right bank, and by garrisons similarly holding the strategic points of the regions.

A neutral zone shall be set up on the right bank of the Rhine between the river and a line drawn ten kilometres (six and a quarter miles) distant, starting from the Dutch frontier to the Swiss frontier. In the case of inhabitants, no person shall be prosecuted for having taken part in any military measures previous to the signing of the Armistice.

No measure of a general or official character shall be taken which would have, as a consequence, the depreciation of industrial establishments or a reduction of their *personnel*.

Evacuation by the enemy of the Rhinelands shall be so ordered as to be completed within a further period of sixteen days—in all thirty-one days after the signature of the Armistice. All movements of evacuation and occupation will be regulated according to the Note.

6. In all territory evacuated by the enemy there shall be no evacuation of inhabitants; no damage or harm shall be done to the persons or property of the inhabitants.

No destruction of any kind to be committed.

Military establishments of all kinds shall be delivered intact, as well as military stores of food, munitions, equipment not removed during the periods fixed for evacuation.

Stores of food of all kinds for the civil population, cattle, etc., shall be left *in situ*.

Industrial establishments shall not be impaired in any way, and their *personnel* shall not be moved.

7. Roads and means of communication of every kind, railroads, waterways, main roads, bridges, telegraphs, telephones, shall be in no manner impaired.

All civil and military *personnel* employed on them shall remain.

Five thousand locomotives, 150,000 waggons, and 5,000 motor lorries, in good working order, with all necessary spare parts and fittings, shall be delivered to the Associated Powers within the period fixed for the evacuation of Belgium and Luxemburg.

The railways of Alsace-Lorraine shall be handed over within the same period, together with all the pre-war *personnel* and material.

Further, material necessary for the working of railways in the country on the left bank of the Rhine shall be left *in situ*.

All stores of coal and material for upkeep of permanent way, signals, and repair shops shall be left *in situ*, and kept in an efficient state by Germany, as far as the means of communication are concerned, during the whole period of the Armistice.

All barges taken from the Allies shall be restored to them. The Note appended regulates the detail of these measures.

8. The German Command shall be responsible for revealing all mines or delay-action fuses disposed on territory evacuated by the German troops, and shall assist in their discovery and destruction.

The German Command shall also reveal all destructive measures that may have been taken (such as poisoning or pollution of springs, wells, etc.) under penalty of reprisals.

9. The right of requisition shall be exercised by the Allied and United States Armies in all occupied territory, save for settlement of accounts with authorised persons.

The upkeep of the troops of occupation in the Rhineland (excluding Alsace-Lorraine) shall be charged to the German Government.

10. The immediate repatriation, without reciprocity, according to detailed conditions which shall be fixed, of all Allied and United States prisoners of war; the Allied Powers and United States of America shall be able to dispose of these prisoners as they wish. However, the return of German prisoners of war interned in Holland and Switzerland shall continue as heretofore. The return of German prisoners of war shall be settled at peace preliminaries.

11. Sick and wounded who cannot be removed from the evacuated territory will be cared for by German *personnel*, who will be left on the spot, with the medical material required.

B.—Clauses relating to the Eastern Frontiers of Germany.

12. All German troops at present in any territory which before the war belonged to Russia, Rumania, or Turkey, shall withdraw within the frontiers of Germany as they existed on 1st August, 1914; and all German troops at present in territories which before the war formed part of Russia must likewise return to within the frontiers of Germany as above defined as soon as the Allies shall think the moment suitable, having regard to the internal situation of these territories.

13. Evacuation by German troops to begin at once; and all German instructors, prisoners, and civilians, as well as military agents, now on the territory of Russia (as defined on August 1st, 1914) to be recalled.

14. German troops to cease at once all requisitions and seizures, and any other undertaking with a view to obtaining supplies intended for Germany in Rumania and Russia, as defined on 1st August, 1914.

15. Abandonment of the treaties of Bukharest and Brest-Litovsk, and of the supplementary treaties.

16. The Allies shall have free access to the territories evacuated by the Germans on their eastern frontier, either through Dantzig or by the Vistula, in order to convey supplies to the populations of these territories or for the purpose of maintaining order.

C.—Clause relating to East Africa.

17. Unconditional evacuation of all German forces operating in East Africa within one month.

D.—General Clauses.

18. Repatriation, with reciprocity, within a maximum period of one month, in accordance with detailed conditions hereafter to be fixed, of all civilians interned or deported who may be citizens of other Allied or Associated States than those mentioned in Clause 3.

19. With the reservation that any future claims and demands of the Allies and United States of America remain unaffected, the following financial conditions are required:—
Reparation for damage done.

While the Armistice lasts no public securities shall be removed by the enemy which can serve as a pledge to the Allies for the recovery or reparation for war losses.

Immediate restitution of the cash deposit in the National Bank of Belgium, and, in general, immediate return of all documents, specie, stocks, shares, paper money, together with the plant for the issue thereof, touching public or private interests in the invaded countries.

Restitution of the Russian and Rumanian gold yielded to Germany or taken by that Power.

This gold to be delivered in trust to the Allies until the signature of peace.

E.—Naval Conditions.

20. Immediate cessation of all hostilities at sea, and definite information to be given as to the location and movements of all German ships.

Notification to be given to neutrals that freedom of navigation in all territorial waters is given to the naval and mercantile marines of the Allied and Associated Powers, all questions of neutrality being waived.

21. All naval mercantile marine prisoners of war of the Allied and Associated Powers in German hands to be returned, without reciprocity.

22. Handing over to the Allies and United States of all submarines (including all submarine cruisers and minelayers) which are present at the moment with full complement in the ports specified by the Allies and the United States. Those that cannot put to sea to be deprived of crews and supplies, and shall remain under the supervision of the Allies and the United States. Submarines ready to put to sea shall be prepared to leave German ports immediately on receipt of wireless order to sail to the port of surrender, the remainder to follow as early as possible. The conditions of this article shall be carried out within fourteen days after the signing of the Armistice.

23. The following German surface warships, which shall be designated by the Allies and the United States of America, shall forthwith be disarmed and thereafter interned in neutral ports, or, failing them, Allied ports, to be designated by the Allies and the United States of America, and placed under the surveillance of the Allies and the United States of America, only caretakers being left on board, namely:—

    6 battle cruisers.
    10 battleships.
    8 light cruisers, including 2 minelayers.
    50 destroyers of the most modern types.

All other surface warships (including river craft) are to be concentrated in German naval bases, to be designated by the Allies and the United States of America, and are to be paid off and completely disarmed and placed under the supervision of the Allies and the United States of America. All vessels of the auxiliary fleet (trawlers, motor vessels, etc.) are to be disarmed. All vessels specified for internment shall be ready to leave German ports seven days after the signing of the Armistice. Directions of the voyage will be given by wireless.

Note.—A declaration has been signed by the Allied delegates and handed to the German delegates to the effect that, in the event of ships not being handed over owing to the mutinous state of the fleet, the Allies reserve the right to occupy Heligoland as an advanced base to enable them to enforce the terms of the Armistice. The German delegates have on their part signed a declaration that they will recommend the Chancellor to accept this.

24. The Allies and the United States of America shall have the right to sweep up all minefields and obstructions laid by Germany outside territorial waters, and the positions of these are to be indicated.

25. Freedom of access to and from the Baltic to be given to the naval and mercantile marine of the Allied and Associated Powers. To secure this the Allies and the United States of America shall be empowered to occupy all German forts, fortifications, batteries, and defence works of all kinds in all the entrances from the Kattegat into the Baltic, and to sweep up all mines and obstructions within and without German territorial waters without any questions of neutrality being raised, and the positions of all such mines and obstructions are to be indicated.

26. The existing blockade conditions set up by the Allied and Associated Powers are to remain unchanged, and all German merchant ships found at sea are liable to capture. The Allies and United States contemplate the provisioning of Germany during the Armistice as shall be found necessary.

27. All naval aircraft are to be concentrated and immobilised in German bases to be specified by the Allies and the United States of America.

28. In evacuating the Belgian coasts and forts Germany shall abandon all merchant ships, tugs, lighters, cranes, and all other harbour materials, all materials for inland navigation, all aircraft and air materials and stores, all arms and armaments, and all stores and apparatus of all kinds.

29. All Black Sea ports are to be evacuated by Germany; all Russian warships of all descriptions seized by Germany in the Black Sea are to be handed over to the Allies and the United States of America; all neutral merchant ships seized are to be released; all warlike and other materials of all kinds seized in those ports are to be returned, and German materials as specified in Clause 28 are to be abandoned.

30. All merchant ships in German hands belonging to the Allied and Associated Powers are to be restored in ports to be specified by the Allies and the United States of America, without reciprocity.

31. No destruction of ships or of material to be permitted before evacuation, surrender, or restoration.

32. The German Government shall formally notify the neutral Governments of the world, and particularly the Governments of Norway, Sweden, Denmark, and Holland, that all restrictions placed on the trading of their vessels with the Allied and Associated countries whether by the German Government or by private German interests, and whether in return for specified concessions, such as the export of shipbuilding materials, or not, are immediately cancelled.

33. No transfers of German shipping of any description to any neutral flag are to take place after signature of the Armistice.

F.—Duration of Armistice.

34. The duration of the Armistice is to be thirty-six days, with option to extend. During this period, on failure of execution of any of the above clauses, the Armistice may be denounced by one of the contracting parties on forty-eight hours' previous notice.

G.—Time Limit for Reply.

35. This Armistice to be accepted or refused by Germany within seventy-two hours of notification.

APPENDIX II (a)

ORIGINAL ORDER OF BATTLE OF 12TH (EASTERN) DIVISION.

35th Infantry Brigade.

7th Battalion the Norfolk Regiment.
7th Battalion the Suffolk Regiment.
9th Battalion the Essex Regiment.
5th Battalion the Princess Charlotte of Wales's (Royal Berkshire Regiment).

36th Infantry Brigade.

8th Battalion the Royal Fusiliers (City of London Regiment).
9th Battalion the Royal Fusiliers (City of London Regiment).
7th Battalion the Royal Sussex.
11th Battalion the Duke of Cambridge's Own (Middlesex Regiment).

37th Infantry Brigade.

6th Battalion the Queen's (Royal West Surrey Regiment).
6th Battalion the Buffs (East Kent Regiment).
7th Battalion the East Surrey Regiment.
6th Battalion the Queen's Own (Royal West Kent Regiment).

Pioneer Battalion.—5th Battalion the Northamptonshire Regiment.

The Royal Artillery.—62nd, 63rd, 64th and 65th Brigades, Royal Field Artillery. Divisional Ammunition Column.

The Royal Engineers.—69th, 70th and 87th Field Companies. Signal Company.

" A " Squadron King Edward's Horse.

9th Motor Machine Gun Battery.

12th Cyclist Company.

The Royal Army Service Corps.—116th, 117th, 118th and 119th Companies.

The Royal Army Medical Corps.—36th, 37th and 38th Field Ambulances. 23rd Sanitary Section.

The Royal Army Veterinary Corps.—23rd Mobile Veterinary Section.

APPENDIX II (b)

SUCCESSION OF COMMANDING OFFICERS, STAFF OFFICERS, Etc.

Divisional Commanders.

Major-General J. Spens, C.B.	Aug., 1914
Major-General F. D. V. Wing, C.B., C.M.G., killed 2 Oct., 1915	Mar., 1915
Major-General A. B. Scott, C.B., D.S.O.	Oct., 1915
Major-General H. W. Higginson, C.B., D.S.O.	April, 1918

G.S.O. (1).

Lieut.-Colonel the Hon. C. J. Sackville-West, C.M.G., K.R.R.C.	Dec., 1914
Lieut.-Colonel C. J. C. Grant, D.S.O., Coldstream Guards	Dec., 1915
Lieut.-Colonel C. J. B. Hay, D.S.O., Corps of Guides	Jan., 1917
Lieut.-Colonel R. S. Allen, Hampshire Regiment	July, 1917
Lieut.-Colonel W. R. Pinwill, D.S.O., The King's Regiment	May, 1918
Lieut.-Colonel J. D. Belgrave, D.S.O., Royal Artillery	Aug., 1918

G.S.O. (2).

Major J. K. Cochrane, Leinster Regiment	Aug., 1914
Major C. J. B. Hay, D.S.O., Corps of Guides	Jan., 1915
Major E. C. W. Conway-Gordon, Skinner's Horse	Jan., 1917
Major C. A. S. Page, M.C., Middlesex Regiment	May, 1917
Colonel R. Burritt, Manitoba Regiment	Oct., 1917
Major C. F. M. N. Ryan, D.S.O., M.C., Royal Engineers	July, 1918

G.S.O. (3).

Major G. de la P. B. Pakenham, D.S.O., Border Regiment	Mar., 1915
Major F. V. Thompson, Royal Engineers	Oct., 1915
Captain A. S. Herbert, The Queen's	Mar., 1916
Captain G. L. Brown, Middlesex Regiment	June, 1916
Captain H. R. Gadd, M.C., Suffolk Regiment	Aug., 1916
Captain T. P. Coe, M.C., Norfolk Regiment	July, 1917
Captain W. B. Anderson, Highland Light Infantry	April, 1918

APPENDICES

A.A. & Q.M.G.

Lieut.-Colonel H. P. Hancox, Royal Inniskilling Fusiliers	Sept., 1914
Lieut.-Colonel E. H. Collen, D.S.O., Royal Artillery	Oct., 1915
Lieut.-Colonel F. R. Burnside, D.S.O., 3rd Hussars	Mar., 1918

D.A.A.G. (formerly D.A.A. & Q.M.G.).

Major A. F. Stewart, Suffolk Regiment	Aug., 1914
Major D. R. Robertson, 12th Lancers, I.A.	Oct., 1915
Major S. A. Mott, Royal Scots Fusiliers	Mar., 1916
Major E. St. C. Gray, M.C., Poona Horse	April, 1916
Major J. St. J. Graham, General List	July, 1917

D.A.Q.M.G.

Major G. B. Coleman, D.S.O.	Aug., 1914
Major W. R. Hughes, M.C.	Feb., 1917

A.D.C.

Captain C. C. Towers, Essex Yeomanry, killed 2 Oct., 1915	Dec., 1914
Lieutenant R. V. Falkner, M.C., 4th Hussars	May, 1915
Lieutenant R. F. E. R. d'Erlanger, M.C., Rifle Brigade	Dec., 1915
Captain J. B. W. Robinson, County of London Yeomanry	Jan., 1917
Lieutenant H. P. Wykeham-Musgrave, Royal Artillery	May, 1918
Lieutenant D. W. Bennett, King's Own	Aug., 1918

35TH INFANTRY BRIGADE.

Commanders.

Brig.-General C. H. C. Van Straubenzee, C.B.	Aug., 1914
Brig.-General A. Solly-Flood, C.M.G., D.S.O., 4th Dragoon Guards	Nov., 1915
Brig.-General B. Vincent, C.M.G., 6th Inniskilling Dragoons	Jan., 1917
Brig.-General A. T. Beckwith, C.M.G., D.S.O., Hampshire Regiment	Aug., 1918
Brig.-General B. Vincent	Sept., 1918

Brigade Majors.

Major Scobell, M.C.	Aug., 1914
Major J. L. Dent, D.S.O., M.C., killed 12 April, 1917	Feb., 1916
Captain M. L. Woollcombe	April, 1917
Captain J. Broadwood, M.C.	July, 1917
Captain J. L. Dickinson	Dec., 1917
Captain C. H. Cooke, M.C.	May, 1918

APPENDICES

Staff Captains.

Captain A. Scott-Murray, M.C.	Jan., 1915
Captain W. R. Creighton	Nov., 1918

7TH BATTALION THE NORFOLK REGIMENT.

Commanding Officers.

Lieut.-Colonel J. W. V. Carrol, C.M.G.	Aug., 1914
Major T. C. Atkinson	Sept., 1915
Lieut.-Colonel F. E. Walter, D.S.O.	Oct., 1915
Lieut.-Colonel R. Gethen, M.C.	Oct., 1917
Lieut.-Colonel H. L. F. A. Gielgud, M.C., killed 30 Nov., 1917	Nov., 1917
Lieut.-Colonel E. T. Rees, D.S.O., M.C.	Dec., 1917
Major G. West	Mar., 1918
Lieut.-Colonel F. S. Cooper, D.S.O.	April, 1918
Major G. West	April, 1918
Lieut.-Colonel R. Gethen, M.C.	April, 1918
Lieut.-Colonel H. A. Scarlett, D.S.O.	May, 1918

Adjutants.

Major R. T. H. Reynolds, M.C.	Aug., 1914
Captain A. N. Charlton, M.C.	Oct., 1915
Lieutenant M. L. Chaland, M.C.	Dec., 1916
Captain M. Tapply, M.C.	July, 1917
Lieutenant M. L. Chaland, M.C.	Sept., 1917
Captain A. N. Charlton, M.C.	Oct., 1917
Captain M. Tapply, M.C.	Dec., 1917
Lieutenant A. F. R. Brown, M.C.	Oct., 1918
Captain H. S. Hobson	Oct., 1918

7TH BATTALION THE SUFFOLK REGIMENT.

Commanding Officers.

Lieut.-Colonel C. D. Parry-Crooke, C.M.G.
Major G. H. Henty.
Lieut.-Colonel F. S. Cooper, D.S.O.
Major J. H. Lindsay, D.S.O.
Lieut.-Colonel G. V. W. Hill, D.S.O.

Adjutants.

Major H. R. Gadd, D.S.O.
Lieutenant G. H. Taylor.
Lieutenant R. J. Lawler.
Captain G. L. Crandon, M.C.

APPENDICES

9TH BATTALION THE ESSEX REGIMENT.
Commanding Officers.

Lieut.-Colonel C. G. Lewes, D.S.O.	Aug., 1914
Major C. J. Ryan, killed 8 July, 1916	July, 1916
Major E. B. Hicker, M.C.	July, 1916
Lieut.-Colonel B. O. Richards, D.S.O.	July, 1916
Lieut.-Colonel H. E. Trevor, killed 12 April, 1917	Nov., 1916
Major J. L. Hackett	April, 1917
Major G. Green, M.C.	April, 1917
Lieut.-Colonel F. V. Thompson, D.S.O., died of wounds 14 Oct., 1917	May, 1917
Major W. Russell Johnson	Oct., 1917
Lieut.-Colonel H. M. de Sales La Terriere, M.C.	Oct., 1917
Lieut.-Colonel G. Green, M.C.	April, 1918
Lieut.-Colonel W. Russell Johnson, D.S.O.	Aug., 1918
Lieut.-Colonel H. M. de Sales La Terriere, M.C.	Nov., 1918

Adjutants.

Captain C. C. Spooner, D.S.O.	Aug., 1914
Lieutenant R. Hickson, M.C.	July, 1916
Captain G. A. L. Graham	April, 1917
Captain H. E. Godin	Mar., 1918
Captain W. E. Wheeler	Sept., 1918
Lieutenant H. Wardall	Oct., 1918
Captain S. R. Whaley	Oct., 1918

5TH BATTALION PRINCESS CHARLOTTE OF WALES'S (ROYAL BERKSHIRE REGIMENT).
Commanding Officers.

Lieut.-Colonel F. W. Foley, D.S.O.	Aug., 1914
Major G. H. Arbuthnot	Dec., 1915
Lieut.-Colonel F. G. Willan, D.S.O.	Feb., 1916
Major T. V. Bartley Dennis	July, 1917
Lieut.-Colonel E. H. J. Nicolls, D.S.O., M.C.	Aug., 1917
Lieut.-Colonel H. T. Goodland, D.S.O.	June, 1918
Lieut.-Colonel E. H. J. Nicolls, D.S.O., M.C.	Oct., 1918

Adjutants.

Captain M. L. Slaughter	Aug., 1914
Captain F. H. Hudson	Sept., 1915
Lieutenant C. A. Gold	Oct., 1915
Captain C. A. Mallam, M.C.	July, 1916
Captain G. E. Collins	Oct., 1918
Second Lieutenant W. H. Ashby	Feb., 1919

This battalion was transferred to the 36th Infantry Brigade in February, 1918.

APPENDICES

1st/1st Cambridgeshire Regiment.

Joined the 12th Division in April, 1918, absorbing the remnants of the 7th Battalion Suffolk Regiment.

Commanding Officers.

Lieut.-Colonel E. T. Saint, D.S.O., died of wounds 29 Aug., 1918	Oct., 1917
Lieut.-Colonel M. C. Clayton, D.S.O.	Aug., 1918

Adjutants.

Captain E. R. Wood, M.C.	Jan., 1918
Captain C. H. Hollis, M.C.	April, 1918
Captain A. Johnson, M.C.	June, 1918
Captain E. Walker, M.C.	July, 1918

36th Infantry Brigade.

Commanders.

Brig.-General H. B. Borradaille, D.S.O., ret. pay I.A.	Aug., 1914
Brig.-General L. B. Boyd-Moss, C.M.G., D.S.O., South Staffordshire Regiment	Nov., 1915
Brig.-General C. S. Owen, C.M.G., D.S.O., Royal Welch Fusiliers	Nov., 1916

Brigade Majors.

Major C. Parsons	Aug., 1914
Major F. G. Willan, D.S.O.	Nov., 1915
Major D. F. Anderson, D.S.O.	Feb., 1916
Captain I. D. Guthrie, M.C.	Jan., 1917
Captain P. G. J. Gueterbock, D.S.O., M.C.	July, 1917

Staff Captains.

Captain S. G. Evans, M.C.	Aug., 1914
Captain N. H. H. Charles, M.C.	Oct., 1916
Captain W. H. C. Hardy, M.C.	April, 1918
Lieutenant H. P. McCabe	Dec., 1918

8th Battalion the Royal Fusiliers (City of London Regiment).

Commanding Officers.

Lieut.-Colonel A. C. Annesley, D.S.O., killed 7 July, 1917	Aug., 1914
Lieut.-Colonel N. B. Elliott-Cooper, V.C., D.S.O., M.C., died of wounds, 11 Feb., 1918	July, 1916
Lieut.-Colonel S. E. Sandars, D.S.O., M.C.	Dec., 1917

APPENDICES

Adjutants.

Captain T. G. Cope, D.S.O.	Aug., 1914
Captain Robertson Walker	Mar., 1916
Captain Ling, M.C.	July, 1916
Captain D. C. Royle, M.C.	Aug., 1916
Captain V. D. Cook	Jan., 1918

This battalion was absorbed in the 9th Battalion in February, 1918.

9TH BATTALION THE ROYAL FUSILIERS (CITY OF LONDON REGIMENT).

Commanding Officers.

Lieut.-Colonel J. C. Robertson.	Aug., 1914
Lieut.-Colonel S. Gubbins, D.S.O.	Aug., 1915
Lieut.-Colonel G. C. R. Overton, D.S.O.	June, 1916
Lieut.-Colonel W. V. L. Van Someren, D.S.O., M.C.	July, 1917

Adjutants.

Captain H. L. Pattinson	Aug., 1914
Captain M. E. Coxhead	Aug., 1915
Captain G. E. A. R. Rawling	Feb., 1916
Lieutenant T. L. Calwell	July, 1916
Captain S. Hilton, M.C.	Nov., 1916
Captain V. D. Cook	Jan., 1919

7TH BATTALION THE ROYAL SUSSEX REGIMENT.

Commanding Officers.

Lieut.-Colonel W. L Osborn, D.S.O.	Aug., 1914
Lieut.-Colonel H. A. Carr, D.S.O.	Aug., 1916
Lieut.-Colonel A. J. Sanson, killed 5 July, 1917	Oct., 1916
Lieut.-Colonel G. H. Impey, D.S.O.	Aug., 1917
Lieut.-Colonel A. L. Thomson, D.S.O.	July, 1918

Adjutants.

Captain R. J. A. Betham	Aug., 1914
Captain H. S. Stocks	Mar., 1916
Captain G. Nagle, M.C.	July, 1916
Captain H. S. Bowley, M.C.	July, 1917
Captain E. S. Ellis, M.C.	Aug., 1918

11TH BATTALION THE DUKE OF CAMBRIDGE'S OWN (MIDDLESEX REGIMENT).

Commanding Officers.

Lieut.-Colonel W. D. Ingle	Aug., 1914
Lieut.-Colonel L. L. Pargiter, D.S.O.	July, 1916
Lieut.-Colonel T. S. Wollocombe, M.C.	Feb., 1917

APPENDICES

Adjutants.

Captain L. L. Pargiter, D.S.O.	Aug., 1914
Captain H. L. MacIlwaine	July, 1916

This battalion was disbanded in February, 1918.

37TH INFANTRY BRIGADE.
Commanders.

Brig.-General C. A. Fowler, C.B., D.S.O.	Aug., 1914
Brig.-General A. B. E. Cator, D.S.O., Scots Guards	Feb., 1916
Brig.-General A. B. Incledon-Webber, C.M.G., D.S.O., Royal Irish Fusiliers	Oct., 1917

Brigade Majors.

Captain W. E. Scafe, D.S.O.	Aug., 1914
Captain H. E. Trevor	Aug., 1915
Captain M. Cradock-Hartopp	Nov., 1916
Captain J. F. Dew, M.C.	Jan., 1917
Captain P. B. B. Nichols, M.C.	April, 1918
Captain Norman Smithers, M.C.	July, 1918

Staff Captains.

Captain L. C. MacD. Stewart	Aug., 1914
Captain J. F. Dew, M.C.	Aug., 1916
Captain P. B. B. Nichols, M.C.	Jan., 1917
Captain Norman Smithers, M.C.	April, 1918
Captain W. Lunn	July, 1918

6TH BATTALION THE QUEEN'S (ROYAL WEST SURREY REGIMENT).
Commanding Officers.

Lieut.-Colonel H. F. Warden, D.S.O.	Aug., 1914
Lieut.-Colonel N. T. Rolls, D.S.O.	April, 1917
Lieut.-Colonel P. Whetham, D.S.O.	April, 1918
Major D. Mann, M.C.	Dec., 1918

Adjutants.

Captain R. A. M. Bassett, M.C.	Aug., 1914
Captain D. Mann, M.C.	Dec., 1915
Captain R. D. C. Webb	Mar., 1918
Lieutenant F. Hakes	Feb., 1919

6TH BATTALION THE BUFFS (EAST KENT REGIMENT).
Commanding Officers.

Lieut.-Colonel W. A. Eaton	Aug., 1914
Lieut.-Colonel H. R. H. Pratt, D S.O.	Dec., 1915
Lieut.-Colonel T. G. Cope, D.S.O.	Mar., 1916
Lieut.-Colonel A. S. Smeltzer, D.S.O., M.C.	June, 1917

APPENDICES

Adjutants.

Captain T. Wheler	Aug., 1914
Captain J. C. Page	Sept., 1915
Captain J. Turk, M.C.	Nov., 1917

7TH BATTALION THE EAST SURREY REGIMENT.

Commanding Officers.

Lieut.-Colonel R. H. Baldwin, D.S.O.	Aug., 1914
Lieut.-Colonel L. D. Scott, M.C.	Dec., 1917

Adjutants.

Captain E. H. J. Nicolls, M.C.	Aug., 1914
Captain L. D. Scott, M.C.	
Captain K. Anns, M.C.	
Captain H. O'D. Macan	Nov., 1917

This battalion was disbanded in February, 1918.

6TH BATTALION THE QUEEN'S OWN (ROYAL WEST KENT REGIMENT).

Commanding Officers.

Lieut.-Colonel Robinson, C.M.G., D.S.O.	
Lieut.-Colonel Evans, C.B.	
Lieut.-Colonel Venables	
Lieut.-Colonel C. S. Owen, C.M.G., D.S.O.	Nov., 1915
Lieut.-Colonel W. R. A. Dawson, D.S.O.	Nov., 1916
Lieut.-Colonel H. Peploe, D.S.O.	Dec., 1918

Adjutants.

Captain G. E. Wingfield-Stratford, M.C.	Aug., 1914
Major W. J. Alderman, D.S.O.	Sept., 1916
Captain W. G. Dove, M.C.	Nov., 1916
Captain E. G. V. Hughes	Feb, 1919

This battalion joined the Army of the Rhine in March, 1919.

5TH BATTALION THE NORTHAMPTONSHIRE REGIMENT (PIONEERS).

Commanding Officer.

Lieut.-Colonel G. A. Trent, C.M.G.	Aug., 1914

Adjutants.

Captain A. C. Pickering, M.C.	Aug., 1914
Captain M. Cathcart, M.C.	April, 1917
Captain L. Potter	Jan., 1919

APPENDICES

Divisional Artillery.

General Officer Commanding.

Brig.-General S. E. G. Lawless	Oct., 1914
Brig.-General K. L. McLeod	Feb., 1915
Brig.-General W. H. Willis, C.B., C.M.G.	Feb., 1916
Brig.-General H. M. Thomas, C.M.G., D.S.O.	Sept., 1917

Brigade Majors.

Major H. K. Gregory	Oct., 1914
Major H. Karslake, D.S.O.	Feb., 1915
Major E. O. Lewin, D.S.O.	Aug., 1915
Major M. H. Dendy, D.S.O.	Feb., 1916
Major W. J. L. Poston, D.S.O.	Oct., 1916
Major C. A. Clowes	Sept., 1917
Major N. R. L. Chance	Jan., 1918
Major H. W. L. Waller	July, 1918

Staff Captains.

Lieutenant O. C. Bevan	Feb., 1915
Captain A. C. Calder	Jan., 1917
Captain A. Fox	Oct., 1917
Captain F. J. Taylor	Nov., 1918

A.D.C.'s.

Lieutenant G. Renwick	May, 1915
Lieutenant G. B. B. Hughes	Nov., 1915
Lieutenant H. E. Simson	Feb., 1916
Captain L. H. Gow	Nov., 1916

62nd Brigade, R.F.A.

Commanding Officers.

Colonel C. F. Blane, C.M.G.	Aug., 1914
Lieut.-Colonel H. Valentine	Nov., 1915
Lieut.-Colonel H. E. S. Wynne, D.S.O.	Mar., 1916

Adjutants.

Captain C. Caddington	Aug., 1914
Lieutenant G. V. Ormsby	April, 1915
Lieutenant the Hon. R. D. Denham	Nov., 1916
Lieutenant H. A. Hambleton	Feb., 1917
Lieutenant G. H. L. M. Samuel	May, 1918
Captain A. G. Johnson	Aug., 1918

APPENDICES

63RD BRIGADE, R.F.A.
Commanding Officers.

Lieut.-Colonel W. A. Short, C.M.G.	Aug., 1914
Lieut.-Colonel L. J. Hext, C.M.G.	Sept., 1916
Lieut.-Colonel R. C. Coates, D.S.O.	April, 1917
Lieut.-Colonel R. G. Thomson, C.M.G., D.S.O.	Jan., 1918

Adjutants.

Lieutenant J. B. Kindersley	Aug., 1914
Lieutenant L. C. Woodward	Sept., 1916
Lieutenant J. N. Bromet	Dec., 1916
Captain D. S. Caldwell	Aug., 1917
Captain E. Freeman	Sept., 1918
Captain G. A. M. Routledge, M.C., M.M.	Oct., 1918

64TH BRIGADE, R.F.A.
Commanding Officers.

Colonel D. Dewar	Aug., 1914
Lieut.-Colonel R. A. C. Wellesley	
Lieut.-Colonel Barton	Oct., 1915

Adjutant.

Captain Duff.

This Brigade became an Army Brigade in December, 1916.

65TH BRIGADE, R.F.A.
Commanding Officers.

Colonel Hutchinson	Aug., 1914
Lieut.-Colonel L. J. Hext, C.M.G.	

Adjutants.

Lieutenant Smithers.
Lieutenant Woodward

This Brigade was broken up in August, 1916, to raise the 62nd, 63rd, and 64th Brigades to six-gun batteries.

DIVISIONAL AMMUNITION COLUMN.
Commanding Officers.

Lieut.-Colonel C. W. M. Knight, D.S.O.	Aug., 1914
Colonel J. F. Craig, C.M.G.	Nov., 1916

Adjutants.

Captain Williams	Aug., 1914
Captain Roberts	Mar., 1917

APPENDICES

Divisional Engineers.

Commanding Royal Engineers.

Lieut.-Colonel S. F. Williams, C.M.G.	Aug., 1914
Lieut.-Colonel W. Bovet, C.M.G.	July, 1916
Lieut.-Colonel A. T. Shakespear, D.S.O., M.C.	July, 1918

Adjutants.

Captain F. V. Thompson	Aug., 1914
Lieutenant E. M. Tabor	May, 1915
Captain F. T. Lee-Norman	Sept., 1916

12th Battalion Machine Gun Corps.

Commanding Officers.

Lieut.-Colonel R. Oakley, D.S.O.	Feb., 1918
Lieut.-Colonel W. G. A. Coldwell	Oct., 1918

Adjutants.

Captain J. Wilkie	Feb., 1918
Captain E. H. Mansell, M.C.	Jan., 1919

Royal Army Service Corps.

12th Divisional Train.

Commanding Officers.

Lieut.-Colonel E. C. L. Fitzwilliams	Oct., 1914
Lieut.-Colonel H. C. Allin	Nov. 1915

Adjutant.

Captain A. Davidson	Oct., 1914

Royal Army Medical Corps.

A.D.M.S.

Colonel J. B. Wilson, C.M.G.	Aug., 1914
Lieut.-Colonel J. P. Silver, D.S.O.	Feb., 1916

D.A.D.M.S.

Captain J. D. Richmond.
Major C. H. Balfour.
Major Ferrie.
Captain E. A. Mills.

APPENDICES

36TH FIELD AMBULANCE.

Major Bridges	Sept., 1914
Lieut.-Colonel H. N. Dunn	April, 1915
Lieut.-Colonel C. H. Turner, D.S.O.	July, 1915
Captain T. S. Eves	Aug., 1916
Captain H. C. E. Rankin	Jan., 1917
Lieut.-Colonel J. H. Fletcher, D.S.O., M.C.	Dec., 1917

37TH FIELD AMBULANCE.

Captain Dunkerton	Oct., 1914
Lieutenant E. T. Glinny	Jan., 1915
Lieutenant K. G. Crawford	Mar., 1915
Lieut.-Colonel N. V. Prynne	April, 1915
Lieut.-Colonel T. C. Phelan, D.S.O., M.C.	Nov., 1915

38TH FIELD AMBULANCE.

Lieut.-Colonel G. H. Goddard, D.S.O.	April, 1915
Lieut.-Colonel W. H. Forsyth, D.S.O.	Mar., 1916

ROYAL ARMY ORDNANCE CORPS.
D.A.D.O.S.

Lieut.-Colonel E. Henderson	1915
Captain Haslam	1915
Captain H. C. Whitaker	Jan., 1916

ROYAL ARMY VETERINARY CORPS.
D.A.D.V.S.

Major O. S. Fisher	1915
Major F. B. Sneyd	June, 1917

ROYAL ARMY CHAPLAINS' DEPARTMENT.
Senior Chaplains.

Rev. F. G. D. Webster	1915
Rev. H. P. Berkeley, M.C.	May, 1916
Rev. P. Middleton Brumwell, M.C.	1915

PROVOST-MARSHAL.

Lieut.-Colonel A. C. Tompkins	1915
Captain J. P. Allix	Oct., 1916

APPENDIX III (a)

SUMMARY OF HONOURS AND AWARDS GAINED.

Victoria Cross	6	Bars to D.C.M.	4
K.C.B.	1	M.M.	1,857
C.B.	3	Bars to M.M.	136
C.M.G.	14	Meritorious Service Medal	154
O.B.E.	2	Promotions	35
D.S.O.	62	Mentions	534
Bars to D.S.O.	9	French Decorations	40
M.C.	430	Belgian Decorations	28
Bars to M.C.	44	Italian Decorations	7
D.C.M.	256	Russian Decorations	6

APPENDIX III (b)

AWARDS OF THE VICTORIA CROSS.

At the Hohenzollern Craters on 6th March, 1916.

No. 6707 Lance-Corporal (Acting-Corporal) WILLIAM RICHARD COTTER, 6th Battalion East Kent Regiment.

For most conspicuous bravery and devotion to duty.

When his right leg had been blown off at the knee, and he had also been wounded in both arms, he made his way unaided for fifty yards to a crater, steadied the men who were holding it, controlled their fire, issued orders, and altered the dispositions of his men to meet a fresh counter-attack by the enemy.

For two hours he held his position, and only allowed his wounds to be roughly dressed when the attack had quieted down.

He could not be moved back for fourteen hours, and during all this time had a cheery word for all who passed him. There is no doubt his magnificent courage helped greatly to save a critical situation.

At the Battle of Arras on 9th April, 1917.

No. 5190 Sergeant HARRY CATOR, East Surrey Regiment.

For most conspicuous bravery and devotion to duty.

Whilst consolidating the first line captured system, his platoon suffered severe casualties from hostile machine gun and rifle fire. In full view of the enemy, and under heavy fire, Sergeant Cator with one man advanced across the open to attack the hostile machine gun. The man accompanying him was killed after going a short distance, but Sergeant Cator continued on, and picking up a Lewis gun and some drums on his way, succeeded in reaching the northern end of the hostile trench.

Meanwhile, one of our bombing parties was seen to be held up by a machine gun. Sergeant Cator took up a position from which he sighted this gun and killed the entire team and the officer, whose papers he brought in.

He continued to hold that end of the trench with the Lewis gun with such effect that the bombing squad was enabled to work along, the result being that 100 prisoners and five machine guns were captured.

Near Monchy-le-Preux on 3rd May, 1917.

No. 55295 Corporal GEORGE JARRATT, late Royal Fusiliers.

For most conspicuous bravery and devotion in deliberately sacrificing his life to save others.

He had, together with some wounded men, been taken prisoner and placed under guard in a dug-out. The same evening the enemy were driven back by our troops, the leading infantrymen of which commenced to bomb the dug-outs. A grenade fell in the dug-out, and, without hesitation, Corporal Jarratt placed both feet on the grenade, the subsequent explosion blowing off both his legs.

The wounded were later safely removed to our lines, but Corporal Jarratt died before he could be removed. By this supreme act of self-sacrifice the lives of these wounded were saved.

In the German Counter-Attack near Cambrai on 30th November, 1917.

Captain (Temporary Lieut.-Colonel) NEVILLE BOWES ELLIOTT-COOPER, D.S.O., M.C., Royal Fusiliers.

For most conspicuous bravery and devotion to duty.

Hearing that the enemy had broken through our outpost line, he rushed out of his dug-out, and, on seeing them advancing across the open, he mounted the parapet and dashed forward, calling upon the reserve company and details of Battalion Headquarters to follow. Absolutely unarmed, he made straight for the advancing enemy, and, under his direction, our men forced them back 600 yards. While still some forty yards in front he was severely wounded.

Realising that his men were greatly outnumbered and suffering heavy casualties, he signalled to them to withdraw, regardless of the fact that he himself must be taken prisoner.

By his prompt and gallant leading he gained time for the reserves to move up and occupy the line of defence.

And

Temporary Lieutenant SAMUEL THOMAS DICKSON WALLACE, R.F.A.

For most conspicuous bravery and devoted services in action in command of a section.

When the *personnel* of the battery was reduced to five by the fire of the artillery, machine guns, infantry and aeroplanes; had lost its commander and five of the sergeants, and was menaced by enemy infantry on the right flank, and finally in the rear, he maintained the fire of the guns by swinging the trails round close together, the men running and loading from gun to gun. He thereby not only covered other battery positions, but also materially assisted some small infantry detachments to maintain a position against great odds.

He was in action for eight hours, firing the whole time, and inflicting serious casualties on the enemy. Then, owing to the exhausted state of his *personnel,* he withdrew when infantry support arrived, taking with him the essential gun parts and all wounded men.

His guns were eventually recovered.

No. 358 Sergeant THOMAS JAMES HARRIS, M.M., 6th Battalion the Queen's Own (Royal West Kent Regiment).

For conspicuous gallantry and devotion to duty near Morlancourt on 9th August, 1918.

During the attack of the battalion the advance was much impeded by hostile machine-guns concealed in the crops and shell holes. Sergeant Harris led his section against one of these, capturing it, and killing seven of the enemy. Later, on two successive occasions, he attacked, single-handed, enemy machine guns which were causing heavy casualties and holding up the advance. He captured the first gun and killed the team, but was himself killed when attacking the second one. It was largely due to the great courage and initiative of this non-commissioned officer that the advance of the battalion was continued without delay and undue casualties. Throughout the operations he showed a total disregard for his own personal safety and set a magnificent example to all ranks.

APPENDIX IV

Summary of Casualties.

Place.	Period.	Killed. Ofrs.	Killed. O.R.	Wounded. Ofrs.	Wounded. O.R.	Missing. Ofrs.	Missing. O.R.
Ploegsteert Wood	Jun. to Sept., 1915.	15	195	46	1,020	—	—
Loos and Quarries	1 to 21 Oct., 1915.	39	541	68	2,237	10	459
Hohenzollern and Givenchy.	26 Oct., 1915, to 18 Jan., 1916.	9	190	44	976	—	11
Hohenzollern Craters	14 Feb. to 25 April, 1916.	27	551	135	3,149	1	157
Ovillers	1 to 9 July, 1916.	30	328	96	2,612	48	1,529
Beaumont Hamel and Pozières.	10 July to 14 Aug., 1916.	21	321	109	2,141	14	363
Arras	27 Aug., to 30 Sept., 1916.	2	19	15	159	—	4
Gueudecourt	1 to 20 Oct., 1916.	43	431	78	2,111	14	634
Arras	21 Oct., 1916, to 8 April, 1917.	12	261	48	902	1	19
Arras	9 to 12 April, 1917.	27	335	74	1,466	—	242
Scarpe	25 April to 18 May, 1917.	21	519	89	2,105	33	827
Monchy-le-Preux	19 June to 23 Oct., 1917.	28	465	99	2,182	13	312
Cambrai	16 Nov. to 5 Dec., 1917.	41	386	102	1,966	87	2,254
Fleurbaix	15 Jan. to 20 Mar., 1918.	2	69	15	393	—	7
Albert	24 Mar. to 22 April, 1918.	24	344	96	1,757	20	684
Mailly Maillet and Bouzincourt.	23 April to 5 June, 1918.	8	243	60	1,483	5	75
Morlancourt to Epéhy.	3 Aug. to 30 Sept., 1918.	80	769	204	4,466	6	704
Sallaumines to St. Amand.	1 to 30 Oct., 1918.	6	110	37	521	3	34
Totals	—	435	6,077	1,415	31,646	255	8,315

Total Casualties (Killed, Wounded and Missing).
Officers 2,105
Other Ranks . . . 46,038

APPENDIX V

THE MEMORIALS.

THE first Memorial to the officers and men of the 12th Division was erected in 1917. After the Battle of the Somme in 1916 a strong feeling arose that the gallant and epic fight at Ovillers should be commemorated. Accordingly a site was selected close to the ruins of the church of Ovillers, and on this spot, sacred for all time to the 12th Division, a simple oak cross was raised. It stands on high ground, and can be seen from far and near, and, notwithstanding the engagements that took place in its vicinity in 1918, the cross remains on that spot to this day, a memorial to the brave men who fell in the great fight in July, 1916.

At the close of the War it was decided to erect two permanent Memorials, one in the vicinity of Arras and one at Epéhy. The former is situated in the Commune of Wancourt, and stands on the ridge by Feuchy Chapel cross roads, on the south of the Arras-Cambrai road, and near the " brown " line captured by the Division in the Battle of Arras. The site of the memorial at Epéhy is at the cross roads, about half a mile south-east of the village, where the road turns to Malassise Farm, a position which will always be remembered by those present at the capture of Epéhy in September, 1918.

The Memorial Crosses are copies of the beautiful cross on York Minster, supported by hexagonal shafts, with six panels on the plinths. On the front panel is inscribed: " In memory of the officers, W.O.'s, N.C.O.'s., and men of the 12th (Eastern) Division, who fell in the Great War for King and Country." On the rear panel is the Victory Emblem, and on the four side panels are inscribed the battle honours of the Division. The base is also hexagonal. On the front is inscribed : " Grant them, O Lord, eternal rest," and on the other sides appear the Divisional Emblem, the Ace of Spades.

The Dedication ceremonies in connection with these Memorials took place on the 24th July, 1921. The first was held at 10 a.m. at the Arras Memorial in the presence of General Maistre (Member of the French Council of War), Major-General Sir Arthur Scott, K.C.B., D.S.O., Major-General the Honourable Sir Charles Sackville West, K.B.E., C.M.G., Military Attaché to the British Embassy in Paris, the Préfet and Sous Préfet of the Pas de Calais, the Mayors of Feuchy, Wancourt, Monchy-le-Preux, Tilloy, and Warlus, together with a representative number of officers of the 12th Division who had proceeded to France specially for the ceremony. General Maistre unveiled the Memorial, and, in an eloquent speech, handed it over to the perpetual care of the inhabitants of the district. The Memorial was then dedicated by the two senior Chaplains of the Division, the Rev. H. P. Berkeley, M.C., and the Rev. P. Middleton Brumwell, M.C. The Last Post and Réveillé were sounded by Sergeant A. Miller (late 9th Battalion, Essex Regiment), after which Major-General Sir Arthur Scott closed the ceremony by an address, in which he recalled and summarised the work of the Division. At the conclusion, a touching demonstration of respect was given by the children from the Commune of Wancourt, who, passing in front of the Memorial, laid wreaths and flowers around it.

The party then proceeded to Epéhy, where it was welcomed by the Mayor and Conseil Municipal of Epéhy, the Préfet and Sous Préfet of the Somme, and General Philipot, Commanding at Amiens. A procession was formed, and, headed by the band of the Epéhy Branch of the Old Comrades Association of the Great War, moved from the village to the site of the Memorial, where some 400 people from Epéhy and the neighbouring villages had gathered to pay the last tribute of respect to the heroic dead. The same ceremony was observed as at Arras, speeches being delivered by General Maistre and Major-General Sir Arthur Scott. Stirring addresses followed from the Mayor of Epéhy, the President of the Epéhy Branch of the Old Comrades Association, and the Préfet of the Somme. The band played the National Anthems of Great Britain and France, and the memorable ceremony came to a close.

MEMORIAL CROSS AT EPÉHY

APPENDIX VI

"THE SPADES."

THE 12TH DIVISIONAL THEATRICAL TROUPE.

DURING 1915, the theatrical talent in the Division was confined to a small, but excellent, number of artistes in the Royal Army Medical Corps and Royal Army Service Corps, and these formed the nucleus of the Divisional Concert Party later on.

Amongst this nucleus were Staff-Sergeant Hammersley, R.A.M.C., Lance-Corporal Watterworth, R.A.S.C., and Private Gilpin, R.A.M.C. who were the stand-by throughout the history of divisional entertainment.

At Christmas a pantomime was given in the theatre at Bethune.

It was after the first phases of the Battle of the Somme in 1916, and after the large development of the canteens and the creation of the Divisional Band that "Q" turned their attention to the formation of a Divisional Concert Party.

In September, 1916, the Division was in the Arras sector, holding a long front, with the three infantry brigades in the line, and the difficulty was to select a site for a theatre sufficiently central for the battalions in reserve. Eventually Berneville was selected and a big theatre commenced, but before it could be finished the Division was on the move again to the Somme. The Concert Party had, however, begun to take shape, chiefly the result of appeals to brigadiers for "talent," and it did some good preliminary work under Staff-Sergeant Hammersley.

In October, the Division fortunately returned to the same area after its third turn in the Battle of the Somme, and the Berneville Theatre was finished by the first week in November. The engine and cinema arrived from England, electric light was installed, scenery painted, a band-pit made, and the afterwards famous Divisional String Band inaugurated.

The Concert Party was now brought up to a high state of efficiency by the energies of Lieutenant Howe, 8th Royal Fusiliers, and his artistes. "Dolly" Clare (Lance-Corporal) was discovered, and at once made an enormous and attractive addition to the caste. New costumes, songs, etc., were bought, and success was instantaneous. Crowded houses (twice daily) helped to swell the finances of the Institutes so considerably that grants in aid of recreations for divisional, brigade, etc., purposes became possible. This continued till December, when the Division went back to the Le Cauroy rest area, and Berneville passed to other Divisions.

The acting of Staff-Sergeant Hammersley, the excellent comic singing of Lance-Corporal Watterworth, the soprano singing and dancing of " Dolly " Clare, and the baritone songs of Private Gilpin, were splendid assets upon which expansion of the Troupe was made possible.

The Le Cauroy rest area, like nearly all rest areas, was not provided with any theatre, but finally Houvin was selected, and a big barn utilised both for the Cinema and Concert Party.

The real success took place as soon as the big attack on the 9th April, 1917, had gained ground outside Arras, and when it became safe to use Arras itself. Although the town was occasionally shelled by long-range guns, divisional theatres throve there. Our Division was fortunate enough to secure the big Arras Theatre, and, after some hard work, renovating and repairing the scenery and pulleys, the " Spades," under Lieutenant Howe and Staff-Sergeant Hammersley, did immense work, while cinema shows were held in the afternoons. The theatre was not allowed to hold more than 800, but crowded houses were the rule. More artistes were necessary to fill the big stage, and several excellent additions were made, in particular, Private Maas (conjuror and card tricks), Private Hall (comic artist), Lance-Corporal (Miss) P. Keele, Private (Miss) Jenkins, Lance-Corporal Strong, Lance-Corporal Sutcliffe. After several excellent revues, " The White Man " was played for about three weeks, the costumes having been obtained from London. The Arras Theatre was occupied until the end of October, 1917.

Owing to the fighting at Cambrai in November, 1917, no concert work was possible till the Division moved up north again to Aire for Christmas, and then to Merville, where a theatre was found and used for a short time before the Division occupied the Croix du Bac area in January, 1918. Here a well equipped theatre was handed over by the outgoing Division, and the " Spades " and cinema were soon hard at work until March, when the German attack put an end to such fixed area luxuries as theatres, etc.

There can be no doubt whatever but that such institutions as Divisional Theatre, Band, Cinema, and Canteens, were of enormous benefit to the men and were fully appreciated by them.

E. H. COLLEN.

THEATRICAL TROUPE

INDEX

Acheville Trench, 216
Acq, 215
Adam Trench, 148
Adams, Lieutenant W. C., 95
— Private T., 118, 119
Aerial torpedo, 27
Aeroplanes, British, 137
— enemy, activity of, 83, 87, 88, 115, 117, 119, 120, 128, 145, 149, 159, 183
— — dropping of pamphlets by, 163
Agnez lez Duisans, 90, 113
Aire, 159, 161, 258
Aladdin, 30
Albert, 49, 56, 59, 159, 167, 169, 170, 172, 174, 177, 178, 190
Albert-Amiens railway, 171
Albert-Bapaume Road, 169
Alderman, Lieut.-Colonel, 120, 121, 139, 245
Aldershot, 3
Alexander, Lance-Corporal, 82
Allen, Lieut.-Colonel R. S., 238
Allenby, Field-Marshal Viscount, 74, 97
Allin, Lieut.-Colonel H. C., 248
Allix, Captain J. P., 249
Ambrines, 89
Amiens, 49, 185, 187, 190, 194, 195
Ammunition dump, 169, 188
— increased supply of, 50
— shortage of, 11, 12
— stores blown up, 124
Ancre River, 169, 170, 171, 172, 178, 182, 190, 191, 192
— valley, 171
Anderson, Major D. F., 242
— Captain W. B., 238
Annequin, 43
Annesley, Lieut.-Colonel A. C., 35, 57, 242
Anns, Captain K., 245
Anson Battalion, 173, 184
Arbuthnot, Major G. H., 241
Armentières, 6, 7, 10, 12, 162, 167
Armistice, signing of, 224, 225
— terms of, 231-6
Army, First, 13, 33, 48, 97, 109, 159, 215
— Second, 5, 12
— Third, 73, 74, 86, 97, 109, 135, 167, 168, 210

Army, Fourth, 49, 50, 79, 81, 189, 190, 195, 210, 213
— Fifth, 56, 73, 81, 109, 167, 168
— French, 187, 189, 190
— New, 3, 11, 13, 31
— of occupation, 228
Army Corps—
Ist, 13, 27, 41, 47, 48
IInd, 62, 70, 73
IIIrd, 49, 50, 55, 134, 135, 189, 190, 195, 213
IVth, 13, 24
Vth, 168, 170, 185
VIth, 74, 79, 85, 90, 92, 103, 106, 107, 108, 114, 115
VIIth, 97, 135, 168, 170, 171
VIIIth, 50, 62, 215
Xth, 16, 18
XIth, 16, 18
XIIIth, 50
XVth, 50, 79, 159, 162
XVIIth, 97, 108, 115, 125, 126, 130
XVIIIth, 106, 114
XXIInd, 185, 187, 197
Arras, 12, 13, 75, 76, 79, 90, 91, 93, 95, 99, 106, 108, 114, 120, 255, 258
— Battle of, 90 *et seq*.
— sector, 74, 75, 79, 86
Arras-Cambrai road, 95
Artillery, co-operation between infantry and, 70
— enemy, increased activity of, 164
— French, 188
Ashby, Second Lieutenant W. H., 241
Atkinson, Major T. C., 240
Auberchicourt, 225, 227
Aubers Ridge, 12
Aubigny, 215
Auby, 217, 218, 219
Auchonvillers, 181, 182, 183, 184
Austin, Lance-Corporal J., 30
Australian Corps, 62, 64, 65, 67, 68, 69, 70, 177, 178, 189, 190, 200
Aveluy, 159, 174, 175, 176, 185
— Bridge, 170, 172, 175
— Wood, 173, 175, 176, 185
Avion, 216

Bailey, Major, 21
Bailleul, 164

INDEX

Baldwin, Lieut.-Colonel R. H., 60, 71, 99, 110, 122, 139, 153, 245
Balfour, Major C. H., 248
Baltic, enemy losses in, 9
Banteux, 135, 137, 150
— Ravine, 150
Bantouzelle, 159
Barnes, Major-General Sir R., 162
Barrages, 82, 94, 95, 98, 99, 108, 109, 122, 124, 125, 126, 186, 192, 196
Barton, Lieut.-Colonel, 83, 247
— Sergeant, 195
Basieux, 50
Basse Noyelles, 217
Bassett, Captain R., 244
Baudains, Captain G. A., 124, 175, 222
Baum, Sergeant, 217
Bayard, Captain, 30
Bayonet Trench, 81, 83, 108
Bazentin-le-Grand, 168
Beames, Second Lieutenant, 100
Beaucamp, 157, 158
Beaucourt, 175, 182
Beaumont Hamel, 62, 172, 182, 183
Beauquesne, 184
Beaurains, 76, 122
Beck, Lieutenant, 37
Beckwith, Brig.-General A. T., 191, 195, 239
Bécordel, 197
Beet Factory, 144
Belcher, Major, 156
Belgium, 132
Belgrave, Lieut.-Colonel J. D., 238
Below Trench, 212
Bennett, Lieutenant D. W., 239
Berger, Lieutenant, 208
Berguette, 161
Berkeley, Rev. H. P., 227, 249, 256
Bernafay Wood, 80, 198, 199
Berneville, 257
Betham, Captain R., 243
Bethune, 28, 29, 47
Betrancourt Camp, 62
Betts, Sergt.-Major, 194
Beuvry, 220
Bevan, Lieutenant O. C., 246
Big Willie Trench, 36, 40
Billy-Montigny area, 216
Bird Cage, 212
Bird Post, 212
Bird Trench, 208, 209
Blackader, Major-General, 161
Blacklock, Major-General, 168
Blackwell, Second Lieutenant, 174
Blake, Company Sergt.-Major, 103
Blane, Colonel C. F., 246
Blangy, 90
Bleak House, 151, 158
— Quarry, 141, 142
— Trench, 148, 149

Boal, Captain, U.S.A., 128
Boeseghem, 5
Bois Bernard, 216
— des Bœufs, 102
— Grenier, 165
— Hugo, 17
— du Vert, 122
Bomb attacks, 18, 19, 24, 121, 148, 150, 154, 183, 203
Bonavis, 136, 139, 141, 153
— Farm, 153
— Ridge, 151, 154, 159
Borrodaile, Brig.-General H. B., 14, 28, 242
Borst, Second Lieutenant C. L., 127
Bosenghem, 27
Boujon, 220
Boulogne, 5
Bouquemaison, 134
Bourne, Second Lieutenant, 98
Bouzincourt, 63, 68, 69, 73, 168
— sector, 185
— Spur, 185
Bovet, Lieut.-Colonel W., 187, 248
Bowley, Captain H. S., 243
Boyd-Moss, Brig.-General L. B., 28, 35, 37, 43, 68, 88, 89, 242
Boyden, Lance-Corporal H. T., 32, 33
Bradley, Private, 41
Braeton Post, 208, 209, 210, 211
Branch, Private, 22
Bray-Albert Road, 170, 171, 172
Bray-Méaulte Road, 195, 196
Breslau Trench, 141
Brétencourt, 75, 76
Bridges, Major, 49, 249
Brigades, artillery—
62nd, 2, 6, 103, 155, 157
63rd, 2, 6, 103, 155, 157
64th, 2, 6, 83
Brigades, infantry—
35th, *passim*.
36th, *passim*.
37th, *passim*.
Brims, Major R. W., 204
Briqueterie, 198, 199, 201
"British Campaign in France and Flanders," 179
Broadwood, Captain J., 145, 239
Brodie, Captain, 21
Bromet, Lieutenant J., 247
Broughton, Major, 155
Brown, Captain G. L., 125, 238
— Private, 24
— Private F. J., 83
Bruce-Williams, Major-General Sir H., 97, 103
Bruille, 223
Brumwell, Rev. P. Middleton, 29, 249, 256
Bull, Lieutenant K. R., 119

INDEX

Burgess, Gunner A., 157
Buridon, 222
Burnside, Lieut.-Colonel F., 239
Burritt, Colonel R., 238
Bushell, Private, 183
Bus-les-Artois, 62
Busnes, 13, 31, 167
Butcher, Corporal, 24
Butler, Lieut.-General, 189, 190, 213
Byng, General Lord, 97, 121, 124, 128, 135, 141, 159, 168

" C1 " Trench, 40
" C4 " Trench, 37
Cable Trench, 153
Caddington, Captain C., 246
Calais, Préfet of, 255
— Sous-Préfet of, 255
Calder, Captain A. C., 246
Caldwell, Captain D., 247
— Private K., 193
Calwell, Lieutenant T., 243
Cambrai, 132, 161, 163, 258
— Battle of, 132 et seq.
— Road, 97, 149, 150, 153, 155, 156, 157, 158, 159
Camouflage, 133, 136
Campbell, Major-General Sir D., 80, 204
— Major, 188
— Private F. T., 141, 142
Camping, Lance-Corporal, 65
Canadian Corps, 6, 13, 97, 189, 190
Canal du Nord, 135, 202, 204
— de l'Escaut, 135, 212, 221, 223
— de la Haute Deule, 217
Canal Valley, 141, 147
Canaples, 189
Canaries, use in mining galleries of, 46
Cannon, Captain, 44
Capper, Second Lieutenant, 116, 121
Carey, Major-General, 215
Carlton, Corporal, 165
Carnoy, 168, 169, 197, 198, 201, 214
— Ridge, 197
Carr, Lieut.-Colonel H. A., 243
Carre, Captain, 17
Carrol, Lieut.-Colonel, 240
Cartridge Trench, 110, 111
Catelet Trench, 211
— Valley, 211
Caterer, Private, 58
Cathcart, Captain, 55, 245
Cator, Brig.-General A. B. E., 32, 39, 43, 90, 97, 110, 125, 126, 244
— Sergeant, 100, 101, 251
Cavalry Corps, 190
Cayley, Brig.-General, 83
Cazelet, Captain G. L., 66
Cemetery Ridge, 149, 157
Cinema film, attempt to take, 99

" Circus, The," 122
Cité St. Elie, 16, 20
Chaland, Lieutenant M. L., 240
Chalmers, Major W., 174
Chance, Major N., 246
Chapel Crossing, 144, 146
— Hill, 104, 144, 147
Chard, Captain R., 37
Charles, Captain N., 242
Charlton, Captain A. N., 149, 151, 240
Charwood, Second Lieutenant, 118
Chateau l'Abbaye, 223
— Thierry, 188
Cheshire Quarry, 148, 150
Chestnut Avenue, 207
Choques, 13, 221
Chord, The, 34, 36, 37, 39, 40, 41
Christmas 1917.. 161
Church work, 102, 104
Clare, Lance-Corporal " Dolly," 257, 258
Clarke, Sergeant C. W., 218
Clayton, Lieut.-Colonel M. C., 199, 203, 207, 226, 242
Clements, Second Lieutenant R. F., 164
— Major-General, U.S.A., 128
Clowes, Major C. A., 246
Coates, Lieut.-Colonel R. C., 155, 247
Cochrane, Major J. K., 238
Cockeram, Second Lieutenant, 111, 112
Coe, Captain T. P., 238
Colchester, 2
Coldwell, Lieut.-Colonel, 248
Coleman, Major G. B., 239
Colincamps, 171
Collen, Lieut.-Colonel, 27, 88, 106, 164, 239
Collins, Captain G. E., 184, 241
— Company Sergt.-Major J., 53
Comber, Second Lieutenant, 174
Communications, difficulty in establishing, 58
Contalmaison, 168
Conan-Doyle, Sir Arthur, 179
Contay, 60
Cook, Captain V. D., 72, 243
Cooke, Captain C. H., 239
Cooper, Lieut.-Colonel, 102, 122, 170, 240
Cope, Lieut.-Colonel, 37, 63, 68, 82, 99, 110, 243, 244
Cordela, 219
Cotter, Lance-Corporal, 40, 251
Cottesmore Trench, 209
Counter attack, Allied, 188 et seq.
Courcelles, 217, 218, 219
Couper, Major-General Sir V., 86
Couturelle, 106
Cox, Sergeant, 182, 183

INDEX

Coxhead, Major, 111
Coyles, Bombardier, 157
Cradock-Hartopp, Captain M., 244
Craig, Colonel J. F., 247
Crandon, Captain, 177, 240
Craters—
   "A," 36, 37, 38, 43
   "B," 37, 44
   "C," 37, 39, 44
   No. 1, 34, 36, 41, 43, 44
   No. 2, 34, 38, 40, 43, 44
   No. 3, 34, 44
   No. 4, 34, 44
   Triangle, 36, 37, 38, 39, 40, 41
   Battle of, 32 et seq.
Crawford, Lieutenant K. G., 249
Creighton, Captain W. R., 240
Crèvecœur, 159
Crinchon, Valley of, 75
Croix du Bac, 258
— de Guerre, presentation of, 188
Crombie, Captain, 59
Cromyn, Sergeant, 36
Cross, Lance-Corporal C., 66
Crowe, Private T., 66
Cruciform Post, 209
Crupez, 220
Cubray, 222
Currey, Major, 22
Currie, Lieut.-General Sir A., 189
Cyclists' Corps, 19, 145, 147

Dados Lane, 209
— Loop, 210, 211
Dainville, 75, 76
Dale, Lance-Coporal, 58
— Trench, 115
Daly, Second Lieutenant E. St. F., 127
Daniels, Captain, 35
Davey, Second Lieutenant R. E., 127
Davidson, Captain, 21
— Captain A., 248
Davies, Private, 24
Dawson, Lieut.-Colonel W. R. A., 9, 20, 99, 112, 127, 153, 154, 170, 192, 208, 211, 222, 245
Day, Lance-Corporal, 22
Debeney, Général, 187, 189
Debeno, Lieutenant G. P., 103
Décours River, 222
Deelish Trench, 207
Deighton, Lieutenant, 22
De Lisle, Lieut.-General Sir H. de B., 83, 106, 113, 135
Dendy, Major M. H., 246
Denham, Lieut. the Hon. R. D., 246
Dennis, Major Bartley, 241
Dent, Major J. L., 239
Dernancourt, 159, 172, 190, 194
Desmaillet, General Brissaud, 188
Deverell, Major-General, 97, 114

Devil's Trench, 110, 111, 112, 117
Dew, Captain J. F., 244
Dewar, Colonel, 247
Dickinson, Captain J. L., 239
Dismounted Cavalry Division, 33
Divisions—
   1st, 4, 18
   2nd, 4, 171, 176
   3rd, 92, 93, 94, 96, 97, 102, 112, 114
   4th, 62, 123, 129
   6th, 135
   7th, 19
   8th, 49, 50, 51, 55, 56, 218, 221, 223
   9th, 13, 50, 157, 168, 171
   11th, 75
   12th—
      commanding officer. See Wing; Scott; Higginson.
      constitution of, 1, 2, 3
      training of, 1, 2, 32, 48, 92, 122, 133, 180
      entraining for France, 4
      marching in France, 5
      disposition of forces of, 6, 14, 60, 80, 97, 158
      casualties in, 8, 21, 24, 31, 38, 39, 46, 61, 74, 83, 95, 106, 113, 120, 123, 128, 140, 159, 176, 177, 179, 182, 184, 187, 212, 254
      working parties from, 10, 11
      system of relief in, 11
      Battle of Loos, 12 et seq.
      preparations for attack, 18, 19
      attack by, 20, 21, 22
      Winter 1915–16..26 et seq.
      relieved by 15th Division, 27
      in reserve area, 27, 28, 31, 47, 89
      Battle of the Craters, 32 et seq.
      mining operations by, 34
      congratulated, 42, 66, 73, 107, 123, 124, 125, 141, 160, 184, 204
      Battle of the Somme, 49 et seq.
      attack on Ovillers, 50
      inspection by H.M. the King, 68, 69, 195
      work on roads and trenches, 80, 81, 84
      Winter 1916–17..86 et seq.
      relieved by 14th Division, 89
      Christmas 1916...89
      Battle of Arras, 90 et seq.
      need for reinforcement of, 126
      relieved by 4th Division, 129
      Battle of Cambrai, 132 et seq.
      winter 1917–18..161 et seq.
      reduction in strength of, 163, 180, 212
      relieved by 57th Division, 166
      stemming German advance, 167 et seq.
      relieved by 38th Division, 179

INDEX 263

Divisions—*continued*.
  12th—*continued*.
    attached to First French Army, 187
    advancing, 190 *et seq.*
    prisoners taken by, 107, 205, 212
    guns taken by, 107, 205, 212
    activities after the Armistice, 225
    Winter 1918–19..225 *et seq.*
    presentations of colours by H.R.H. the Prince of Wales, 226, 227
    demobilisation, 228, 229
    original order of battle of, 237
    honours and awards gained by, 250–3
    memorials to officers and men of, 255, 256
    theatrical talent in, 257–8
  14th, 4, 79, 86, 89
  15th, 13, 24, 27, 47, 92, 93, 97, 100, 104, 127
  16th, 47
  17th, 108, 171, 176, 177, 184
  18th, 186, 187, 190, 191, 192, 194, 197, 198, 202, 206, 208, 211, 212
  19th, 49, 51, 53, 55
  20th, 81, 83, 134, 135, 140, 147, 150, 152, 153, 154, 215
  21st, 80, 204
  35th, 170, 185
  38th, 161, 179
  47th, 169, 170, 171, 177, 190, 192, 197, 201, 204
  48th, 63, 73
  49th, 62, 69, 70
  50th, 13
  51st, 127
  57th, 162, 166
  58th, 126, 189, 190, 194, 197, 205, 207, 209, 217, 222
  63rd, 169, 171, 173, 174, 177, 184
Divisional Ammunition Column, 2, 25, 188
— artillery, 10, 12 15, 17, 1 9,21, 24, 25, 36, 39, 41, 48, 49, 55, 57, 60, 63, 64, 69, 70, 73, 76, 84, 89, 92, 93, 95, 96, 98, 99, 103, 106, 115, 120, 122, 123, 125, 126, 127, 128, 133, 136, 137, 143, 155, 157, 161, 165, 168, 171, 174, 178, 183, 186, 189, 208, 211, 212, 223, 246, 247
— band, 48, 226, 257
— canteen, 27, 43, 258
— cinema, 29, 257, 258
— concert party, 11, 28, 79, 88, 114, 257, 258
— Field Companies, R.E., 2, 16, 55, 106, 127, 145, 147, 152, 178, 204, 219, 224

Divisional front, 8, 14, 93, 95, 114, 142, 171, 189, 208, 215, 223
— headquarters, 6, 8, 14, 19, 26, 27, 28, 33, 47, 49, 50, 51, 60, 61, 63, 69, 73, 75, 80, 86, 89, 90, 96, 106, 129, 132, 134, 143, 144, 148, 152, 159, 161, 162, 166, 168, 169, 177, 179, 225
— Institute, 29
— school, 27
— Signal Company, 2, 18, 25, 179
— sports, 48, 89, 114, 225, 226
— staff, 41, 106
— train, 3
Douai, 111, 225
Douai-Orchies Road, 220
Dougal, Captain Roney, 157, 188
Douglas Smith, Major-General, 81, 135
Doullens, 73, 106, 134
Dourges, 218
Dove, Captain W. G., 139, 140, 245
Drocourt, 216
Du Cane, Lieut.-General Sir J., 79, 159
Dudeney, Lieutenant E. A., 187
Duff, Captain, 216, 222, 247
Dug-outs, construction of, 93, 96, 98
— enemy traps in, 105
Dunkerton, Captain, 249
Dunn, Lieut.-Colonel, 249
Dunsly, Private, 58

East Reserve Trench, 115
Eastbourne, 3
Eastern counties, patriotism in, 1
Eaton, Lieut.-Colonel W., 244
Ecquedecques, 27
Edginton, Lance-Corporal, 116
Edwards, Lieutenant F., 67
Ellard, Lieutenant H., 217
Eleu dit Leauvette, 215
Eley, Lieut.-Colonel, 155, 157
Elliott, Second Lieutenant W. J., 127
Elliott-Cooper, Lieut.-Colonel N. B., 36, 63, 83, 110, 127, 150, 151, 152, 242, 252
Ellis, Captain E., 243
Englebelmer, 182
Epéhy, 204, 205, 206, 207, 214, 255, 256
Erlanger, Lieutenant R. d', 239
Erre, 225, 226
Escaut River, 210
— Valley, 210
Estaires, 164, 166
Evans, Captain S. G., 242
— Lieut.-Colonel, 245
— Second Lieutenant, 72
— Sergeant, 20, 21
Eves, Captain T. S., 249

INDEX

Falkner, Lieutenant R., 239
Fanshawe, Lieut.-General Sir E., 170
— Major-General R., 63
Farm Ravine, 152
Faubourg St. Saveur, 90
Faulkner, Sergeant J., 67
Faunthorpe, Major, 99
Favière Wood, 198, 199, 201
Fellowes, Lieutenant, 95
Ferguson, Major, 145
Fergusson, Lieut.-General Sir Charles, 97, 108, 115, 130
Ferrie, Major, 248
Festubert, 29
Feuchy Chapel, 255
— — Redoubt, 97, 102
— Mayor of, 255
— Road, 102, 103, 104
— Switch, 100
Field Ambulances—
  36th, 3
  37th, 3, 105, 106
  38th, 3, 39
Fifoot, Second Lieutenant E. L., 66
Findlay, Lieutenant, 20
Fins, 134
— Valley, 147
Fire, liquid, 67
Fisher, Major O. S., 249
Fisher's Keep, 207
Fiske, Lieutenant, 211
Fitzwilliams, Lieut.-Colonel E. C., 248
Flack, Lance-Corporal, 195
Flagnies, 221, 222
Flammenwerfer, 66, 67, 116, 120, 121
Flers, 80, 81
Fleselles area, 49
Fletcher, Lieut.-Colonel J. H., 38, 105, 106, 249
Fleurbaix, 164, 180
— sector, 161, 162
Flines, 220
Flood, Brig.-General A. Solly, 27, 45, 83, 86, 239
Flowers, Lieutenant, 146
Foch, Maréchal, 13, 188
Foley, Lieut.-Colonel F. W., 241
Football, 32, 225
Forceville, 73
Forsyth, Lieut.-Colonel, 249
Fosse 4..218
— 7..218
— 8..14, 17, 18, 26, 34, 35, 38
Foster Lane, 150, 158
Fouquières, 216
— lez Bethune, 13, 24, 27
Fourth Avenue, 63, 64, 65
Fowler, Brig.-General C. A., 14, 24, 32
Fox, Captain A., 246
Franks, Major-General, 168
Freeman, Captain E., 247

French, Field-Marshal Viscount, 14,15
French Army, Sixth, 50
— civilians, kindness of, 49
— — release of, 140
— — welcome British troops, 219, 220
— forces, co-operation of British and, 12, 13, 16, 50, 57, 81, 187
— General Headquarters, warning from, 177
Fresnes, 216
Frévent, 134
Fricourt, 80
Furley, Major, 21

Gadd, Captain H. R., 238
Gale, Lance-Corporal, 184
Garnet, Captain, 72
Garnier du Plessis, Général, 188
Gas attacks, 14, 47, 86, 87, 109, 110, 167, 178, 179, 184, 196, 202, 210
Gauche Wood, 144, 145, 146
Gentelles Wood, 189
German forces—
  strong position of, 13, 14, 50, 76, 99, 100, 133, 208
  counter attack by, 14, 20, 143 *et seq.*, 159, 160, 186, 187, 196, 203, 211
  bombardment by, 14, 20, 58, 72, 113, 123, 125, 148, 158, 165, 177, 178, 182, 187, 191
  bombardment of, 50, 57, 63, 68, 70, 84, 94, 98, 122, 126, 127, 186
  casualties sustained by, 17, 44, 59, 176
  bomb attacks by, 23, 30, 32, 37, 52
  mining by, 30, 33, 43, 44
  capture of supplies from, 60, 61
  prisoners captured from, 65, 86
  night raids by, 88, 93, 94, 162, 163, 165, 166
  retreat of, 102, 190 *et seq.*
  guns captured from, 103, 173, 205
  traps left by, 105, 224
  reinforcement of, 165
  advance of, 167
  efficiency of artillery of, 182
German Fusilier Guards, 199
Gethin, Lieut.-Colonel, 102, 127, 240
Gielgud, Lieut.-Colonel H. L., 148, 149, 240
Gilfillan, Second Lieutenant, 94
Gillespie, Major, 155
Gilpin, Private, 257, 258
Gin Avenue, 152, 155, 156
Givenchy sector, 29, 30
Glinny, Lieutenant E. T., 249
Goddard, Lieut.-Colonel, 249
Godin, Captain H. E., 241
Godley, Lieut.-General Sir A., 185, 204
Gold, Lieutenant C. A., 241

INDEX

Gonnehem, 13
Gonnelieu, 143, 145, 149, 152, 155, 156, 157
— Cemetery, 156
— Ridge, 148, 149
Goodland, Lieut.-Colonel H. T., 226, 241
Gordon, Major Conway, 238
Gorringe, Major-General Sir G., 169, 192
Gough, General Sir Hubert, 13, 27, 32, 41, 43, 56, 65, 69, 73
Gould, Gunner F. C., 157
Gouzeaucourt, 144, 146, 147, 148, 149, 156, 158
Gow, Captain L. H., 246
Graham, Captain G. A. L., 241
— Major J., 239
Granatenwerfer, 127
Grandcourt, 172
Grande Rullecourt, 89
Grant, Lieut.-Colonel C. J. C., 89, 238
Gray, Major E., 239
Grease Trench, 84
Green, Lieut.-Colonel C., 23, 191, 194, 241
Green Lane, 116
— Switch, 152, 158
Gregory, Major H. K., 246
— Captain J. N., 184
— Private, 82
Grenades, 18, 19, 30, 35, 36, 59, 60, 66, 141
Grenouillère Bridge, 153, 159
Grid, 80
— Support, 82
Guards Division, 14, 18, 19, 24, 26, 146, 147
Gubbins, Lieut.-Colonel, 35, 243
Guémappe, 108
Gueterbock, Captain P. G., 242
Gueudecourt, 80, 82
Gunther, Second Lieutenant, 111, 112
Gun Trench, 16, 17, 18, 20, 22, 23, 110, 112, 113
Guthrie, Captain I. D., 242
Guyencourt, 204, 205, 206

Habarcq Trench, 100
Hackett, Major J. L., 241
Haig, Field-Marshal Earl, 13, 31, 228
Hairpin Trench, 23
Hakes, Lieutenant F., 244
Haking, Lieut.-General Sir R., 16, 18, 23
Haldane, Lieut.-General Sir J., 74, 90, 97, 107, 114
Hale, Private, 58
Hall, Private, 258
Ham, 27
Hambleton, Lieutenant H. A., 246

Hamel, 170, 175
— Work, 100
Hammersley, Staff-Sergeant, 257, 258
Hancox, Lieut.-Colonel H., 239
Hangest Trench, 100
Hardecourt, 198, 199, 214
Harding-Newman, Captain, 221
Hardman, Lieutenant, 221
Hardy, Captain W. H., 242
Harris, Sergeant, 193, 253
Hart Work, 100
Haslam, Captain, 249
Haucourt Trench, 101
Hautallaines, 134
Haute Rive, 222
Havrincourt, 135
Hay, Lieut.-Colonel C. J. B., 89, 106, 238
— Ian, 2
Hayward, Captain, 98
Hazebrouck, 5
Heath, Lieutenant, 17
Hedgman, Corporal J., 108, 109
Hédauville, 73
Hédauville-Bouzincourt area, 62
Hem, 220
— Trench, 100
Henderson, Lieut.-Colonel, 249
Heneker, Major-General, 218
Hénencourt, 50, 51, 176
Henin Liétard, 217
Henty, Major G. H., 22, 52, 148, 240
Herbert, Captain A. S., 238
Heron Works, 100
Hesdin, 132
Heudecourt, 134, 142, 144, 147, 159, 205
Hewat, Lieutenant, 20
Hext, Lieut.-Colonel, 103, 247
Heythorp Post, 208, 209
— Trench, 209
Hicker, Major E., 241
Hickson, Lieutenant R., 241
Higginson, Major-General H. W., 182, 188, 205, 223, 226, 238
Hill 70..13, 14
— 105..195
— Trench, 115
Hill, Lieut.-Colonel G., 240
Hilton, Captain S., 243
Hindenburg line, 133, 135, 140, 149, 155, 158, 160, 202, 206, 210
— support line, 133, 136, 139, 153, 154
— Trench, 139, 150, 154
Hoare, Company Sergt.-Major, 174
Hobbs, Second Lieutenant, 187
Hobson, Captain H. S., 240
Hohenzollern Redoubt, 14, 18, 26, 33, 43, 47
Hollis, Captain C. H., 192, 242
Holt Work, 100, 101

INDEX

Home counties, patriotism in, 1
Honnecourt, 143, 156
Honours gained by 12th Division, 250–3
Hook Trench, 114, 115, 116, 117, 119, 120, 121
Horne, General Lord, 97, 159, 215
Horse Post, 208
Houlette, 100, 101
Hounslow, 2, 3
Houplines, 8, 10, 11
Houvin, 258
Howard, Sergeant W., 157
Howe, Lieutenant, 88, 257, 258
Howitzers, 2, 36, 103, 110
Hubbard, Captain, 72
Hudson, Major-General Sir H., 49
— Captain F. H., 241
Hughes, Captain E. G., 245
— Lieutenant G. B., 246
— Major W. R., 239
Hulloch Road, 18
Hunter-Weston, Lieut.-General Sir A., 62, 215
Hutchinson, Colonel, 247
Hythe, 3

Impey, Lieut.-Colonel G. H., 126, 150, 170, 175
Infantry, co-operation of artillery and, 70, 157
— — tanks and, 137, 138
— Lane, 119, 125
Ingle, Lieut.-Colonel W. D., 33, 243
Ingouville-Williams, Major-General, 49
Isham, Captain, 68
International Post, 162
Iron Cross, capture of supplies of, 61
Irvine Lane, 146, 147, 158
" It," 87
Italian Attaché, visit to Divisional Headquarters of, 27
Italy, troops sent to, 132

Jackson, Private, 58
Jacob, Lieut.-General C., 62, 69
Jacqvenne Copse, 205
James, Second Lieutenant C. S., 178
Japanese Attaché, visit to Divisional Headquarters of, 27
Jarratt, Sergeant G., 111, 252
Jarrott, Sergeant, 101
Jenkins, Private, 258
Jeudwine, Major-General Sir H., 135, 143
Joffre, Maréchal, 31
Johnson, Captain A., 242
— Captain A. G., 188, 246

Johnson, Lieut.-Colonel Russell, 144, 241
— Private, 203
Johnson's Provisional Battalion, 144

Karn, Second Lieutenant, 53
Karslake, Major H., 246
Kearney, Lance-Corporal, 58
Keele, Lance-Corporal P., 258
Kekewich, Lieutenant S. B., 158
Kelan, Second Lieutenant, 55
Kennifick, Lieutenant E. H., 53
Kenyon, Lance-Corporal, 202
Ketteringham, Second Lieutenant, 76
Kildare Avenue, 209, 211
— Post, 206
Kindersley, Major, 157, 204, 247
King, H.M. the, inspection by, 68, 69, 195
— Colonel, U.S.A., 128
— Private, 9
— Edward's Horse, 3, 19
Kirkbridge, Private, 119
Knight, Lieut.-Colonel, 247
Knights, Second Lieutenant, 164
Knoll, The, 210

La Bassée, 12, 13
La Boisselle, 50, 51, 53, 55, 59, 169
Labour Companies, 81
La Bourse, 13
La Gorgue, 164
Lambton, Major-General Hon. Sir W., 62, 123
Landas, 221
Langley, Sergeant, 220
La Piéterie, 220
Lapigny, 48
La Placette, 220
Lark Post, 210, 211
Lateau Wood, 136, 139, 140, 141, 147, 153, 154, 159
La Terrière, Lieut.-Colonel de Sales, 148, 170, 226, 241
La Vacquerie, 149, 150, 152, 157, 158
— — Valley, 154
Laventie, 167
Lawford, Major-General, 82
Lawless, Brig.-General S. E., 246
Lawrie, Major-General, 169
Leach, Lieutenant, 24
— Sergeant, 59
Leavers, Private, 195
Le Cauroy, 113, 114, 129, 257, 258
Lecelle, 221
Lee, Major-General Sir R., 186
Lee-Norman, Captain, 96, 248
Le Forest, 200, 201
Leipzig salient, 51, 56

INDEX

Le Maroc, 221, 222
Lens-Canal, 215
Lens-La Bassée Road, 16
Le Quennet, 136, 139
—— Farm, 154
Levins, Sergeant, 210
Lewes, Lieut.-Colonel C. G., 241
Lewin, Major E. O., 246
Lewis, Captain, 58, 59
Lieramont Cemetery, 204
Ligny, 80
Lindsay, Major J. H., 240
Ling, Captain, 243
Lillers, 13, 27, 31, 47, 48
Little Priel Farm, 206, 208, 209
— Willie Trench, 39
Llewellyn, Lieutenant, 156
Lœuilly, 188
Longeau, 49
Long Trench, 114, 115, 116, 117, 118, 119, 120
Longueval, 81
Loos, 13, 14, 25
— Battle of, 12 et seq.
— salient, 48
— sector, 45
Lord's cricket ground, 3
Lunn, Captain W., 244
Lys River, 6, 162, 164, 165

Maas, Private, 258
Mabel Corons, 216
McAllister, Private, 103
Macan, Captain, 245
McCabe, Lieutenant H. P., 242
McCallum, Captain, 183
— Second Lieutenant R. B., 124
McCarthy, Lieutenant, 184, 185
Machine Gun Battalion, 170, 174, 178, 194
—— Corps, 147
— guns, inadequate supply of, 11
MacIlwaine, Captain H. L., 244
McKenna, Private, 38
Mackenzie, Captain, 157
McLeod, Brig.-General K. L., 32, 246
Maddison, Second Lieutenant, 149
Mailly-Maillet, 181, 182, 184
Main Sewer, 92, 96
Maison Rouge, 102
Maistre, Général, 255, 256
Malassise Farm, 206, 207, 255
Mallam, Captain C. A., 241
Maltzhorn Farm, 198, 199
— Ridge, 198, 199
Mametz, 169, 189, 197, 198
Manancourt, 134, 202, 206
Manicon, Second Lieutenant J. H., 127
Mann, Major D., 227, 244
Mansell, Captain E. H., 248

Mantle, Gunner J. W., 157
Mapston, Private, 116
Marchant, Lieutenant S., 200
Marcoing, 135
Marden, Major-General, 135
Margots, Captain, 17
Maricourt, 50, 168, 198, 214
Marindin, General, 185
Marshall, Major-General, 224
Martinpuich, 49
Martinsart, 173
— Wood, 175
Mash Valley, 50, 53, 56, 57
Masnières, 135, 139, 140
Masnières-Beaurevoir line, 133
Masny, 225, 228
Mason, Captain, 37
Maulde, 221
— Fort, 221
Maurepas, 200, 214
— Ridge, 204
Maxse, Lieut.-General Sir I., 106, 113
Maxstead, Company Sergt.-Major, 82
Maynard, Captain, 94
Mazingarbe, 16
Méaulte, 168, 172, 196
Memorial crosses, design of, 255
Memorials to officers and men of 12th Division, 255, 256
Mericourt, 216
Mersey Street, 150
Merville, 161, 164, 166, 180, 258
Mesnil, 170, 173, 185
Meteren, 5
Millencourt, 50
Miller, Sergeant A., 256
Mills, Captain E. A., 248
Minenwerfer, 41, 43
Mining—
  British, 33, 34, 35, 36, 45
  enemy, 30, 34, 43, 44, 45
  charges used for, 35
Moakes, Corporal G., 100
Mobile Veterinary Section, 3
Moislains, 134
Monchy-le-Preux, 97, 104, 105, 108, 114, 115, 124, 129, 255
Monro, General Sir C., 33, 34
Mons, retreat from, 15
Montauban, 80, 168, 169, 197, 198
Montdidier salient, 195
Mont de la Justice, 221, 223
Montenescourt, 113
Montigny, 217
Moore, Lieutenant, 58, 59
Moorhouse, Sergeant, 32
Morlancourt, 192, 194, 195, 201, 212, 213, 214
Morland, Lieut.-General Sir T., 56
Moreuil, 188
Motor Machine Gun Battery, 3

INDEX

Mott, Major S. A., 239
Mount, The, 122
Mouquet Farm, 64, 69
Mule Trench, 209
Munro, Major, 188

Nagle, Captain G., 243
Nash, Captain, 164
Neuve Chapelle, 165
New Street, 109
Newton Post, 148
New Zealand Division, 171, 172, 181
Nichols, Captain P. B., 244
Nicol, Major, 155
Nicolls, Lieut.-Colonel E. H. J., 148, 170, 184, 241, 245
Nieppe, 6, 8, 11
Nightingale, Private, 166
Nock, Lieutenant, 203
Nœux les Mines, 13, 15
No-Man's-Land, 34, 56, 57, 58, 61, 78, 87, 92, 96, 99, 166, 183
Northampton Trench, 38
Nossworthy, Private, 58
Nouvel Houplines, 9
Noyelles, 43, 216
— Godault, 217, 218
No. 12 Copse, 208
Nurlu, 202, 203, 204, 214
— Ridge, 204

Oakhanger Wood, 200
Oakley, Lieut.-Colonel, 170, 194, 248
Observation Ridge, 99, 100
Ockenden Trench, 208
Old Copse, 207
Onslow, Lieutenant Sir Robert, 68
Oosthove Farm, 11
Oppy, 215
Orange Hill, 102, 103, 104
Orchies, 220
Ormsby, Lieutenant G. V., 157, 246
Osborn, Lieut.-Colonel W. L., 57, 58, 60, 243
Ossus Wood, 212
Ottar, Captain, 21
Overton, Lieut.-Colonel G., 57, 82, 99, 243
Ovillers, 50, 51, 56, 59, 60, 163, 169, 170, 255
Owen, Brig.-General C. S., 53, 72, 82, 89, 97, 110, 135, 150, 177, 191, 195, 226, 245

Page, Captain J. C., 245
Pagen, Captain, 82
Paish, Captain A. L., 144, 193
Pakenham, Major G., 238
Palmer, Company Sergt.-Major, 44

Pam Pam Farm, 136, 139, 153
Pargiter, Lieut.-Colonel, 243, 244
Parker, Private, 195
Parminter, Second Lieutenant, 127
Parry, Company Sergt.-Major, 218
— Crooke, Lieut.-Colonel C. D., 240
Parsons, Major C., 242
Passchendale, 126
Patterson, Captain H., 7
Pattinson, Captain H. L., 243
Peizières, 134, 204, 205, 206, 207
Pelican Trench, 141, 142, 149, 150, 151
Pelves, 109
Pennel, Sergeant R. H., 223
Pentelow, Sergeant, 78
Peploe, Lieut.-Colonel H., 227, 245
Perceval, Major-General, 62
Pereira, Major-General, 171
Pernois, 189
Pèronne, 134
Perris, Private L. W., 22
Perry, Corporal, 116
Petite Rue, 221
Phelan, Lieut.-Colonel, 249
Phillips, Captain the Hon. R., 36, 37
Philomel, 47
Philosophe, 19, 25
Phyall, Private S., 17
Pick Avenue, 120
Pickering, Captain A. C., 245
Pike, Captain J. M., 20, 127
Pim, Lieutenant, 88
Pinwill, Lieut.-Colonel, 238
Ploegsteert Wood, 6
Pollard, Lieutenant, 21, 22
Pollington, Sergeant, 166
Pommiers Redoubt, 80, 197
Pont à Sault, 217
Portuguese troops, 162, 168
Poston, Major W., 246
Potter, Captain, 245
Pottinger, Lieut.-Colonel, 155
Pozières, 62, 169
— Trench, 63
Pratt, Lieut.-Colonel, 244
Prince of Wales, H.R.H. the, 68, 69
— — — presentation of colours by, 226, 227
—Reserve, 207, 208
Prior, Private W. H., 117
Proyart, 215
Prynne, Lieut.-Colonel, 249
Puchevillers, 73, 184
Pulteney, Lieut.-General Sir W., 49, 55, 134, 135
Purfleet, 2

Quality Street, 14
Quarries, the, 14, 16, 18, 21, 22, 23, 24, 32, 33, 34, 45, 178, 210, 211
Quarry Post, 141, 148

INDEX

Quéant-Drocourt line, 216, 217
Quentin Mill, 144
— Ridge, 146, 155, 156, 157
Querrieu Chateau, 195

Raincheval, 184
Ramsay, Major-General, 189, 217
Rankin, Captain H., 249
Ration Trench, 63, 64, 65, 66, 67, 68, 69, 70
Rawling, Captain G. E., 243
Rawlinson, General Lord, 13, 49, 189, 190, 214
Reday, Lieutenant J. M., 103
Redford, Lieutenant, 58
Reed, Major-General, 97, 104
Rees, Lieut.-Colonel E. T., 170, 174, 176, 240
Reeves, Sergeant R. C., 207
Regiments—
  Artists' Rifles, 174
  Bedfordshire, 174
  Buffs. *See* East Kent.
  Cambridgeshire, 1st, 180, 191, 194, 195, 196, 198, 199, 203, 206, 207, 208, 215, 217, 218, 221, 226, 242
  City of London. *See* Royal Fusiliers.
  Duke of Cambridge's Own. *See* Middlesex.
  Durham Light Infantry, 147
  East Kent, 2, 6, 20, 21, 39, 40, 41, 43, 51, 56, 63, 64, 68, 77, 82, 83, 99, 110, 111, 116, 123, 133, 139, 153, 154, 166, 170, 173, 183, 185, 187, 189, 192, 194, 195, 196, 197, 198, 200, 204, 207, 211, 212, 215, 220, 222, 223, 227, 244
  East Surrey, 2, 7, 16, 20, 39, 44, 51, 55, 56, 59, 60, 71, 99, 100, 110, 122, 133, 139, 153, 154, 163, 245
  Essex, 2, 23, 24, 51, 52, 53, 56, 59, 60, 69, 70, 72, 76, 84, 85, 101, 102, 103, 104, 109, 116, 118, 125, 148, 149, 150, 158, 163, 165, 166, 170, 172, 174, 177, 178, 184, 191, 194, 195, 196, 197, 199, 200, 203, 206, 207, 210, 215, 217, 220, 226, 241
  Hampshire, 85
  Manchester, 59
  Middlesex, 2, 6, 24, 32, 33, 39, 58, 60, 83, 94, 99, 104, 105, 136, 139, 140, 142, 143, 144, 146, 163, 243
  Newfoundland, 84
  Monmouthshire Pioneers, 147
  Norfolk, 2, 21, 22, 30, 51, 69, 70, 76, 84, 88, 101, 102, 108, 120, 127, 129, 148, 149, 150, 164, 165, 170, 172, 174, 175, 176, 191, 195, 196, 203, 206, 207, 215, 218, 219, 220, 221, 226, 240

Regiments—*continued*.
  Northamptonshire, 3, 5, 16, 20, 44, 48, 55, 65, 81, 96, 106, 121, 133, 146, 147, 152, 172, 174, 175, 176, 178, 191, 204, 207, 208, 224, 225, 226, 245
  Northumberland Hussars, 145, 147
  Pioneers. *See* Northamptonshire.
  Princess Charlotte of Wales. *See* Royal Berkshire.
  Queen's. *See* Royal West Surrey.
  Queen's Own. *See* Royal West Kent.
  Royal Berkshire, 2, 21, 51, 52, 67, 78, 94, 101, 102, 103, 104, 108, 109, 119, 141, 148, 149, 163, 170, 175, 176, 177, 178, 183, 184, 194, 195, 196, 198, 203, 206, 207, 209, 210, 215, 226, 241
  Royal Fusiliers, 2, 7, 8, 9, 16, 23, 28, 29, 32, 35, 36, 38, 39, 55, 56, 57, 58, 60, 63, 64, 65, 66, 82, 99, 100, 110, 111, 115, 124, 139, 140, 141, 142, 148, 149, 150, 151, 152, 158, 163, 170, 172, 175, 176, 178, 194, 195, 196, 199, 200, 203, 206, 207, 209, 210, 215, 216, 217, 221, 223, 226, 242, 243
  Royal North Lancashire, 144
  Royal Sussex, 2, 24, 30, 39, 57, 58, 59, 60, 63, 64, 65, 99, 104, 110, 111, 112, 115, 119, 120, 126, 142, 147, 150, 152, 164, 170, 175, 176, 194, 195, 196, 197, 198, 203, 206, 209, 215, 217, 219, 220, 223, 226, 243
  Royal West Kent, 2, 9, 16, 17, 18, 20, 21, 41, 43, 53, 64, 72, 82, 99, 101, 112, 118, 119, 120, 121, 127, 139, 147, 153, 163, 164, 165, 166, 169, 170, 173, 176, 186, 187, 192, 193, 196, 197, 198, 199, 205, 208, 209, 211, 215, 216, 220, 221, 222, 227, 228, 245
  Royal West Surrey, 2, 6, 20, 44, 51, 52, 53, 64, 77, 83, 87, 98, 99, 118, 120, 125, 127, 140, 142, 143, 144, 145, 146, 147, 165, 166, 169, 170, 173, 176, 186, 187, 191, 192, 193, 194, 197, 200, 201, 207, 208, 211, 215, 216, 221, 224, 227, 244
  South Lancashire, 60
  Suffolk, 2, 22, 51, 56, 59, 67, 68, 94, 101, 102, 109, 122, 141, 148, 149, 150, 165, 170, 172, 174, 176, 177, 180, 240
  Worcester, 84
Reliefs, system of, 79
Remiencourt, 188
Renwick, Lieutenant G., 246
Revelon, 144

INDEX

Revelon Farm, 145, 146, 147
— Ridge, 145, 146, 147, 159
Reynolds, Major R., 240
Rheims, 190
Rhineland Bridgeheads, 225, 228
Ribecourt, 190
Richards, Lieut.-Colonel B. O., 70, 85, 241
Richmond, Captain J. D., 248
Richthofen Squadron, 120
Rider, Private, 106
Ridge Reserve, 206
Rifle Trench, 108, 109
Rifleman's Crater, 30
Riverside Wood, 202
Roads, bad condition of, 80, 81
Robecq, 13
Roberts, Captain, 247
Robertson, Major D. R., 239
— Lieut.-Colonel J. C., 108, 243
Robinson, Captain J. B., 239
— Lieut.-Colonel, 245
Robson, Lieutenant, 78
Rockets, 53
Rœux, 108, 109, 110, 112
Rolfe, Lieutenant, 64
Rolls, Lieut.-Colonel N. T., 99, 127, 140, 144, 244
Ronssoy, 208
Ronville, 92
Room Trench, 208
Rosenthal, Major-General, 189
Rosult, 221
Rouse, Private L., 66
Routledge, Captain G., 247
Routley, Second Lieutenant, 64
Rouvroy, 216
Royal Air Force, 73, 92
— Army Medical Corps, 3, 25, 38, 55, 106, 248
— — Service Corps, 3, 25, 45, 248
— Engineers, 2, 10, 16, 25, 35, 42, 46, 48, 49, 55, 69, 81, 96, 106, 115, 121, 123, 127, 133, 147, 152, 178, 187, 204, 212, 219, 224, 248
— Field Artillery, 2, 16, 32, 83, 103, 155, 157, 158, 171, 176, 177, 187, 213
Royle, Captain D. C., 243
Rumball, Private, 22
Rumilly, 135
Russell, Major-General, 171
Russia, defection of, 162
Russian Attaché, visit to Divisional Headquarters of, 27
— Sap, 44
Ryan, Major C. F., 283

Sackville-West, Major-General the Hon. Sir Charles, 238, 255

Sailly la Bourse, 26, 27, 33, 47
Saint, Lieut.-Colonel E. T., 180, 191, 192, 199, 242
St. Amand, 221, 222
St. Elie Avenue, 22
St. Hilaire, 27
St. Omer, 5, 166
St. Patrick's Avenue, 209
St. Quentin, 95
St. Sauveur, 92
Sallaumines, 216
Salvage, 225
Samèon, 221
Sammons, Lance-Corporal, 218
Samuel, Lieutenant G., 246
Sandars, Lieut.-Colonel S. E., 242
Sanitary section, 3
Sanson, Lieut.-Colonel A. J., 99, 243
Sap 9...43
Sap 9a...43
Sap 12...44
Sargeant, Corporal J., 184
Saulcourt Wood, 204
Sauvagerie, 220
Savernake Wood, 200
Savill, Private H., 117
Savy, 215
Saxons, non-aggressive attitude of, 9
Scabbard Trench, 110, 112
Scafe, Captain E., 244
Scarlett, Lieut.-Colonel H. A., 191, 220, 226, 240
Scarpe River, 90, 108, 109, 221, 222, 223
Scobell, Major, 239
Scott, Major-General Sir Arthur, 16, 23, 27, 42, 55, 68, 69, 97, 101, 104, 107, 112, 120, 130, 133, 141, 159, 160, 181, 225, 238, 255, 256
Scott, Lieut.-Colonel L. D., 44, 245
Scott-Martin, Lieutenant, 118, 119
Scott-Murray, Captain A., 240
Secrecy, methods of guarding, 134, 135
Senlis, 60, 68, 168, 169, 170
Shakespear, Lieut.-Colonel A. T., 187, 248
Sharp, Major J. S., 95
— Company Sergt.-Major M., 37
Shave, Private, 129
Shells, tear, 43, 47
Shorncliffe, 2
Short, Lieut.-Colonel W. A., 247
Shrapnel Trench, 115
Shute, Lieut.-General Sir C., 185, 187
Siege Batteries, 36
Sievers, Captain, 145
Signal Corps, 137
Silver, Lieut.-Colonel J. P., 106, 248
Simencourt, 113
Simson, Lieut. H., 246
Sixth Avenue, 63, 64, 69, 70

INDEX

Skey, Major C. O., 188
Slade, Second Lieutenant G. B., 127
Slaughter, Captain M. L., 241
Smart, Lance-Corporal, 24
Smeltzer, Lieut.-Colonel A. S., 139, 153, 154, 170, 173, 192, 211, 223, 227, 244
Smith, Private A., 129
— Second Lieutenant M. Bell, 127
— Brig.-General K. J. Kincaid, 213
— Lieutenant Lea, 41
— Captain L. C. R., 127
— Lieut.-Colonel M., 103
— Private S. A., 38
— Sergt.-Major, 212
Smithers, Lieutenant, 247
— Captain Norman, 244
Smoke Screens, 12, 13, 18, 20, 58, 127, 151, 188, 191
Sneyd, Major F. B., 249
Snipers, camouflaging posts of, 7
Snow, Lieut.-General Sir T., 97
Soames, Major, 21
Soissons, 190
Somme, Battle of, 49 et seq., 255, 257
— Préfet of, 256
— Sous-Préfet of, 256
Sonnet Farm, 135
Sorel le Grand, 134
— Wood, 204
Sound ranging, invention of, 93
Souvain, 225, 226
"Spades, The." See Divisional Concert Party.
Spens, Major-General J., 3, 238
Spies, 10, 28, 29
Spoon Trench, 119, 120, 125, 126
Spooner, Captain C., 241
Stamer, Sapper W. J., 127
Stamper, Major, 157, 188, 208
Stansfield, Private H. P., 106
Steenwerck, 5
Stephenson, Private E., 216
Stewart, Major A. F., 239
— Captain MacD., 244
Sticky Trench, 44
Stocks, Captain H. S., 243
Stone Lane, 211
— Trench, 211
Strap Trench, 117, 124
Stratford, Captain Wingfield, 245
Strong, Lance-Corporal, 258
Sunken Road, The, 51, 53, 56, 153, 154, 155
Sutcliffe, Lance-Corporal, 258
Sutherland, Major, 155
Sutton, Sergeant J., 165
Swallow Trench, 211

Tabor, Lieutenant, 248

Tamblin, Corporal, 82
Tank Corps, 139, 141
Tanks, 96, 100, 102, 104, 132, 133, 135, 136, 137, 146, 190, 192, 193, 194, 196
Tapply, Captain M., 240
Tara Usna Line, 59
Taylor, Captain F. J., 246
— Lieutenant G. H., 240
— Second Lieutenant, 78
Telephones, tapping enemy, 9
Tétard Wood, 207
"The First Hundred Thousand," 2
Thiennes, 161
Thiepval, 176
— area, 62, 64
Thilloy, 80
Thomas, Captain, 118, 119
— Lieutenant H. G., 219
— Brig.-General H. M., 125, 188, 246
Thompson, Lieut.-Colonel A. L., 195, 226, 243
— Lieut.-Colonel F. V., 128, 238, 241, 248
Thomson, Lieut.-Colonel R. G., 247
Thun, 222
Tilloy, Mayor of, 255
Tino Trench, 211
Tomkins, Captain, 20
Tompkins, Lieut.-Colonel A. C., 249
Toulorge, General, 188
Toutencourt, 179
Tower, Captain C. C., 15, 239
Traitoire River, 222
Trenches, conditions in, 29, 26, 115
— enemy, night raids on, 76, 77, 78, 87, 88, 93, 98, 115, 116, 163, 164, 165, 166, 183, 184, 185
— — photography of, 92
— improvement of, 14, 92, 93, 121, 162, 164
Trench Mortars, 30, 36, 57, 116, 121, 123, 127, 141, 177, 185, 192, 193, 196
— warfare, end of, 190
Trent, Lieut.-Colonel G. A., 27, 69, 86, 96, 172, 178, 191, 226, 245
Trevor, Lieut.-Colonel H., 102, 241, 244
— Sergeant, 196
Trones Wood, 198, 199
Tuckey, Lieutenant, 156
Tuffil, Corporal S., 202
Tunnelling Company, 35, 41, 42
Turk, Captain, 245
Turner, Lieut.-Colonel, 249
— Lance-Corporal W. G., 88
— Quarry, 142, 147
Tutt, Private, 58
Twin Copses, 115

INDEX

United States Army, 164, 192, 194, 210, 212
Upward, Lieutenant, 37

Valentine, Lieut.-Colonel H., 246
Van Someren, Lieut.-Colonel W. V. L., 150, 170, 226, 243
— Straubenzee, Brig.-General C. H., 14, 21, 27, 239
Varennes, 60
Varney, Sergeant F., 183
Vaucellette Farm, 134, 143, 144, 145, 147, 158
Vaux Wood, 206
Venables, Lieut.-Colonel, 245
Vendhuile, 208, 212, 215
Verey Lights, 77
Vermelles, 14, 16, 43
Vermelles-Hulloch Road, 16
Verquin, 13
Victoria Cross, awards of, 251-3
Vignacourt, 189
Villers Bretonneux, 189
— Guislain, 143, 144, 145, 146, 148, 149, 155
— Plouich, 152, 155, 157
Vimy Ridge, 97
— sector, 215
Vincent, Brig.-General B., 93, 97, 135, 144, 145, 146, 147, 168, 191, 216, 226, 239
Vine Lane, 116

Wagnonlieu, 96, 106
Wail, 132
Wailly, 76
Waite, Company Sergt.-Major, 67
Walker, Captain E., 242
— Captain Robertson, 243
Wall, Lance-Corporal, 116
Wallace, Private R. H., 193
— Lieutenant S. T. D., 156, 157, 252
Waller, Major H., 246
Wallis, Captain, 192
Walter, Lieut.-Colonel F. E., 70, 101, 120, 121, 240
Walters, Lieutenant, 23
Wancourt, Commune of, 255, 256
Wancourt-Feuchy line, 97, 104
Ward, Captain R., 68
Wardall, Lieutenant H., 241
Warden, Lieut.-Colonel H. F., 53, 244
Wardrop, Lieutenant, 37
Warloy, 60, 168, 177
Warlus, 75, 86, 255

Warner, Lieutenant S. A., 163
Warren, Private, 57
Warsaw, capture of, 9
Watterworth, Lance-Corporal, 257, 258
Webb, Captain R., 244
Webber, Brig.-General Incledon, 126, 139, 152, 169, 170, 192, 227, 244
Webster, Rev. F., 249
Wellesley, Lieut.-Colonel, 247
West, Major G., 240
— Captain J. R., 241
— Private, 116
Whaley, Captain S. R., 241
Wheeler, Captain W. E., 241
Wheler, Captain T., 245
Whetham, Lieut.-Colonel P., 170, 191, 244
Whippets, 171, 190, 197
Whitaker, Captain H. C., 249
White, Lieutenant, 146
"White Man, The," 258
Wilcox, Second Lieutenant H. P., 139
Wilkie, Captain J., 248
Willan, Lieut.-Colonel F. G., 51, 102, 104, 241, 242
Williams, Captain, 247
— Lieut.-Colonel, 248
Willis, Brig.-General E. H., 32, 93, 103, 125, 126, 246
Wilson, Major A. H., 7
— Colonel J. B., 32, 248
Wing, Major-General F. D. V., 3, 15, 238
Wire, destruction of, 94, 98, 136, 139, 186
— difficulties in negotiating, 77, 78, 84, 203, 207, 208
Witham, Captain, 157
Wollocombe, Lieut.-Colonel, 99, 139, 144, 169, 243
Wood, Captain E. R., 242
Woodward, Lieutenant L. C., 157, 247
Woollcombe, Captain M. L., 239
— Lieut.-General Sir C., 75
Wykeham-Musgrave, Lieutenant H. P., 239
Wynne, Lieut.-Colonel H., 103, 155, 157, 246

Yates, Lieutenant, 17
Ypres, 120
Ypres salient, 5, 12, 204

Zinc Works, The, 223

GENERAL MAP OF WESTERN FRONT.

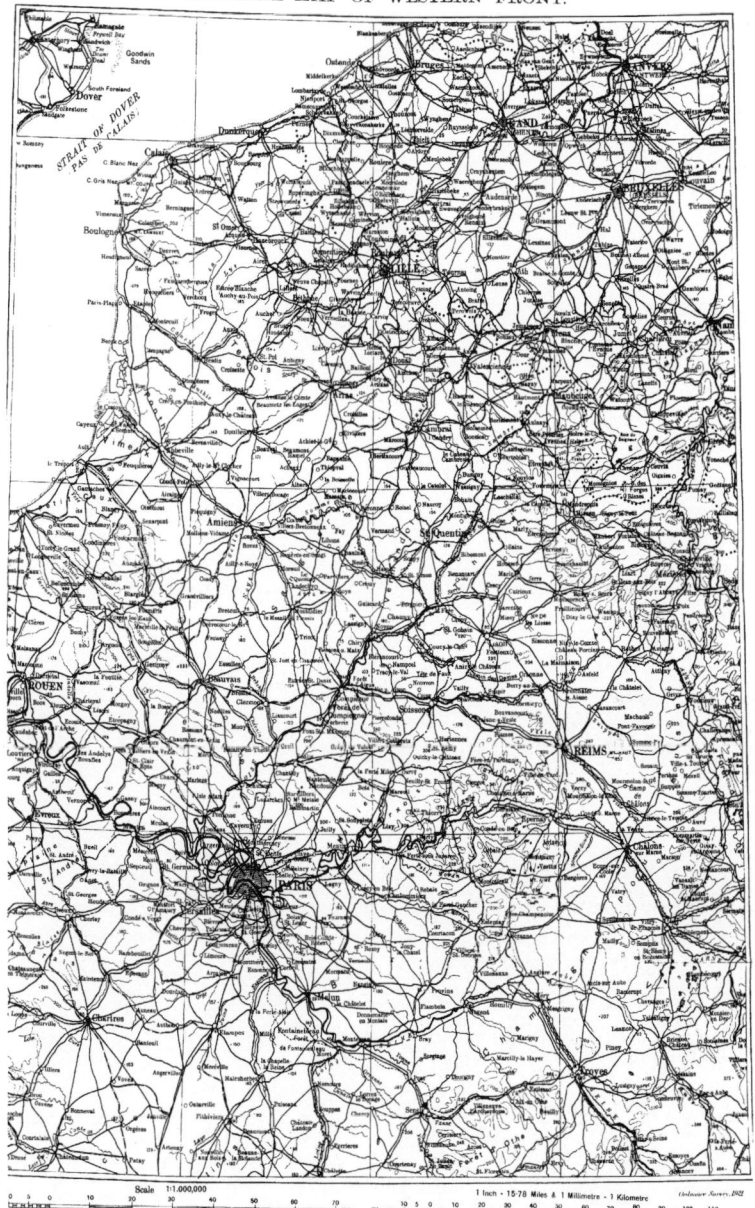

Printed in Great Britain by
Amazon.co.uk, Ltd.,
Marston Gate.